2004

Why there is Something rather than Nothing

Why there is Something rather than Nothing

Bede Rundle

CLARENDON PRESS · OXFORD

OXFORD
UNIVERSITY PRESS

Great Clarendon Street, Oxford OX2 6DP

Oxford University Press is a department of the University of Oxford.
It furthers the University's objective of excellence in research, scholarship,
and education by publishing worldwide in

Oxford New York

Auckland Bangkok Buenos Aires Cape Town Chennai
Dar es Salaam Delhi Hong Kong Istanbul Karachi Kolkata
Kuala Lumpur Madrid Melbourne Mexico City Mumbai Nairobi
São Paulo Shanghai Taipei Tokyo Toronto

Oxford is a registered trade mark of Oxford University Press
in the UK and in certain other countries

Published in the United States
by Oxford University Press Inc., New York

British Library Cataloguing in Publication Data

Data available

Library of Congress Cataloging in Publication Data

Data available

ISBN 0–19–927050–3

1 3 5 7 9 10 8 6 4 2

Typeset by Newgen Imaging Systems (P) Ltd., Chennai, India
Printed in Great Britain
on acid-free paper by
Biddles Ltd, King's Lynn, Norfolk

PRAESIDI SOCIISQVE COLLEGI SANCTAE ET INDIVIDVAE
TRINITATIS

Preface

The question, 'Why is there something rather than nothing?', has a strong claim to be philosophy's central, and most perplexing, question. As providing a possible starting point for a proof of the existence of God, its centrality is assured, and it has a capacity to set one's head spinning which few other philosophical problems can rival. The principal answers which it receives are of two kinds. First, as just indicated, we have the theist's response: the existence of anything at all can be explained only if we can suppose that there is a being, God, who exists of necessity and is the source of all being. Second, and ever more commonly, it is held that physics will provide the answer. Cosmological theories are being continually developed and refined to such a point that we can expect an eventual explanation of why our universe exists, and hence of the more general fact that something exists, to arise out of such a theory

Both these responses are problematic. Our remarkable success in devising scientific explanations, in resolving what have initially appeared impenetrable mysteries, may make for a presumption that favours the naturalistic alternative, but there are many, scientists as well as non-scientists, who believe that we must look beyond science if we are to find a final explanation. The province of cosmology is nothing short of the whole universe, but it is difficult to see how enlightenment might be found *within* that province. One way or another, the existence of something seems always to be presupposed. On the other hand, if the origins of what is of concern to cosmology are not a question for cosmology itself, it is not clear that theology can fare any better, given the problems associated with the very concept of God. The universe does not appear to be self-explanatory, but it has yet to be made clear how a genuine explanation could be given by invoking a being outside space and time, as God is customarily conceived to be.

In the face of the difficulties presented by these two solutions, we may be drawn to a reluctant acceptance that the existence at which we marvel is just a matter of brute, inexplicable, fact. Reluctant, since as a response that disowns rather than offers the possibility of enlightenment, this is not a happy resting place. However, while it may be difficult to see where else to turn, there is a further possibility. Neither of the answers touched upon gives what might be considered a typically philosophical solution, a solution which proceeds by showing that the troublesome questions rest on mistaken assumptions. A distinctive feature of philosophical questions lies in the way they transform under scrutiny, giving way, as the nature of the issue becomes clearer, to a series of sub-questions often not obviously related to the original query. This is one reason why, to the beginner in the subject, much philosophy is found baffling; to someone ignorant of the history of the problem, it is not evident why the issues being addressed are felt to be relevant, let alone important. This development often has, in addition, a deflationary aspect: the initial question is superseded by those that follow because it is revealed to harbour a misconception. If, for instance, the mind–body problem is conceived of as a problem of understanding how two kinds of 'stuff', the mental and the physical, can interact, it is not going to meet with an answer which does not fault the formulation. Likewise in the present instance: if there is something improper about assumptions behind our seemingly unanswerable questions, if what is perceived as an intractable problem is no more than a confusion, then a resolution may take the form of an exposition of the misconceptions, a rejection of the questions, and a consequent dispelling of our perplexity. This, I suggest, is what we meet with at crucial points in the enquiry that follows.

The main lines of our argument are straightforward. After expounding difficulties, largely familiar, in the theist's approach, we consider two possible answers to the question why there is something rather than nothing. There is, first, the relatively modest observation that there has to be something or other, and second, the more traditional claim that there is some particular being that has to be. The former recommends itself over the latter as being weaker, yet able to provide an answer to the initial question, and we offer reasons for thinking it correct. At this point we also bring to bear our deflationary considerations, arguing that the notion of beginning to be has no application to the universe, and hence that there is in this instance no coming into existence for which we have to find a cause. More generally, it is suggested that when talking about the universe we get into difficulties not altogether dissimilar from those encountered in talking about God. In either case, the concepts we invoke have a clear application within the universe, but they break down when extrapolated either to a supposedly transcendent being or to the universe itself. However, while it is seemingly inconceivable that there should have been nothing at all, it is far from clear why there is what there is. Our response is to argue that if there is anything at all, there must be matter; nothing else has the kind of existential independence required. The domain of the immaterial offers us, principally, the abstract and the mental. We do not have to reject either category but, if neither enjoys an independent existence, matter remains unchallenged. But even if matter can be assured, we are still left wondering why the universe is, more specifically, as it is. It is at this point that most of the issues pass from philosophy to physics, but certain questions, such as those concerning the way in which explanations may come to an end and the possibility that the universe has existed for an infinite time, have sufficient philosophical content to fall within the scope of our investigation.

When the universe is our subject-matter, the number of topics clamouring for attention is daunting: God, causality, space, time, essence, existence, necessity, infinity, explanation, mind—practically all the concepts of interest to metaphysics. A theory of everything is not our business, but a philosophy of just about everything philosophy dreams of is needed, and the analyses that follow patently fail to meet that need. In some cases I am able to refer to elaborations I have given elsewhere, but my main concern is to present the key considerations in outline, to give an indication of what might be possible in areas where it is so easy to think that we have come to a dead end. And it is only what *might* be possible. I cannot claim that the arguments on key points—as with the central thesis that there has to be something—are compelling. It is, rather, that good reasons can be given in support of the position advocated, and that the case for that position gains further in credibility from the apparent lack of any remotely plausible alternative.

Trinity College, Oxford

Contents

I

Theology and Meaning

Our starting point is the theist's attempt to account for the existence of the universe. The supposition of a transcendent being provokes a range of problems, but we shall give greatest attention to those which relate to God's supposed action on, or in producing, the world—the key conception on which the theist's case turns. The issues are introduced in conjunction with the positivist's challenge to theism, a challenge which we find only partially successful. In general, it does not require subscription to a contentious account of what makes for meaningfulness to find good reason for attributing serious incoherence to the theist's position. In particular, it proves difficult to see how the crucial concept of explanation can have any application to the otherworldly.

I.I MEANING AND VERIFICATION

The principal philosophical threat to theology in the twentieth century is commonly held to have come from logical positivism, with its refusal to allow that metaphysical claims, and those of theology in particular, are meaningful, let alone true. In sanctioning beliefs which purport to go beyond what experience can decide, metaphysics would appear to be at the heart of philosophy: what is there left of the subject if this heart is torn out? The positivists' rejection of metaphysics rested on the verification principle, which laid down that a proposition is meaningful if and only if it is either analytic or empirically verifiable. Linguistic forms deemed acceptable in terms of this principle include everyday propositions about the world along with the more sophisticated propositions of science, in so far as these can have their truth established by observation and experimentation; in addition, propositions of logic and mathematics are admissible, since they can be recognized as true by pure reason. Claims about God, however, are not like descriptions of tables and chairs, nor even electrons; nor do they compare with theorems of pure mathematics. Having no place in either of these favoured categories, they are, for the positivist, to be dismissed as nonsense, forms of words having the appearance of meaningful utterances, but in reality being no better than strings of nonsense syllables. Theological pronouncements are seen to be casualties of this attack even before the question of truth can be raised in their regard. That is, if neither empirical verifiability nor purely logical support can be granted, there is nothing for us to consider even as a possibility. As failing on both counts, the pivotal proposition, 'God exists', does not bear enough sense even to be false.

The theological response to A. J. Ayer's *Language, Truth and Logic*, in which this position was vigorously advanced, was twofold. There was little by way of positive rehabilitation of traditional theism in the face of Ayer's onslaught. Some tried to argue that crucial theological propositions could be found to be true, even if this discovery had to wait until we were dead— 'eschatological verification'—but most sought either to find fault with positivism, or to adjust the interpretation of theological propositions in such a way that these were no longer in the line of fire. The approach commonly followed by those who found fault was largely a matter of trying to demonstrate that the verification principle did not conform to its own demands: it was not based on experience, yet if it were in the category of the logical, it would, on Ayer's showing, 'simply record our determination to use words in a certain fashion' (1952: 84).

This analysis makes it appear that the only alternative to construing the principle as an empirical generalization is to take an arbitrary stand on a question of meaning. However, if we might equally say that the non-empirical alternative concerns logical connections between concepts of meaning, understanding, and verification, it would appear that this category is just the one where the principle, if warranted, could be expected to find its justification. Indeed, to suggest that the issue could be anything other than conceptual might well now strike us as extraordinary; as about what makes sense, it is pre-eminently a 'grammatical' matter, in Wittgenstein's extended sense of the term, according to which grammar encompasses rules of use quite generally, semantic as well as syntactic. Whether a particular use of language requires the possibility of verification is surely to be decided by ascertaining just what that use involves, and whether the relevant considerations vindicate a more general requirement of verifiability is a question to be pursued by extending this conceptual enquiry. However, given that the alternative to the empirical was thought of in the disparaging terms indicated, it is understandable that those who wished to impale the verification principle on the logical/empirical dilemma considered themselves to be on firm ground. At all events, even if the ground is not as firm as it appeared, that does not help with the problem, as urgent as ever, of making sense of theological discourse.

Before elaborating this point, it is worth mentioning a stronger reason for querying the positivist's appeal to the verification principle. Consider the suggestion that the universe might suddenly double in size; a development which, it is said, would inevitably elude all observation and measurement, and which can accordingly be ruled out as meaningless by the principle. When there is something which remains constant, something relative to which other objects may be described as increasing in size, we can make sense of expansion, but take away any such fixed point and the concept ceases to have application. With expansion, as with motion generally, we are dealing with a *relational* notion, and when one term of the relation is denied us, the conditions requisite for applying the concept do not obtain. It is preferable to put it this way rather than say that the expansion would be undetectable; that comes too close to conceding that it makes sense to speak in these terms, as with Waismann's comment on the supposition: 'this remarkable change of our world could not be verified in any way, it would remain completely unnoticed by us' (1965: 326). But the crucial point is that there would be nothing *to* notice. What is lacking is definition, not observability. By contrast, the gravitational attraction which a marble exerts upon the earth is infinitesimal, but it is at least defined—unmeasurable, certainly, but not incalculable.

Just why the possibility of finding out about the putative expansion is denied us is made clear in this account, but if we conclude that the hypothesis is accordingly nonsensical or meaningless, this verdict has to be consistent with the consideration that it is only by reflecting on the meaning of the words that we come to appreciate that verification is ruled out. That need not be a problem. We commonly condemn as nonsense propositions that stand no chance of truth—'The Government can be counted upon not to raise taxes'—but in the positivist's mouth this condemnation is tantamount to the claim that what has been said is totally unintelligible, nothing better than mere gibberish, and that, surely, makes nonsense of the procedure whereby we come to our dismissal. 'The universe might double in size' makes enough sense for us to be able to argue that the ostensible possibility eludes verification. However, what we have may still be classed as a failure of meaning, in that there is a lack of definition of key terms when applied in the context envisaged. That, plus forms of incoherence close to, or actually involving contradiction, is the pattern which, I suggest, is most often to be met with when theological propositions are found wanting.

If at least a modicum of sense must be granted before questions of verification can be addressed, the lesson to be learned from a lack of verifiability will not be the positivist's, though that is not to say that there is nothing to learn from this failure. This topic is usefully pursued via a consideration of Wittgenstein's views on verifiability.

In his transitional period, Wittgenstein was firmly wedded to verificationism: 'The verification is not *one* token of the truth, it is *the* sense of the proposition' (1975: §166; cf. 1979a, *passim*); 'To show what sense a statement makes requires saying how it can be verified and what can be done with it' (1979b: 19). However, this uncompromising position eventually gave way to the weaker claim that an account of how a proposition is verified has the role only of a *contribution* to the grammar of that proposition. That is, our understanding of a proposition may be elucidated by explaining what findings, if any, would show it to be true, but questions of meaning are not exhausted by such considerations. In keeping with his contention that meaning is use, the emphasis shifts from condemning forms of words which the positivist would proscribe to asking how those words are going to be used. This stance is evident in the following passage from *Remarks on the Philosophy of Psychology* I:

366. We read in a story that someone had a dream and did not tell it to anyone. We don't ask how the author could learn it.—Don't we *understand* it, when Strachey makes surmises about what Queen Victoria may have seen in her mind's eye just before her death? Of course—but didn't people also *understand* the question how many souls there was room for on the point of a needle? That is to say: the question whether one understands this does not help us here; we must ask *what* we can do with such a sentence.—*That* we use the sentence is clear; *how* we use it is the question.

(1980: §366)

Granting understanding is granting meaning, but a positivist thesis could still lurk in the requirement that a use be specified. It is noticeable that Wittgenstein acknowledges a use or uses for much religious language, but it is precisely because these are invariably non-metaphysical that there is little comfort here for a traditional theist, who yearns for a use of assertoric utterances which in some way extends the range of fact-stating language. Indeed, I should have thought that the essentials of the positivist's position could be secured if we could justify his refusal to allow this extension (cf. Ayer 1959: 16). And, if that is right, it would seem that the further characterization of metaphysical propositions as meaningless need be no part of his main purpose, but an unnecessary distraction. His concern is, after all, with 'cognitive' or 'factual' meaning, so he can afford to be generous in his use of 'meaningful', so long as the domain of the factual does not outstrip that of the verifiable. Compare Hume's closing remarks in the *Enquiry*, where he dismisses any forms of reasoning that fall outside the categories of 'abstract reasoning concerning quantity or number' and 'experimental reasoning concerning matter of fact and existence' (1902: 165). This passage has been taken—by Ayer, for instance (1952: 31, 54)—to show Hume to be a precursor of positivism, but it is noteworthy that the offending forms are not dismissed as meaningless. None the less, given that they are thought by Hume to qualify as 'sophistry and illusion', there is little comfort here for the metaphysician.

The positivist has, then, a case against the theist if he can justifiably charge the latter with ascribing to his claims a use to which their metaphysical status does not entitle them; most notably, the kind of use proper to an empirical proposition. Here we may note that, while the contention that use is sufficient for meaning makes for a liberal position on what counts as meaningful, we do not find Wittgenstein offering us more than the empirical and the grammatical as defining the possible status of a given form of words. There are occasions when both are refused, as with avowals of present feelings or states of mind—'I'm fed up', 'I'm afraid'—but these exceptions are of no more help to the metaphysician than is the acknowledgement of performative utterances, such as 'Thank you' or 'Congratulations', as a species which escapes the true–false category. Far from regarding metaphysical propositions as a significant further category, Wittgenstein characterizes these as grammatical propositions masquerading as empirical—ostensible truths about the world which prove to be stipulations about the uses of words. Someone who says, 'A penny for your thoughts', clearly considers the question of what another is thinking to be empirical, suitably answered by an honest declaration from the person addressed. It is very much to the point to make the request, since although the response may be untruthful, in many circumstances there will be no reason not to take what is said at face value. A philosopher who holds that we can never tell what another is thinking appears to be saying that an empirical possibility is being denied us, but it is likely to emerge that for him, unlike most of mankind, nothing could conceivably *count* as finding out the thoughts of another.

As another illustration, consider how views concerning time may be mistakenly advanced as competing metaphysical hypotheses. So, on one natural approach, time is treated as a dimension introduced to accommodate change. We can allow that the swimming pool is both deep and shallow at the same time, since it can be deep at one end, shallow at the other. Symmetrically, we can allow that the pool is both deep and shallow in the same place—at the same end—since it can be deep and shallow at different times. However, we might also have reconciled the latter ascriptions by thinking of the pool as comprising not only spatial, but also temporal 'parts', one of which involves being deep, the other being shallow. Which approach is correct? There is surely no call to dismiss the familiar way of speaking, but so long as the temporal parts view can be coherently formulated, it gives us a variant way of speaking to be assessed in terms of, say, its utility for some purpose. It may be a rival at this level, but we are talking about alternative grammars, systems of concepts, not alternative theories. That bodies have temporal parts is not a hypothesis, empirical or otherwise. The complaint of the person who rejects this conception is not that his prolonged searches have failed to find such parts, nor is their advocate triumphantly going to disclose something that had been overlooked in his searches; rather, for the one party there is nothing to be dignified with the term 'part' in this connection; for the other, the term can be said to enjoy a legitimate extension of its standard use. What might be called the metaphysical approach, however, regards the alternatives as substantive views about the world, at most one of which is correct—theories about the nature of time in a way that makes a comparison with physical theory appropriate.

Does our repudiation of this approach rest on the supposition of a well-defined distinction between conceptual and empirical issues, or between analytic and synthetic propositions? If so, is it not relying on a distinction that has been thoroughly discredited, most notably by W. V. Quine? For Quine, an analytic proposition is one that is immune to revision, that is held to be true come what may (1961). An ascription of analyticity is accordingly akin to a prediction, and an unsafe one at that: we cannot be sure that our proposition will not be revised at some future date. However, why should the future history of a given form of words, *P*, concern us? We may be so using *P* that nothing is allowed to count against it, or we may not.

There can be a damaging lack of clarity if we have not decided what standing our words are to have, but we are not required to take a decision which we and others must stand by for all time. That enduring stance is required only for an enduring ascription of analyticity; a current attribution of that status is not dependent on its future continuation. Likewise with respect to the distinction between the conceptual or grammatical and the empirical.

A relevant lack of clarity may infect theological claims, which have often been criticized on the grounds that they are advanced as, in effect, empirical propositions, but not treated as subject to the laws of evidence appropriate to such status. Thus, a model for a verificationist critique of such claims took shape in the parable of the garden in John Wisdom's article 'Gods'. Two people return to their long-neglected garden, finding both signs of neglect and apparent signs of a gardener's attention. One of them insists against the other that there has indeed been a gardener, but, in the absence of any sightings of him, retreats to the view that he is invisible to mortal eyes. Evidence that a gardener does come and evidence to the contrary continue to accumulate, but eventually the gardener hypothesis ceases to be experimental, there being no difference in the expectations of the one who accepts and the one who rejects it: 'The one says "A gardener comes unseen and unheard. He is manifested only in his works with which we are all familiar", the other says "There is no gardener." ' (1944: 192).

This parable was used by Anthony Flew to illustrate his contention that theological propositions are liable to suffer 'death by a thousand qualifications'. The believer in God, like the believer in the gardener, will not accept anything as counting against his belief, but since there is nothing which this contradicts, nor is there anything which it affirms. His assertion of existence is not really an assertion at all (1955: 14–15). Wisdom presents the parallel as showing how an explanatory hypothesis, such as that of the existence of God, may start by being experimental and gradually become something quite different (1944: 191). Clearly, a hypothesis which aims to qualify as experimental invites criticism on verificationist grounds. However, it is not clear to what extent key theological propositions are so intended; nor, even, is it altogether clear what the logic is behind this style of criticism. Let us look further at this latter point.

Suppose that some unobservable entity is postulated as the cause of certain happenings. Although the conjectured cause is unobservable, it could be that the theory which postulates it is open to refutation, the cause being taken to bring about changes in certain specified conditions only.

If, the changes not being forthcoming, subsidiary hypotheses are introduced ad hoc, with nothing in their favour apart from their power to protect the theory from refutation, then we shall have a procedure which can be reckoned arbitrary, and which threatens to deprive the theory of content. In Wisdom's parable, retreat to the supposition that the gardener is invisible is a step in this direction, but if it were a demand of a physical theory that something it postulated could be known only by its effects, then this would not figure as an ad hoc hypothesis. On the contrary, it might be as absurd to speak of observability as it would be to speak of an atom as green and juicy. And that—a being known only through its effects—is how many would think of God.

Imagine we have a film of a gardener at work—turning over the soil, planting seeds, laying compost, watering plants, pruning trees, and so forth. Suppose now that we airbrush the gardener from our film, filling in the blanks where he had been with the background which he then occluded. What the gardener did would be left unchanged, and would constitute happenings crying out for explanation, an explanation which, it would seem, might conceivably deserve the description: postulating an invisible gardener. If we had to do with no more than the difference between the two possibilities just sketched, I imagine we should not feel that the hypothesis of such a gardener posed an impossible strain either on our comprehension or on our credulity. After all, if our invisible gardener can push a wheelbarrow, he could presumably make his presence felt by pushing us, when the evidence we should have of him would be comparable with what a blind person has of physical objects. Indeed, when the sense of touch is in question there need be no opposition between the notions of direct knowledge of an object and knowledge of it through its effects. One of the problems with the parable as recounted by Wisdom lies in the conflicting or partial character of the evidence, pointing as it does in opposed directions: there are signs of neglect but also signs of caring intervention. But the major difficulty with the theistic hypothesis is not that it postulates something that is not directly observable, but that what it postulates is at such a remove from the physical world, it is difficult to see how it might be said to bring about happenings within that domain. Compare poltergeist phenomena, where some have thought we have reason to acknowledge an invisible agent responsible for moving furniture about. There are clearly problems here, but the central consideration is that the strange phenomena surely direct us to look for an answer *within* the known world. Things, after all, are shifting about, so we want something that can push, pull, lift, and otherwise do what it takes to affect an object's position in space.

When a being, if it exists at all, exists or acts at a particular location, then the supposition of its existence or action will generate expectations which may be fulfilled or disappointed, and if nothing is allowed to count against the supposition, it could be considered vacuous. Some propositions about God may have to meet this challenge, but it is not clear that Wisdom's gardener provides a relevant model for dealing with a proposition affirming God's existence, rather than with a hypothesis about an action or intervention on God's part at a particular time, since this proposition may be held to be true of necessity, true however our world may be. If that is its standing, then of course nothing will count against it, just as nothing will count for a proposition that is logically false. It is of interest that, in the article cited, Wisdom vacillates between talking of God and talking of gods. It would seem that it is on the latter, which present problems similar to those posed by poltergeists, fairies, and leprechauns, that his remarks have most bearing.

However, there is no lack of theological assertions which invite confrontation with evidence. Take the claim that God answers our prayers. If, in an attempt to support this claim, a believer draws attention to occasions when what was prayed for comes about, but ignores those cases where it does not, can we not accuse him of being selective with respect to the evidence? Or suppose that, taking no chances, he holds that God will assuredly answer our prayers, though not necessarily in a way we should expect or, indeed, even understand. Kai Nielsen cites a particularly egregious example, due to E. L. Fackenheim, of this way out: 'Good fortune reveals the hand of God; bad fortune, if it is not a matter of just punishment, teaches that God's ways are unintelligible, not that there are no ways of God' (Fackenheim 1964: 55; Nielsen 1982: 143). If there were occasions on which it was evident that God had answered our prayers, then occasions when he seemingly has not could be admitted. The difficulty lies in the total lack of assured instances; when we are let down, we have *only* a range of stratagems for seeking to minimize the damage to God's standing as one who answers prayers. Likewise with the attempt to reconcile God's goodness with the incalculable suffering that has been endured by human beings and animals over the ages. And it is not because the ways of God are mysterious that the clear cases are lacking. Given the opacity of the claim that God, an immaterial spirit, acts upon the material world, it is difficult to see how there could *be* cases which gave proof of his agency.

To raise difficulties concerning God's intentions is to treat the relevant beliefs as akin to empirical beliefs about human beings, where questions of verification are pertinent. The objections may carry considerable weight, but to envisage the beliefs in this way is very much a matter of playing the believer at his own game. As has just been made plain, the deeper objection remains that we have no idea what it means to speak of God as intervening in the affairs of this world. True, the superficial approach may be thought to take us as far as we should wish. Thus, suppose that our objections are countered by saying that the disregard for the evidence shows only a failing on the part of the believers, not a failing in the beliefs themselves. In that case, we might argue, the appropriate conclusion, based on a more even-handed consideration of the evidence, is that the beliefs are simply false. And, indeed, it is hard to see how anyone could regard the pain and misery in this world as consistent with the existence of an all-powerful, all-knowing, and omni-benevolent deity. But this approach, and the conclusions, remain superficial, crediting the 'beliefs' with more significance than they merit. Or again, let us try to make out the best case possible for the efficacy of prayer. So, we suppose that a carefully conducted experiment reveals that when people suffering from 'incurable' illnesses are prayed for, a significant percentage of them make an unexpected recovery, while those in a control group, not prayed for, succumb to the illness in great numbers—neither group knowing that such an experiment is taking place. It is a reasonable hypothesis that *something* is at work that favours those prayed for, but the claim that a divine agency is responsible, rather than some as yet unknown natural cause, is a real contender as an explanation only if we can make sense of the implication that the relevant changes have been effected by a being that makes no physical contact with those who recover.

Verificationist criticisms may, then, be to the point, but without taking us to the heart of the matter, to the deeper incoherences that theological language harbours. We quoted earlier a passage where Wittgenstein grants sense to the question of how many souls there is room for on the point of a needle, and the following comments are in similar vein:

36. Certain considerations may lead us to say that 10^{10} souls fit into a cubic centimetre. But why do we nevertheless not say it? Because it is of no use. Because, while it does conjure up a picture, the picture is one with which we cannot go on to do anything.

(1978: 135)

On the one hand, if there is nothing we can do with what is said, little is being conceded in granting it sense, but in these and similar instances we may well feel that even that is to concede too much. How might we apportion souls, beings without spatial dimensions, to volumes of space? What grounds could we possibly have for speaking of a soul, or angel, as *on* a needle—so as *touching* it—rather than as hovering above it, or being a centimetre to one side? Given the apparent irreconcilability of the notions of being a soul and having a spatial location, Wittgenstein's accommodating view surely stretches tolerance to the limits.

This is, of course, an eccentric proposition, but difficulties of coherence and definition are readily found with more serious theological concepts and assertions. Someone who insists that God, though lacking eyes and ears, watches him incessantly and listens to his prayers, is clearly not using 'watch' or 'listen' in a sense we can recognize, so while the words may be individually meaningful and their combination grammatical, that is as far as meaningfulness goes: what we have is an unintelligible use of an intelligible form of words. God is not of this world, but that is not going to stop us speaking of him as if he were. It is not that we have a proposition which is meaningless because unverifiable, but we simply misuse the language, making an affirmation which, in the light of our understanding of the words, is totally unwarranted, an affirmation that makes no intelligible contact with reality. The positivist's diagnosis may be in error, but that does not make for a significant lessening of pressure on the theologian to clarify his pronouncements.

Some of the more incoherent of these pronouncements defy even grammar. For instance, it is claimed that 'if there is a God identified initially as a first cause, then *that* he is and *what* he is are one and the same reality' (J. J. Haldane in Smart and Haldane 1996: 147). But the different ways in which the phrases 'that God is' and 'what God is' may be completed show that any talk of the same reality is incoherent. That God is can be said to be true, but not what God is, whereas 'What God is is benevolent' makes sense, but not 'That God is is benevolent'. Similarly, if even more absurdly, the proposal that God is an ethical principle, namely, that value ought to come into existence, that he is the creatively ethical need that there should exist a good world, mismatches a supposed being, God—something which, without riding roughshod over the superficial grammar, we can at least describe as a creator—with something, a principle or proposition, which patently cannot be spoken of in this way (see Haldane ibid., 28; Leslie 1989: 167). These are among the more serious of the objections to theism, since they bear upon propositions which are thought to get to the heart of God's nature, to the extent that this is possible for human beings.

However, it would surely be wrong to say that 'God' is simply meaningless, on a par with a nonsense word. We can say much about its usage, even if the clearer aspects of that usage relate to what God is *not*—as Aquinas would be the first to agree (*Summa contra Gentiles*, I, 14, 30). The term is sufficiently meaningful for us to be able to say that it is understood differently in different systems of belief—in polytheism, monotheism, and pantheism, for instance—though the meaningfulness of 'God' at this level is consistent with the notion of God proving ultimately self-contradictory. Compare words such as 'heaven', 'hell', 'limbo' and 'purgatory'. The *literal* use of 'hell' is surely the theological one, not one derived by some figure of speech from a use in which a more familiar region is denominated. Even 'transubstantiation' is in some sense a meaningful term, and someone who does not know that a battle was waged over *homoousios* and *homoiousios* may be as ignorant of meaning as of history. Is it in place to speak of degrees of meaningfulness? The many unanswered questions about what 'God' means, together, perhaps, with inconsistent patterns of usage in its regard, stand in the way of reckoning it fully intelligible, but propositions in which 'God' figures are not to be dismissed as mere verbiage. On the other hand, it is not a matter of the sort of nonsense that we meet with in such forms as 'The mouse sought an injunction against the cat' or 'The bookcase has a guilty conscience', where none of the component words presents problems of intelligibility. With propositions in which 'God' figures we have a term which is the focus of just such a problem. Once more, however, the difficulties that arise before the question of possible verification is broached, being conceptual rather than epistemic obstacles to a coherent hypothesis.

Similar seemingly unresolvable problems arise with other terms relating to the otherworldly. Take 'angel' and 'devil'. These are familiar enough words of our language, and it would be hard to deny them all meaning, problematic though they may be. Interestingly enough, it is again their literal meaning that is the more problematic, not some use that is an extension thereof. We have no problem with a description of people as angels or devils. We can say *something* about angels—even naming their orders, as cherubim and seraphim—and while requests for further clarification are unlikely to get us far, perhaps the little we do have is enough to dismiss most of what is said about angels in a way that compares with finding an inconsistency, their distinctive angelic nature logically precluding the other characteristics, as of personality and a relation to the physical, which have been allotted to them. Certainly, we do not have to go as far as to deny all meaning to discern a tension between the idea of being an angel—an 'immaterial spirit'—and having the spatial location required to be on the point of a needle, or indeed to be a bearer of messages. Much of the difficulty with talk of God likewise derives from our insistence in making him in our likeness, and so attributing to him a mind, and even a personality—everything except the body needed to give it all sense.

The problem of meaning is sometimes overlooked by those who seek to make theistic hypotheses more acceptable by expanding the range of allowable *proofs*. Thus, it is acknowledged that a rigorously deductive demonstration proceeding from observed phenomena is powerless to establish such a hypothesis, and the regularities required to sustain an inductive proof are simply not there to draw upon. However, while other approaches, such as inference to the best explanation, cumulative case arguments, probabilistic reasoning, or locating the hypothesis in a coherent set of beliefs, may in general offer a broader range of possibilities, they do nothing to remove uncertainties in the meaning of the conclusions which they aim to support.

1.2 ANALOGY AND GOD'S ATTRIBUTES

It is commonly thought that what theological discourse requires is a suitable doctrine of analogy. Words used of God's creatures cannot be used in exactly the same sense when transferred to God, yet there must be some relation between the two uses, not mere equivocation. The presumption appears to be that we cannot introduce a word *ab initio* to apply to God, but must adapt our given non-theological vocabulary to that end. This may appear inescapable, but it is not clear that a word could not enjoy a theological use from the outset. That could conceivably be so with 'incorporeal', say, a term which, we may note, would appear to apply in a literal sense to God—though it is significant that it belongs in the category of negative predicates. We may also note that the use of a term which, like 'omnipotent' or 'omniscient', is not transferred from non-theological to theological contexts, none the less relies on an understanding of words which, like 'do' and 'know', have their home in the more mundane setting.

Two species of analogy have been thought of particular importance in this connection: analogy of proportionality and analogy of attribution.

Analogies of the first kind conform to the pattern, 'A is to B as C is to D'. Aristotle gives us the example 'As old age is to life, so is evening to day' (*Poetics*, 1457b), and the theological applications profess to see the relation between a term predicated of God and God's infinite nature mirror the relation between the same term predicated of man and the latter's finite nature. With analogy of attribution we have a comparison between a primary and a derivative use. This may take two forms. In the one case, a relation to a being to which the term applies in its primary use enters into the very meaning of the term in its derivative use, as 'healthy applied to animals comes into the definition of *healthy* as applied to medicine, which is called healthy as being the cause of health in the animal' (*Summa Theologiae*, I, Q. 13, Art. 6). In the other case, the description is transferred from, say, cause to effect, but we should not introduce a reference to the causal relation into the term's meaning when elaborating the derivative use. Examples here might be 'witty' or 'perceptive' as applied to a person, and in a derivative way, as applied to a person's remarks. Distinguishing the two cases may be difficult, but a variety of relations is possible in either, including those of cause, effect, sign, symptom, and manifestation. At all events, the theological applications seek in this pattern a justification for transferring to God descriptions used of his creation, usually on the grounds that God is causally responsible for the features described.

Analogy of proportionality has been considered inadequate to an elucidatory role on the grounds that, in its theological forms, it presents us with two 'unknowns'. It is said that God's goodness is to his nature as man's goodness is to man's nature, but that brings enlightenment only if we have some hold both on the divine goodness and the divine nature. The comparison does not serve to confer enlightenment. It might also be added that the clause, 'man's goodness is to man's nature', while less problematic than its theological counterpart, is itself far from clear, and it is correspondingly not clear what of value or significance we should have learned were this relation a basis for explaining 'God's goodness is to the divine nature'. A more perspicuous formulation might propose that, just as man is good in a way that is appropriate to his nature, so God is good in a way that is appropriate to his, but it remains uncertain how an under-standing of the former relation can throw light on the latter. However, this is just one example—and not necessarily one that we might wish to set much store by. A more relevant proportionality is given with: 'God is to the universe as a sculptor is to his sculpture'; or: 'God is to the universe as an artist is to his painting.' If either analogy is fitting, there will be at least something positive that can be said about the all-important relation of God to the world.

Before taking this further, we may note that consideration of non-theological examples suggests that a surprising amount can be based on the most exiguous information within this scheme. Take the analogy, 'Colour is to sight as sound is to hearing', and consider how this might be developed in tackling the question whether a person blind from birth could have a concept of colour. On narrow empiricist principles, this may appear an impossibility, but on these principles the blind would be bandying about words of which they had no understanding whatsoever, and, as the linguistic competence of those such as Helen Keller demonstrates, this is altogether too harsh. And it is not difficult to see how a degree of understanding could be attained by a blind person. Such a person will, after all, have some conception of a perceptual sense, and will appreciate that some senses require contact with the object perceived, while with others we may become apprised of objects at a distance. Sight, we may explain, is of the latter kind, so in this respect is like hearing rather than touch. The person may also come to appreciate that the information yielded by sight includes information concerning location, shape and size, properties of which he may well have some knowledge, and we can do something towards locating colour in our conceptual scheme by explaining its standing as a 'proper' object of vision: just as sounds can only be heard, smells only smelled, so colours can only be seen. Again, we may point out that colours have aesthetic qualities—they may, like sounds, be harmonious or discordant—and we can give an indication of the kind of information that colour can supply about coloured objects. Since none of this explanatory detail will put the blind person in a position to make firsthand judgements of colour, it can justly be said that one of the main aspects of possession of the concept is denied him. However, having a concept is not an all-or-none affair, but consists in a cluster of abilities, and the blind person may be in possession of enough of these for it to be quite unwarranted to say that he simply has no concept of colour.

With the example of sight and colour there is no doubting the intelligibility of the terms and their relations, and, while there may be a problem for the unsighted, there is no question of two unknowns as far as the sighted are concerned. This calls to mind I. M. Crombie's suggested appeal to authority in dealing with theological claims. Crombie considers that we can believe 'God made the world' to be true even though we have no conception of the reality which this reports, likening this circumstance to 'the way in which a man born blind can know it is true that green is a restful colour, though he has no conception of what green is, nor of what it is for one's eyes to find repose. That is, by some kind of authority' (1987: 175). A blind man could know on authority that the proposition 'Green is a restful colour' was true without even knowing what it meant, but to say that he could know that green is a restful colour while having *no* conception of what green is looks like a flat contradiction. Still, perhaps this does not affect Crombie's main point, namely, 'we have it on trustworthy authority that we shall not go religiously astray if we think of God as if he were a finite being of whom certain truths hold; we shall not go wrong in the matters with which religion deals if, with certain reservations, we put a finite being having certain properties into that gap in our understanding which constitutes the notion of the divine' (1987: 175).

So, apparently, the consequences of the religious belief are much the same as they would be if that belief had a more mundane interpretation, as with respect to a very powerful and wise person, let us say. However, the 'authority' would appear to enjoy an understanding which is beyond us, an understanding that enables him to say that we do not do a great injustice to the facts if we think in this way, yet it does not seem that it is a matter of a more privileged understanding of 'God made the world', since Crombie has admitted to grave doubts about the programme of removing human limitations from concepts normally used to speak about human beings, and claiming that something remains when this is done: 'I sympathize with those who say that when you take away the human limitations you take away everything of which we have any conception' (1987: 175). This does not appear to clarify the problem of meaning: if our words do not apply literally, or indeed intelligibly, when used by us, nor will they when used by another, and if the words are given a different interpretation, we shall no longer be dealing with the issue on which we sought enlightenment.

When we explain sight by drawing on a knowledge of other senses, and relate colour to sight by invoking an already understood relation between hearing and sound, the major unknown proves to be colour. 'Proportionality' is invoked in explaining colour, but the explanation of sight rests on a more direct comparison with other senses. If the pattern is to extend to God, we shall have to go beyond considerations of proportionality and appeal to a more direct comparison between God and, presumably, his creatures. Take 'God is to the universe as an artist is to his painting.' The comparison may be aimed at elucidating 'God', or the relation between God and the universe. Since, if the former is our aim, we are simply drawing attention to God's creative role, there is little to choose between this emphasis and a concern to elucidate the relation, and in this instance that relation is not one that can be thought immediately transferable from the more familiar case. On the contrary, given that God is thought of as an immaterial being outside space and time, the problem is to see how his production of the universe could usefully be compared with the artist's production of his painting. Hume makes the general point forcefully: 'But this method of reasoning [from analogy] can never have place with regard to a Being, so remote and incomprehensible, who bears much less analogy to any other being in the universe than the sun to a waxen taper' (1902: 146). Analogy of proportionality is thought unhelpful if it presents us with too many unknowns, but enough may be known for it to be clear that an analogy does not hold.

If the traditional doctrine of analogy offers any hope to theology, it will presumably be with respect to analogy of attribution, which may seek to provide the more direct comparison that we have seen to be necessary. This form exploits the consideration that what we may know of God we are obliged to learn from his effects, so offers the possibility of a firmer grounding in what is given in experience. True, it cannot be said that, if God is the ultimate cause of a creature's being F, that invariably warrants us in saying that he himself is F, even in some merely analogous sense of the term—think of descriptions such as 'hot and clammy'—but analogy of attribution need not be confined to this pattern. Our model might be the use of such terms as 'benevolent', 'merciful', and 'wise' as applied both to agents and to their acts: if an action can be taken as manifesting benevolence, mercy or wisdom, the ascription of benevolence, mercifulness or wisdom to its author is an immediate inference. Focusing on God's effects rather than on God is focusing on something we can describe without doing violence to our understanding of the language; the problem lies with the attribution of authorship, with the standing of the relevant happenings as brought about by God. A being's virtues do not exist just in the abstract, as it were, but they are made known in what that being does and says. If we could be confident that we were witnessing a divine action or hearing a divine voice, we might be able to pronounce without further ado on God's goodness or wisdom on that occasion, using these terms in a familiar way. It is the absence of anything by way of a clear manifestation of these virtues that makes for our difficulty, and that in the two ways already identified. First, the conception of God as at work in the world is problematic; second, the claim of his handiwork to be described in the superlatively positive terms called for—as testifying to a God of infinite benevolence, say—is also questionable.

In passing, depending on the conception of God invoked, the difficulties posed by the existence of pain and suffering may be joined by other problems with a moral dimension. Consider the belief that God will commit the souls of the damned to everlasting torture. If that belief is integral to a creed which also maintains that God has as much as a shred of goodness in his nature—let alone that he is infinitely good and merciful—we surely have in it a knockdown argument against that creed. Likewise, if less emphatically, with a religion which denies salvation to those who, through no fault of their own, have failed to undergo some baptismal rite. Again, what could we make of a religion which insisted that God is to be worshipped or adored? Here we may be inclined to lodge the following protest. If you are going to make your god in the image of man, you might at least filter out some of the less desirable human traits. God should be above any sort of attention-seeking behaviour, for instance, and an insistence on being told how unsurpassably wonderful one is does not rate highly. As Hume, in the figure of Philo, observed: 'It is an absurdity to believe that the Deity has human passions, and one of the lowest of human passions, a restless appetite for applause' (1947: 226). True, this objection assumes that God commands us to worship him in order to gratify some self-regarding desire on his part, when it could be that the point of singing God's praises was protective—to propitiate a God who could be angry or jealous, for instance—but this hardly shows God in a better light. It may be said that worship need amount to no more than showing God the respect due to a benefactor. In general, we could hardly quarrel with the desirability of showing respect, but this surely falls far short of worship. Moreover, the threat of the problem of evil persists, many people having endured a degree of suffering which makes it difficult to see how the being ultimately responsible for their wretched lives could be regarded as a benefactor.

Note that, difficult though it may be to conceive of a state of affairs which could be said to reveal God at work, it is no less difficult to make sense of moral attributions to him if we imagine there to be no physical universe, just an eternal unchanging inactive deity. What could the goodness, let alone the mercifulness, of such a being consist in? To take this further, the picture which dominates traditional western theology is that of God as an eternal, unchanging being for whom being just and merciful is a matter of being one in whom the universals justice and mercy are eternally present; however, since we are denied access to the divine nature, we have no adequate grasp of what these virtues amount to in their divine embodiment, and have to make do with analogy. My objection is not to an unexplained sense of 'merciful' as applied to God, but to the conception of God as merciful which presumes to understand this attribution in such a way as to divorce it from any action, if only hypothetical, on God's part—as if the quality of mercy were to be detected by some form of inspection, only an inspection which, in this instance, our inadequate powers prevent us from making. So, it is lamented that finite beings are incapable of knowing what mercifulness or justice are as they exist in God. That lament may be well placed if it is a confession of ignorance as to what God might, from his perspective, reckon a truly just or merciful act, but I do not know what these virtues are as they exist in my neighbour, let alone in God, since I do not know what it is for them to exist *in* my neighbour—though I have a good enough idea what it is for him to *be* just or merciful. This is not, as I see it, where the real difficulty lies, but that is to be found in the conception of God, an immaterial being, as a recognizable agent of change in the natural world. If sense could be made of such an engagement, to the point that we might identify happenings which testified to the virtue in question, the attribution of mercifulness would make as much sense as a description of what God was doing as exemplifying mercy—mercy as we understand this in actions having a merely human agency behind them. Analogy of attribution is not misplaced in this context; it is just that it rests on the notion of God as an agent interacting with the world, and this presents difficulties of intelligibility.

Similar points hold for non-moral attributes, such as omnipotence and omniscience. Omnipotence is not some species of introspectible trait, but a limitless *capacity* for action, and knowledge, whether limitless or otherwise, is analogous. Omniscience does not consist in the contemplation of an endless range of truths, but in an *ability* to advance every truth authoritatively, or to recognize any truth as such. Note, too, the complication which the doctrine of the divine simplicity introduces, a doctrine to the effect that there is no distinction in God between his various attributes, as, say, of timelessness, omniscience and infinite justice, and, indeed, no distinction between these attributes and God himself. Once more, for these to be the same is not for something 'in' God to be one, but nor does it appear to make sense to say that being timeless and being infinitely just could be the same for God any more than they could for any other being. Peter Geach has attempted to clarify this puzzling doctrine by drawing on an analogy with mathematical functions:

"The square of—" and "the double of—" signify two quite different functions, but for the argument 2 these two functions both take the number 4 as their value. Similarly, "the wisdom of—" and "the power of—" signify different forms, but the individualizations of these forms in God's case are not distinct from one another; nor is either distinct from God, just as the number 1 is in no way distinct from its own square.

(Anscombe and Geach 1961: 122)

However, this comparison presumes a uniformity in the behaviour of 'God' and phrases designating his attributes which is not to be had. 'God's wisdom is unsurpassable' would appear to be simply a stylistic variant of 'God is unsurpassably wise', whence it is unclear how 'the wisdom of God' could be a phrase which turns out to have God as its reference. So long as this way of speaking is maintained the difficulty persists, even if it is held, as with Aquinas (*Summa Theologiae*, I, Q. 3), that the doctrine of divine simplicity is intended to tell us what God is not—a being with distinguishable properties—rather than what he is. Note, too, that this approach cannot even begin to handle such incongruous identities as 'God is not only true, He is truth itself' (*Summa contra Gentiles*, I, Q. 61).

Once more, however, the theist need not adopt the conceptions which give rise to these difficulties. In particular, he is not obliged to agree that what has to be established is identity of *reference* for the relevant predicates. Consider the relation between omnipotence and omniscience. A being who can do anything whatsoever, provided only that it is not ruled out by logic, can give a correct answer to any question put to him, so there is nothing he does not know. He is thus omniscient. Similarly, there is an immediate inference from a being's perfection to either of these attributes, and perhaps also to his timelessness and immutability. If our chain of implications can be placed in a circular formation, we shall have every attribute of God entailing every other, which is as good an interpretation of mutual identity among attributes as one could wish for. Whether the circle can be closed is, of course, an issue of some complexity, and there is some doubt as to whether certain of the divine attributes are even mutually consistent, but at least the way in which the problem is formulated need not be incoherent.

I.3 OTHER MINDS AND RELIGIOUS EXPERIENCE

It has been claimed that belief in God's existence is evidentially on a par with belief in other minds: 'I conclude that belief in other minds and belief in God are in the same epistemological boat; hence if either is rational, so is the other. But obviously the former *is* rational; so, therefore, is the latter' (Plantinga 1967: viii). It would be surprising if this claim could be sustained, since, given that God is supposed to have desires and intentions, to be capable of love and anger, he thereby presents us with a variant of the problem of other minds in addition to the difficulties which his transcendence brings. Think of the problem of descrying a good will behind the suffering that men and animals endure. For anyone attracted by this comparison, the evidence to focus on would be that in which God is, as it were, as close to his effects as possible; not like the deist's God who, having got the universe under way, then leaves it to its own devices, but where his continuing presence might be discerned in Nature. However, it is noticeable that there is nothing here that plays the role of a *criterion* which human behaviour offers in respect of other minds. The 'laws of evidence' into which this notion enters may suffer from an indeterminacy not found in more favoured areas, but this does not stand in the way of an overwhelming presumption that, in appropriate circumstances, a person is upset, disappointed, angry, or bored. There is nothing approaching this weight of evidence in the theological case.

The topic of other minds gives us the opportunity to reinforce an earlier point. It was suggested that, without endorsing the verification principle, we might none the less insist that certain uses of language make verificationist demands. That this is Wittgenstein's position emerges in his treatment of psychological concepts, as when, in *Last Writings* II, he writes:

Someone groans under anaesthesia or in sleep. I am asked "Is he in pain?" I shrug my shoulders or say "I don't know whether he's in pain". Sometimes I acknowledge something as a criterion for it, but sometimes I don't.

Well, do I mean nothing by this? Oh yes: I am making a move in an existing game. But this game wouldn't exist if there weren't criteria in other cases.

Something turns out to be pain or pretence. And that is essential to the concepts 'pain' and 'pretence', even if it is not evident in every single one of their applications.

(1992: 57)

If nothing ever turned out to be pain or pretence, if there were no criteria for their occurrence, the use we make of the relevant words would not be possible. Compare 'The game we play with the word "toothache" entirely depends on there being a behaviour which we call the expression of toothache' (1968: 290). Something can be recognized as a sign or evidence for a mental state only if there is a more direct proof of that state—very much part of a verificationist evidential framework, but again it can be said that the game we play with the relevant concepts, rather than an across-the-board requirement of verifiability, is what makes this demand. So, we come to regard a shifty look, along with various forms of body language—covering one's mouth with one's hand, for instance—as signs that a person is being untruthful, but we could not ascribe them that status unless we had found them to be associated with untruthfulness. And, indeed, there are occasions when the liar's guilt is undeniable. So, two points of relevance to our concerns. First, other minds are not impenetrable to a degree that might give comfort to those seeking to show that our knowledge of God is no worse. Second, finding fault with the verification principle does not mean that an insistence on verifiability is always misplaced, but any attempt to liken theological propositions to empirical propositions risks falling foul of this demand.

What of arguments from religious experience, which may be held to exploit empirical considerations? Criticism here often highlights the unshared character of the experience. Different people may hear ostensibly non-human voices, but since there is no significant convergence— no reports of identical messages received—the experience is thought ultimately explicable in terms of something peculiar to the given individual's make-up, or to such factors as drugs, oxygen deprivation, and so forth, rather than one that obliges us to look heavenwards. This does not strike me as the most useful focus, but is reminiscent of Hume's discussion of miracles, where the attention given to the question of the credibility of witnesses tends to distract us from the principal issue: supposing there to be no doubt about the empirical facts concerning honesty, reliability, and so forth, where do matters stand with the non-empirical issues? Or, indeed, suppose that we ourselves witness the relevant events, so do not have to rely upon testimony. It is much more fruitful to entertain the strongest possible case in these terms—one, that is, where doubts as to testimony are quite unreal, or cannot even arise—and consider what we might then have to acknowledge by way of happenings out of the ordinary. Hume's approach is indeed curious: as if he thought the notion of a miracle sufficiently transparent that the hypothesis of a miraculous occurrence would be a real possibility if the relevant testimony could not be faulted. Similarly with respect to the unshared character of an experience. Some people are said to be able to hear radio signals as a result of chemicals in their teeth behaving like the crystal in a crystal set and rectifying the signal. Even if the source of the signal could not be traced, and if the individual were unique in having this experience, the content of the messages—full news summaries, complete symphonies— would surely be strong evidence of an external origin. What would again remain problematic is the identification of the originator of a message as divine. However awesome or overwhelming the experience, however strong the sense of another being's presence, there is surely nothing in such an experience that obliges us to look beyond the natural world for its source. There are so many intermediate possibilities, so much at a purely naturalistic level that is consistent with the individual's experience, and such a problem in making sense of a divine origin, this latter again struggles to achieve recognition as even a coherent possibility, and appealing to a religious dimension of the experience does not lessen the difficulties involved in the attempt to explain it in this way.

It is perhaps not too much of an over-simplification to conclude that theological language, in so far as it merits the title 'meaningless', does so essentially through taking words whose meaning we should explain by reference to familiar items of our experience—notably human beings— using them in a way that does not respect the conditions in terms of which we understand them, and failing to explain how their extended use is to be justified. Either that, or we have to do with a contradiction, explicit or implicit. To the extent that this gives an accurate diagnosis, it is vain to hope that theological discourse can be rescued by finding deficiencies in a positivist account of meaning. Contradictory character is, of course, an incapacitating defect, but it is important to stress that a failure in definition is more devastating than a failure to be verifiable. This emerged when we were considering the suggestion that everything might be expanding uniformly. While being beyond the limits of the observable is something we may be able to make sense of—there can, after all, be good physical reasons why this should be so—it does not matter how fruitful a physical theory may be, if its application is not defined in certain cases, it simply makes no sense to speak of it as being true in those cases.

Note that to treat certain phenomena as evidence for global expansion presupposes an understanding of what such expansion would be; there is a lacuna at this point which it takes more than an *empirical* relation—as provided by an indirect ground—to fill. Again, we are not being stubbornly verificationist, but the point concerns definition rather than knowability. Likewise with respect to the supernatural. Supposedly indirect evidence for a theological proposition carries no probative weight so long as questions of meaning have not been resolved.

It was suggested that a theological hypothesis which purports to be experimental might thereby expose itself to difficulties centring on verification. Claims that God answers our prayers, for instance, or that he has ordered Nature in accord with his infinite goodness, appear to have observable consequences, however ill defined. In some cases, as the problem of evil testifies, theological claims fare pretty poorly as experimental hypotheses, but in others the difficulties are ones that mirror incontrovertibly real difficulties. Thus, it must be allowed that in some circumstances an explanatory conjecture may remain a genuine possibility despite wide variations in behaviour. This is not unknown in the realm of human action, where we may be able to hold to a claim that an agent is acting with a certain intention, since the action ostensibly in pursuit of some goal may, while counter-productive or otherwise unexpected, be put down to differences in the agent's beliefs as to what will lead to the desired end. What appears as neglect of a garden could conceivably be part of a plan which ultimately resulted in a better garden but which required an intermediate period of disorder. However, in the theological case there are forever in the background problems, not merely of evidence, but of the intelligibility of the conclusion to which the evidence is held to point. There may be no final challenge from verificationism, but no lessening of the pressure to show that apparent nonsense is only seemingly such.

It might reasonably be said that, logically rather than historically, logical positivism has not made much difference to theology—a somewhat surprising conclusion, given that the positivist has been viewed by many a theologian as his major twentieth-century enemy. The positivist was right to insist that questions of truth and falsity in this domain are premature, that questions of meaning have first to be clarified. We may also credit him with drawing attention to the theologian's misguided propensity to treat theological propositions as if they were empirical, to misappropriate notions of evidence, confirmation, probability, and so forth, but this is not to say that the positivist's account of what makes for nonsense in the very foundations of theology is correct. The failures, which are met with before any questions of verification can be broached, are such that no doctrinaire approach to meaning is needed to expose them.

2

God and Explanation

The gods of the ancient Greeks could be described in largely down-to-earth terms, sufficiently down-to-earth for their existence to be an empirical hypothesis, and a hypothesis for which the evidence was less than compelling. Since the Christian God is thought of as a supra-sensible being, the supposition of his existence does not risk proving an empirically gratuitous hypothesis, but this gain is more than balanced by the problems of meaning that transcendence generates. It is not just that something unobservable is postulated; so remote is God from the physical world, we are hard-pressed to understand how he might bear any relation to that domain, whether of creation or of intervention. The consequent difficulty of invoking God in any kind of explanatory role will now be considered with respect to the possibility of miracles, along with other phenomena thought to testify to divine agency.

2.1 MIRACLES AND DESIGN

It is often held that, to be a miracle, a happening must constitute a violation of some natural law. If it is enough, for such violation, that we should have an exception to a well-founded generalization—water never turns into wine, people never rise from the dead—then this is acceptable, and it is also true that, were anything with a claim to the description 'miraculous' to occur, there would have to be a departure from any naturalistically explicable pattern of events. However, this is not so much a matter of familiar conditions now giving rise to an extraordinary outcome, since a further, extraordinary, factor—the intervention of a supernatural agent—is supposed all-important in producing the happening on this exceptional occasion. It is accordingly more a matter of natural laws not being applicable in the circumstances, since they have nothing to say about the enlarged set of conditions. A 'uniform experience' against the violation of a law need not mean a 'uniform experience' against a naturalistically inexplicable event. Rather than adopt a Humean definition, with its requirement that a law be transgressed, we might follow Aquinas: 'Things that are divinely accomplished, apart from the generally established order in things, are customarily called *miracles*' (*Summa contra Gentiles*, III, 101). If God had carried out any of his threats against the Israelites, then, on this definition, what he did would have counted as a miracle even if, as with a plague, there had been many precedents. Humean scepticism about testimony might well appear misplaced in such a case, since it would not be the reported happening that was in doubt, only its causation.

Another misconception concerns the destruction of miraculous character allegedly wrought by repetition. Surely, if God can work a miracle once, he can work it many times. There are *descriptions*, as 'last in series', which are determined as appropriate by subsequent happenings, but causation is not thus determinable. If some event could qualify as a miracle, subject only to remaining unique, that would not tell you anything about the causation of the episode on any of the occasions of its occurrence; it would simply tell you something, of no great interest, concerning the proposed usage of 'miracle'. True, to the extent that an event recurs, that event will not be out of the ordinary, but it could still be extraordinary in its causation, the crucial consideration. It may be that there is some confusion as to just what is to be reckoned out of the ordinary, or perhaps that a regularity account of causation is in the background, frequency of occurrence being taken to be sufficient to establish a natural law. However, no explanation is given with mere regularity, but it has to be a matter of a regular *causal* relation, and if God's agency features in such a relation, then what is regular is a miraculous intervention.

Is the hypothesis of a miracle intelligible? Suppose we are witness to an extraordinary happening in circumstances which give no reason to doubt that we have observed what we claim. So, a person who has lost a leg bathes in the waters at Lourdes, whereupon the limb regenerates before our eyes. If all the expert testimony, reinforced by filmed records and other checks, offers unconditional support to this account, are we not forced to treat the hypothesis of a miraculous cure as at least a possible explanation for what we have observed?

It is no doubt rational to look for a weak point in the seemingly incontrovertible evidence and testimony in such cases, but insistence that there had been fraud or the like could become increasingly difficult to sustain if the evidence mounted up without the remotest indication of error or deceit. And, after all, it is only being suggested that a miracle has to be acknowledged as a *possibility*. How could this little be dismissed?

Modest though the claim may appear, however, there is something of substance in the contention that, when all naturalistic forms of explanation are found wanting, we can look to a supernatural agency for the explanation of a remarkable event. To concede as much as a possibility in this respect is to take a substantive step. Not just anything will count as an explanation. Our familiar explanations for the changes we observe invoke a range of chemical, electrical, and other physical phenomena. No doubt varying greatly in kind, but anything which earns the title of *cause* in producing such changes will have to be capable of standing in one of certain identifiable relations to the body affected. We can no doubt envisage extensions of the familiar relations, extensions which may take us even further away from the ordinary than does our invisible gardener, but if we are presented with *nothing* we could recognize as an agent interacting with, for instance, the limb being transformed, how could we possibly claim to have even the beginnings of an explanation? The event to be explained may be truly remarkable, quite without precedent in human experience, but then a lasting explanation which appeals to the supernatural is equally without precedent. After all, the division of cells is familiar enough—that is how the limb developed in the first place—and not such that a proportionate explanation might be expected to invoke nonphysical forces. And even if we could make sense of such forces, what could give us grounds for an extension to the utmost possible extreme, as furnished by God, a being to whom the very existence of the universe is supposedly due? How could postulating an infinite power be a more acceptable hypothesis than supposing an out-of-the-way but highly knowledgeable worldly agent capable of exploiting properties of matter?

We may well have to broaden our conception of what this universe contains; why should there not be many species of being more intelligent than us, some of whom make their presence felt locally from time to time? However, such a concession leaves us within the physical universe. The difficulty with a supernatural agent is that it requires one foot in both domains, so to speak. To qualify as supernatural it must be distanced from any spatio-temporal character which would place it in our world, but to make sense to us as explanatory of changes therein it must be sufficiently concrete to interact with material bodies, and the more convincingly a case is made for the former status, the greater the difficulties put in the way of the latter. Grant that it has a physical dimension, and there is the risk that what appeared to be a miraculous cause will become a familiar and more or less comprehensible denizen of the natural world. Rule that out as a possibility and we appear to have nothing which would qualify as a potential perpetrator of terrestrial change. The regeneration of a limb immersed in water cries out for explanation, so if all the usual possibilities are exhausted, it seems only rational to look in less well-charted directions. However, an unshakeable belief that there must be an explanation does not ensure that the proposed supernatural hypothesis genuinely counts as one, that in calling something a miracle we are doing anything more than attaching a label inscribed 'Awaiting Explanation'.

But if the natural sciences offer no explanation of some extraordinary happening, can we not be warranted in looking beyond the physical by invoking considerations concerning the specific kind of phenomenon and the context in which it occurred, as when religious significance can be ascribed to virgin births, stigmata, deliverance from imminent danger and cures of illnesses? But such considerations are of no assistance at the point that concerns us; they do not advance our understanding of *how* things could come about in the way claimed. To claim that God said, 'Let there be light', leaves us not one jot the wiser as to how light came about. Likewise, being told that God cured an illness or parted the waves of the Red Sea gives us no inkling as to how the transformation was effected or what 'curing' and 'parting' might mean when stripped of the implications that commonly give them sense. 'God parted the sea' may seem a minor elaboration of 'The sea parted', but the gulf between the two is immeasurable.

Compare attempts at proving the existence of God by appeal to the apparent design confronting us on all sides. It may seem remarkable that, before Darwin had devised his theory of evolution by natural selection, it should have been supposed that anything less than a supreme intelligence could have been responsible for the diverse life forms found on this planet, given the staggering complexity involved, the extraordinary adaptation of the senses and other organs of men and animals to the roles which they perform in their lives, to the various ends serving the creatures' well-being. Some dissent from the view that this order was ordained solely for man's benefit could be expected, but that it should be ordained, and not just pure chance, understandably struck many as evident, as in this passage from Cicero's *De Natura Deorum*:

Who would regard a human being as worthy of the name, if upon observing the fixed movements of heaven, the prescribed dispositions of the stars, and the conjunction and interrelation of all of creation he denied the existence of rationality in all these, and claimed that chance was responsible for works created with a degree of wisdom such as our own wisdom fails totally to comprehend?

(1997: 82)

Even a thinker as sceptical as Voltaire found the inference to a cosmic designer difficult to resist, and it is accordingly of interest that some— Hume, for instance—considered the evidence to fall short of what is required for the theist's conclusion. Hume was insistent that any inferred cause should be proportioned to the known effect, that, if the universe shows a particular degree of goodness or wisdom, no more than a degree of these perfections adapted to the effect may be inferred (1902: 144–5). But even with this restriction, and even when there appears to be no alternative to this reasoning, such inferences do not take us far towards a final explanation: if we are impressed and baffled by the characteristics of animate beings, how much more impressive, baffling, and in need of explanation will we find the nature of any being possessed of the attributes needed to design and create such beings? This is not to say that there is no such being—and Hume appears to have subscribed to an attenuated form of deism—but postulating a divine architect simply adds to, rather than solves, the problem: where before we had the creatures in the natural world crying out for explanation, now we have augmented the problematic totality with one further being, we know not what, which surpasses all these in the problems it poses (cf. Hume 1947: 160–4). With human beings we have some understanding of the characteristics and capacities in which intelligence and creativity are grounded, and some inkling of how these might have come about. With God these are just two of his traits concerning which we are told: you cannot ask for any further explanation of the divine attribute; that God is pure mind or spirit is thought enough to show that, in his case, such attributes need no explanation.

In retrospect, the postulation of a cosmic designer can be seen as a highly primitive form of explanation. Although it speaks of a God, it cannot really see beyond the pattern of explanation which applies at a familiar human level. Indeed, it is of a piece with attempts more generally to mould God in man's likeness, and is not to be excused through its invocation of *mind*, as though this somehow took us out of the natural order. The evolutionary alternative—appeal to random mutations together with the selection of features having adaptive utility—may not be without difficulties, but it has at least the merit of breaking out of the circle in which the argument from design is trapped, pointing to a genuine form of explanation rather than simply repeating the problematic pattern, but now referred to an incomprehensible domain. Once more, then, the pressure to find an explanation should not lead us to accept uncritically just any hypothesis having a superficial claim to provide an answer. The status of explanation is one that has to be earned. The supposition that each biological species originated in a special act of divine creation is hardly calculated to invite this accolade, and while the argument from 'fine tuning'—the form which the design argument has taken in recent times—is of greater sophistication, there is no real progress if this, too, is linked to the conception of an all-powerful and all-knowing being modelled on man.

2.2   FINE TUNING

However, if our concern is with why the universe is as it is, then, whether or not they can be invested with theological significance, considerations relating to 'fine tuning' cannot be ignored. If the values of certain basic physical constants, such as Planck's constant, had been even infinitesimally different from their actual values, a universe hospitable to life would not have been possible. Indeed, if the rate of expansion of the universe after the Big Bang had varied more than one part in 10^{55}, then the universe would have either collapsed or expanded so quickly as to render the formation of galaxies, and hence our solar system and planet, impossible. Surely this bespeaks the guiding hand of a creator concerned to foster intelligent life? Some have attempted to defuse the mystery which this poses by appeal to the 'anthropic principle', which states that 'what we can expect to observe must be restricted by the conditions necessary for our presence as observers' (Carter 1974: 291). How could we fail to find ourselves in a world which had what was required for us to exist? The principle is indeed correct, but not the basis for any substantive conclusions, though it may underlie a useful cautionary precept. Thus, as an application of the principle, John Barrow and Frank Tipler note that 'our observations are biased towards finding a disproportionately large fraction of very bright galaxies compared to the true state of affairs' (1986: 2). The relevant precept might take the form: limitations in our observational powers and situation may result in the acquisition of data which are not truly representative, and we should be advised to take this into account when extrapolating from such findings.

To the question why the universe is the age it is, the anthropic principle yields the answer: because it must be at least this old to allow for the evolution of beings capable of asking such questions. But not every true proposition which furnishes an adequate basis for inferring that such and such is so provides a reason *why* it is so. The kettle is whistling, so the water in it is boiling. The whistling gives us a reason for believing that the water is boiling, but it does not explain why it is, how the boiling came about. The fact that we are here has far-reaching implications for the age and size of the universe, and enables us to place constraints on the possible values of key physical constants, but we have still to explain why the universe is as it is in these as in other respects, where the question is one as to how the universe *came* to be as it is. Statements, or applications, of the principle are often unclear as to whether a reason for believing or a reason for being is at issue. Thus, Stephen Hawking declares that 'the reason why the big bang occurred about ten thousand million years ago is that the universe must be old enough so that some stars will have completed their evolution to produce elements like oxygen and carbon, out of which we are made' (2001: 86). The reason given is not a reason why the Big Bang occurred when it did, but a reason for concluding or believing that it occurred then. One would hope that the latter is what is intended, but other applications of the principle are more difficult to defend, as with the following from Barrow and Tipler: 'Many observations of the natural world, although remarkable *a priori*, can be seen in this light as inevitable consequences of our own existence' (1986: 219). Similarly, '. . . the isotropy of the universe and our existence are both results of the fact that the Universe is expanding at just about the critical rate. Since we could not observe the universe to be different if we were not here, one can say, in a sense, that the isotropy of the Universe is a consequence of our existence' (Collins and Hawking 1973: 317). It is doubtful whether 'in a sense' can rescue this conclusion.

Again, we can readily agree that it is not in the least surprising that we find conditions suitable for life to be satisfied, yet still hold that it is surprising that such conditions should have been satisfied. There is no inconsistency, since the background assumptions are different. Given that we exist, it is in no way surprising that we find the conditions satisfied, since this is a necessary condition for us to exist, and to find anything. But that there should have been the conditions which made life possible generally, and ours in particular, may remain a matter for surprise. To argue that life or consciousness is *inevitable*, since there have to be sentient beings if the world is to be observed, adds a further modal fallacy to the argument: there could not, logically, have been observations without observers, but that is not to say that observers could not but have been.

This last argument may represent an application of the 'strong' anthropic principle, in contrast to the 'weak' version which we have been considering. According to the strong principle, 'The Universe must have those properties which allow life to develop within it at some stage in its history' (Barrow and Tipler 1986: 21). Here, too, there is an ambiguity. If it is simply the presence of life that provides the basis for the inference to the properties which allow life to develop, we have a repetition of the trivial principle: if *A* is necessary for *B*, then if *B* is true, so too is *A*. If, however, it is being maintained that the universe could not but have had those properties, we have a substantive claim. This claim could be true, but even then it would be difficult to argue that it was *because* they allowed life to develop that the properties in question had to be possessed by the universe—rather than that the properties were somehow fundamentally bound up with character as physical.

Philosophers and physicists are nowadays disposed to think of a universe as a determinate species of thing, something of which there may be many. This is in contrast to an older tradition which was less hospitable towards the view that there might be even a single additional universe (see Aquinas, *Summa Theologiae*, I, Q. 47, Art. 3). Roughly speaking, the older view acknowledged *the* universe, as comprising everything there is, or everything physical, but had no use for *a* universe, as a kind of thing or system of things. A common response to the challenge posed by fine tuning exploits the modern conception. Supposing that numerous universes have existed and will exist, a super-abundance of worlds in which the multitude of possible values of fundamental constants could have been realized many times over, it is then not contrary to chance that the values suited to the emergence of life should have obtained in at least one universe, and it is in one such that we happen to find ourselves. It is, again, no objection to this to protest that it is then quite remarkable that we should find ourselves in this exceptionally favoured universe. That observation would be to the point if it were a matter of intelligent life setting off in search of a universe in which it might flourish and being fortunate enough to chance upon this propitious, but rare, environment, when, of course, we are the *outcome* of conditions favourable to life, not antecedent to them; what would be remarkable—remarkable to the point of absurdity—would be to find ourselves in a universe not of this kind.

However, there is a difficulty in the ad hoc character of the 'multiverse' response: we have no reason to suppose that there are, or have been, *any* other universes, the same or different from ours. Fashionable though it may be, to postulate even one further universe is to take an enormous step. Postulating a million million universes, or whatever is needed to raise to an acceptable level the likelihood of this universe coming about, looks to be an expedient of unparalleled desperation. Merely possible worlds can be postulated at no cost whatsoever—we have only logic to answer to, not reality—but aleph-zero possible worlds are as nothing when set against one actual universe, however exiguous. Furthermore, talk of *a* universe will require that the system of things conjectured be unified in some way, most naturally through membership in a common spatio-temporal reference frame. So, for instance, two bodies may be deemed to be in the same universe if and only if it is possible to establish some form of connectedness in space and/or time, however attenuated, between them. As we shall see, this requirement makes it difficult to speak of another universe as existing *now*, or being otherwise temporally located, which may be an embarrassment if it is required that a multitude of worlds be, or have been, realized.

However, we do not face the same difficulty if we can speak in terms of successive phases in the history of a single universe, namely, ours. And it need not be an ad hoc suggestion to suppose that there have been untold preceding eras when different values reigned, since it could conceivably be demonstrated how phases in which other values had been realized would, through their instability, have been superseded by phases in which different values held, this evolutionary process culminating in the current universe. We shall return to this way of reasoning shortly. Note that it is not necessarily true to say that, given any sufficiently long period, any genuine possibility will eventually be realized; not necessarily true that 'When there is an infinite time to wait then *anything* that can happen, eventually *will* happen' (Barrow 2000: 317)—a consideration sometimes held to guarantee the existence of a multiplicity of universes. A device could generate natural numbers for as long as you wish without generating any odd numbers, the even numbers being by themselves sufficiently numerous to sustain the endless possibilities required. Again, it may be possible to accommodate a large number of variations in spatial terms. So, it has been suggested that, if there are different vacuums, different domains where different amounts of inflation have occurred, then the constants which measure the strengths and properties of the forces of Nature may have been variously determined elsewhere (Barrow 2000: 265).

I have suggested that, while it is no matter for surprise that we *find* conditions suitable for life to be satisfied, it may be a matter for surprise that the conditions should have been as they are. Similarly, whether or not the supposition of other universes makes sense, there is still the question as to how our universe came to have the laws it has. If the many-worlds hypothesis is coherent, we can perhaps expect *some* universe to be fine-tuned for life, but the legitimacy of that consideration, or even its inescapability, does not furnish us with an explanation of how a universe that is in fact fine-tuned comes to be of that character. Postulate as many universes as you wish, you will not thereby do away with the need for such an explanation with respect to our universe. Indeed, it is not clear that the *actual* existence of many universes does anything more to make the life-favouring conditions of this universe less surprising than would their merely *possible* existence. Suppose we have a million pieces of paper with a different number, ranging from 1 to 1,000,000, inscribed on each. The chance that an arbitrarily selected piece of paper bears the number 601,327 is just the same as if there were only a single piece of paper on which an arbitrary selection from the numbers 1 to 1,000,000 had been inscribed.

The claim that there is, in the present context, some reason to accede to a plurality of universes, would appear to be fatally undermined by this last consideration. However, there is an important underlying assumption that is still to be addressed. The belief that a multitude of universes is called for is based on the supposition that, by dint of its provision of conditions in which living things can come to be, our universe is somehow special. This supposition is in need of scrutiny. Suppose that dealing a thoroughly shuffled pack of cards produces all the suits in order. The odds against this happening are astronomical, and we should surely insist that the pattern cries out for explanation; yet another distribution, though equally improbable, is not perceived to make the same explanatory demand. Why not? The two distributions are indeed on a par, but what needs explaining is a certain *match*: why it is that a previously specified or familiar ordering— whether it be 'regular' or 'irregular'—has been reproduced. Suppose someone has a game which gives a special place to an ordering which we find of no significance. If the cards were dealt in this order it would not strike us as in the least remarkable, yet for the person to whom the order meant something it would demand an explanation.

Consider now some physical constant whose exact value is crucial for the emergence of life, say the gravitational constant N. Once more it may be argued that the possible values for N are in fact greatly restricted: since we are here to raise the question, they must be confined to those which allow life to come about in the universe. Yes, because there is life we know that the actual value is thus restricted, but it does not follow that it is impossible that the value *should have been* outside this range—when, of course, there would have been no life. If we had plucked a value for N out of the air at random, it would be extraordinary if it were found to match its actual value, but that N has the value it in fact has is no more extraordinary than if it had had some other. Whatever possible universe one might contemplate, it can be considered just as improbable that it should exist as should our own. But, it will be objected, N's having the value it has has enormous consequences for life. True, but other values will have other consequences; it is just that this consequence is of particular concern to us. Consider possible universes $U_1, \ldots, U_n, \ldots$, in each of which N has a different value which, for each U_i, makes for some distinctive feature F_i, that is, some feature not associated with a significant number of other values of N. Then it is not in the least remarkable that U_i has the feature F_i, and this holds if U_i is our universe and F_i is the feature of making life possible. That is, that there should be life in our universe is no more remarkable than the fact that N has its actual value, and that is no more remarkable than any other value would have been. If the range of possible values of N is truly as great as is alleged, then it would be remarkable if we were to encounter another universe in which N had the same value as here, but there is nothing more remarkable about our universe's having that value than there is of any universe's having whatever value it has. But it does not require the actual existence of other universes for this point to be valid.

It may be argued, as in Schlesinger (1988: 124–38), that this argument does not do justice to the rarity of a universe which is capable of sustaining life. That a given physical constant should have the value it has is no more remarkable than the possession of any other value would be, but we are talking not of one but of a whole series of parameters, each of which can have only a narrow range of values if life is to come about. The chances that *all* should have been as they are are infinitesimal. However, the same point can be made. Another selection of values would have given rise to a universe which, we may suppose, would have been distinctive in some other way. It is just that, in all probability, it would be a way which did not hold the same significance for us as does the existence of living things.

A person finds the arrangement of cards remarkable because it is one that is already familiar, which has special significance for him. We find it remarkable that the conditions for life are satisfied in our universe, because we are already intimately familiar with life. We think there is a contrary-to-chance match, but what we are familiar with is a consequence of these fundamental conditions. No one has given an advance characterization of a universe and then found that, contrary to chance, this universe conforms to the characterization, the characterization invoked being one *derived* from the given universe. But if no order has been initially specified to which things are found inexplicably to correspond, there is no call to postulate an intelligence to account for this otherwise inexplicable match.

When fine tuning is enlisted to theological ends, the intelligibility of divine design remains the key consideration. Suppose we have a hypothesis *H* which, if true, would increase the probability that physical constants should have values favourable to the emergence of life. If it is otherwise extremely unlikely that these values should have obtained, then the fact that they have is good evidence that *H* is true. Such Bayesian reasoning is invoked by Richard Swinburne (1979) in arguing that various phenomena are more to be expected if there is a God than if there is not; and, indeed, if 'God exists' can be reckoned a suitable choice for *H*, the argument may well be thought persuasive. However, we have still to confront the problem of making sense of the divine creative activity on which its suitability turns; not only that, but the probability that the design hypothesis is true will remain small if its prior probability was negligible.

2.3 LAWS OF NATURE

Traditional arguments from design are at risk from the possibility that the life to be explained is simply the outcome of developments governed by purely physical laws, with evolutionary considerations playing a particularly important role. The appeal to such considerations is sometimes held simply to push the argument a stage back: might it not be part of God's plan that we should have a universe in which evolution is possible? In one way, this will not do: evolution could be expected to take place in *any* universe, in that it does not take special conditions to ensure that organisms which acquire a feature that favours their survival tend to survive. On the other hand, that is to suppose conditions which are such as to allow the possibility of living organisms, and we cannot count upon these being satisfied in every universe. Arguments from fine tuning to a fine tuner do not appear to account for the laws which favour such conditions, so what might? How is it that we have the laws we have? Here are some considerations which have a bearing on the problem.

First, it is wrong to regard laws of Nature as basic. That status goes to whatever it is—the characteristics and behaviour of particles, gases, and so forth—that the laws codify. Indeed, the notion of a natural or physical law, or at least the use to which this is put, is often questionable. Not because there is no place for the notion, but because those who insist on the reality of such laws tend to model them on legal laws, as if the natural variety likewise enjoyed an independence of the actual behaviour of individuals, to the point even of antedating and dictating that behaviour. Legal laws can be said to have a guiding role, to be determinants of human behaviour, but it is not as if God might rewrite the laws of Nature and inanimate things, being now differently governed, would thereupon proceed to behave differently—though just some such view was in no way foreign to the seventeenth-century conception of laws of Nature as divine commands. With legal laws there is an intelligible relation between the law and behaviour: understanding a law, and having a motive to act in accordance with it, we act. Substitute inanimate bodies for comprehending agents and we sever any such intelligible tie; the law is in no sense instrumental in bringing about accord with it.

The conception of laws of Nature just criticized still has some currency, especially among theologians. Keith Ward writes:

The existence of laws of physics does not render God superfluous. On the contrary, it strongly implies that there is a God who formulates such laws and ensures that the physical realm conforms to them.

(1996: 55–6)

What would God have to do to ensure that atoms, say, behave the way they do? Simply create them to be as they in fact are. Atoms having just those features which we currently appeal to in explaining the relevant behaviour, it does not in addition require that God formulate a law prescribing that behaviour. How, after all, could that possibly help? If there were a number of wayward atoms needing to be prodded into conformity, then some form of agency might conceivably bring them into line, but making atoms as atoms are is an easier way of achieving this end.

Of course, our readiness to appeal to a law in judging whether particular cases are likely to be as claimed may make it seem that the law has priority over individual happenings. And it may well be reasonable to presume a greater likelihood for experimental error than for a falsification of the law. But it has to be supposed that the weight of individual cases justifies us in treating the law in this way—as, in Wittgenstein's terminology, a rule for testing rather than as something to be tested—that we have a body of evidence giving good inductive grounds for thinking that the fault lies with the account or interpretation of the particular case than with the putative law.

It is often objected that cosmological theories which purport to show how the universe could come from nothing do not live up to their minimalist claims. The objection is justified if, for instance, some form of energy or quantum activity is presupposed, but it is surely inappropriate to list pre-existing laws of Nature among such defeating presuppositions. Thus, with respect to the Hartle–Hawking model, which some have taken to show how creation out of nothing may be realized, it is objected that we 'must still grant the existence of quite a body of pre-existing laws of Nature in order to get away with this trick' (Barrow 1988: 231; cf. Worthing 1996: 102–3), and even laws of mathematics are sometimes held to present a similar obstacle. What we have is that, from the moment that there are events at all, lawlike descriptions of these can, we may suppose, be given, but nothing *prior* to these events needs to be assumed, only a uniformity of behaviour that makes possible such descriptions. And laws of mathematics or logic? What had to be so to ensure that 6 plus 7 would be greater than 8? Certain conditions had to be satisfied if we were to *apply* mathematics—to count and to measure, for instance—but nothing is required to rule out a state of affairs that is at odds with mathematical or logical truths. As inconceivable, such states of affairs rule themselves out.

A related misconception is found with the introduction of the notion of compulsion, when the question why we have regularities is construed as a question about what *makes* things march in step. Thus, Kip Thorne, in *Black Holes and Time Warps*, writes that when contemplating certain sequences of laws, 'most physicists are driven to believe that these sequences are converging towards a set of ultimate laws that truly governs the Universe, laws that *force* the Universe to behave the way it does, that *force* rain to condense on windows, *force* the Sun to burn nuclear fuel, *force* black holes to produce gravitational waves when they collide, and so on' (1994: 85). And again, '. . . I shall use the phrase *physical law* with its firm connotation of truly ruling the Universe, that is, truly forcing the Universe to behave as it does' (ibid., 86). As well as introducing a notion of forcing which has no business here, this puts things around the wrong way. It is not the law that is the source of the uniformity, but the uniformity is a prerequisite for us to be able to speak of lawlike behaviour. Compare Paul Davies' observation: 'Central to Milne's whole approach was the conviction that the laws of physics ought to follow from the nature of the universe and not the other way about, as is conventional' (1995: 141). It is high time this convention was abandoned.

It is argued by John Foster that it would be an astonishing coincidence if the past history of gravitational behaviour—stones falling, planets following elliptical orbits—were merely accidental. Clearly, such behaviour calls for explanation, but what is that explanation to be? 'Surely it must be that gravitational behaviour is the product of natural necessity; bodies have hitherto always behaved gravitationally because it is a law of nature that bodies behave in that way' (1983: 89). I am happy to say that the movement of a body will deviate from a straight path because there is a massive body in its vicinity, but not because there is a law of Nature to which the movement conforms. To be told that the movement exhibits lawlike rather than random behaviour is, of course, to be told something about the character of the movement, but it is not to be told *why* the body moves as it does—any more, I might add, than when it is pointed out that *all* bodies behave in that way.

But *why* is there such remarkable regularity in the physical world? Why do the laws of Nature continue to hold from millennium to millennium?—questions often asked as a prelude to calling upon God to account for the orderliness which the universe exhibits. The problem can be usefully approached in the following way. Consider how it is that birds in a flock all wheel in unison. A natural supposition is that each bird conforms its movements to those of another or others—apart from the leading bird, which has the role of setting the course. However, this is not the only possibility. There is, we might surmise, little, if anything, to choose between one bird and another, so if we knew what guided a single bird, we could simply generalize this explanation to the behaviour of its fellows. If a given bird varies its course in accordance with such and such environmental cues, then we may suppose that our question is answered by finding out just how this is effected, the extension to the other members of the flock being immediate, given the sameness both of the birds and of their environment.

It is this latter case, when the birds act independently, yet in the same fashion, that is the model to follow with our present problem. When I press the 'Caps Lock' key on my computer, the same consequences always follow: until the command is cancelled, lower-case letters henceforth appear in upper case. There is nothing remotely remarkable about this uniformity. An explanation can readily be given as to how the change comes about, and it is exactly the same explanation that applies in general as applies with respect to a single episode. The question 'How is it that pressing the Caps Lock key has this effect?' poses no greater problem if understood in general terms than if understood in reference to a particular key press. No special power, charged with securing uniformity, is called for, nothing which would ensure that a given key press might somehow take into account the preceding consequences so as to conform the present episode to these. More generally, uniformity of behaviour is not a puzzling aspect of the universe which has to be accounted for if, first, we have an explanation which fits an individual case and, second, that case is typical, the others being comparable in respect of what is being explained. So long as these two conditions are satisfied, we shall have an explanation why 'same cause, same effect' holds. The explanation why A behaves in the same way as B is simply that the explanation of the way A behaves is the same as the explanation of the way B behaves.

We also raised the question, why do the laws of Nature *continue* to hold? Why, to take an example of a well-established regularity, does water continue to boil at 100°C? Because, dare we say it, nothing about water, heat, or anything else of relevance, has changed in such a way as to result in a different boiling point. And why have there been no such changes? If such changes could be expected, this would be because the properties of water were subject to influences which were likely to operate, in which case we should wish to know what has happened to inhibit their operation. However, if there is no reason to expect a change, there is nothing to be countered. Compare 'Why are there not more uncaused events?' This query may strike us as misconceived: how *could* there be an explanation? However, suppose that uncaused events are associated with particles of a certain kind. In that case, a suitable answer is given by noting the rarity of those particles. And why are they so rare? This may have an answer— perhaps the particles are highly unstable—but it may also be that there is no presumption to counter, in which case there is nothing here that calls for explanation. Note that, had there been changes which resulted in, say, a different boiling point for water, this would normally mean, not that a law had been falsified, but that conditions had become such that a different law, or a refinement of the old law, now applied.

The question why we have the laws we do is secondary to the question why bodies behave as they do, where we have in mind the behaviour that might be described by a law. One form of explanation for such behaviour—perhaps anticipated by Hume (1947: 184–5)—might be found by appealing to the theory of evolution by natural selection (cf. Smolin 1997: ch. 7). Suppose that in the description of some physical phenomenon we make use of a particular constant N, and we wonder why it is that N has the value it has—N is of course not defined numerically, but as, say, 'the constant of gravitation'. One approach to answering this question is the following. Repetition of the question 'Why?' commonly leads us to trace explanations back through a series of more general explanations, but the search which I am proposing will take us back in time. So, suppose we can specify some earlier state of the universe in which none of the interactions occur which a law making use of N would describe; suppose, too, that there is a variety of ways in which this situation may change, and that not all of these will give rise to conditions in which N will have the same value. As a result of random motions in these N-less states, particles (say) eventually emerge which are such as to behave in a way that conforms with a law in which N crucially figures, and where it receives the value v_1. However, suppose now that these novel particles prove unstable, and fail to survive in that form, though the original N-less states continue to form and randomly to throw up further novel particles, now such that a law which specified their behaviour would require that N be assigned the value v_2. And so on through successive values, v_3, v_4, . . . This development might be repeated many times before a stable situation took shape, a situation which persisted and was describable by a law in which N has its current value, v_n. Such an account immediately raises the question as to how the values of any constants occurring in descriptions of the primordial states are to be accounted for, but at least we get some idea of how a stable universe, with its laws, might evolve, perhaps with some reduction in the range of constants to be explained. Moreover, if principles of natural selection are, as it would appear, essentially trivial, then the dependence of laws of nature on such a principle will not be dependence on anything which is itself such a law.

Many philosophers would consider there to be something absurd about much of the preceding discussion. The idea that religious belief involves commitment to certain distinctive forms of explanation of events in the physical universe, forms in competition with what scientists might offer, is surely a superstition which does not merit the attention we have given it, attention which risks conceding that the theologian presents us with a case to answer. Have we not reached a stage where religious language can be seen for what it really is, language with a genuine use, but one which is essentially moral; certainly not one which seeks to *inform* anyone of anything? Here, of course, we are put in mind of Wittgenstein. Initially, Wittgenstein considered that, construed as factual, religious claims simply made no sense, and more or less left the matter there; subsequently, he sought to dissociate such beliefs from any reading that made nonsense of them, advancing a more sympathetic interpretation in terms of the adoption of certain *pictures*, where the use of the pictures is said to be regulative, a matter of interpreting and responding to events and experiences in a certain way; decidedly not a use to represent a state of affairs. So, someone may take everything that happens to him as a reward or punishment, whereas another—and Wittgenstein in particular—does not: 'I think differently, in a different way. I say different things to myself. I have different pictures' (1970: 55).

While Wittgenstein does not dismiss beliefs which, like a belief in the Last Judgement, may in some way guide one's life, the earlier criticism is not retracted. He appeared to have little time for those who demand a literal reading of propositions about God, and then find them wanting on that reading—as if talk of the Eye of God were misplaced so long as questions about God's eyebrows could not be answered (1970: 71). On the other hand, he was equally unsympathetic to those who consider that such propositions can, so taken, be reckoned acceptable, apologists who, like Father O'Hara, would talk of evidence, of reasonable belief, being dismissed as 'ludicrous' (1970: 58). Objections which might fault the believer on the first basis are accordingly dismissed and, on the other hand, any empirical grounding which a belief might conceivably enjoy is considered irrelevant:

Suppose, for instance, we knew people who foresaw the future; make forecasts for years and years ahead; and they described some sort of a Judgement Day. Queerly enough, even if there were such a thing, and even if it were more convincing than I have described, belief in this happening wouldn't be at all a religious belief.

(1970: 56)

It is true that we can discern in Wittgenstein a robust empiricism, a no-nonsense attitude towards matters of fact, but while there may be much to be said for the alternative which he espouses, it does not recommend itself as an account of anything to be found in traditional Christian belief, and even more general talk of *religious* belief may be questioned. Consider the matter of different 'pictures'. There are some who are uneasy when good fortune comes their way, since they feel it is sure to be balanced, sooner rather than later, by misfortune. It is not difficult to see how life's vicissitudes might, though need not, be fitted into this scheme. On the other hand, as with reward and punishment, it is not clear why this would deserve to be styled *religious* if there is no suggestion of an agent, supernatural if not divine, in the background. Wittgenstein considered philosophy, as practised by him, to be heir to what had traditionally gone by the name. I suspect that religion as traditionally understood and religion as he would have us understand it are equally far apart.

Wittgenstein's conception of religion as constituting an autonomous language game, a system of beliefs, practices and ways of speaking not to be assessed on the basis of criteria appropriate to other language games, is sometimes appealed to as a way of protecting religious belief. However, to say that religious beliefs are immune from the kinds of criticisms which scientific hypotheses may invite is just a way of emphasizing the incomparability of the 'claims' that religions and science make. There would be solace here for the traditional believer only if the immunity from criticism could be maintained side by side with a belief in the explanatory character of religious propositions, and that Wittgenstein does not allow. At all events, while we may be at risk of conceding too much sense to hypotheses so ill-starred they do not deserve to be styled 'hypotheses', the continuing attachment to the traditional conception of science and religion as somehow continuous in the way Aquinas, say, thought, means that there is still a way of thinking to be challenged.

3
Causation and Necessity

It was mentioned above that there are many, scientists included, who believe that we must look beyond science to find ultimate explanations, but it often proves that what they hanker after is a quasi-scientific explanation, one that makes crucial use of concepts which have proven of value in enabling us to understand the natural order. One such concept is that of causation, and it will be useful to subject it to scrutiny before considering its theological and cosmological roles. We shall also take the opportunity to look more closely at necessity, an ostensible feature of causation and natural laws which has been thought to be rich in metaphysical, if not theological, implications. Analyses of causation traceable back to Hume continue to enjoy a prominent place in contemporary writings on the subject, and we shall make this tradition our starting point.

3.1 HUME, CAUSES, AND NECESSITY

A Humean account of causation involves both a negative aspect—the rejection of any necessary connection between cause and effect—and a (marginally) more positive contribution: we can look to constant conjunction to furnish the substance of the causal relation. I say 'Humean', since an account with these features customarily attracts this description, but it is questionable whether the account is the historical Hume's. If he can be said to have adopted a 'regularity' theory, it would appear to be restricted to causation only in so far as we can know about it, and not to causation as it is in the objects themselves. It is not so much that Hume cast doubt on the view that there is something like causal power in the world; he merely questioned our ability to arrive at substantive conclusions about its nature (see Strawson 1989). However, whatever Hume's true position, to many there has seemed to be no escape from the austere account of causation which he advances as comprehending as much as can be known. What do we see when we observe fire consuming a piece of wood? Flames licking around the wood, the wood giving off smoke, gradual changes in colour and texture and, eventually, a pile of ashes where the wood had been. Further, closer, observation will doubtless enable us to describe the successive states in greater detail, but, as far as what is given to present observation is concerned, this is all we have to work with in constructing a causal relation. However more closely we inspect our burning wood, however much we embellish our description of the successive phases which go to make up the transformation of wood into ash, the cause–effect relation will remain a matter of brute fact, not a relation which, once the requisite detail is filled in, may become transparent to reason. Thus Hume:

> It appears that, in single instances of the operation of bodies, we never can, by our utmost scrutiny, discover any thing but one event following another, without being able to comprehend any force or power by which the cause operates, or any connection between it and its supposed effect. . . . All events seem entirely loose and separate. One event follows another; but we never can observe any tie between them. They seem *conjoined*, but never *connected*.
>
> (1902: 73–4)

In so far as there is more to be said, it involves, for Hume, the adoption of a broader perspective: what constitutes A as cause of B is to be found in the circumstance that objects similar to A have, more generally, been followed by objects similar to B. It is their standing as an instance of this recurrent pattern that earns the individual happenings the right to be characterized as cause and effect. That is the only way in which a genuine causal relation differs from a mere succession.

Alongside his breakdown in terms of regular succession, Hume also presents an account of causation in which a condition relating to necessity is added, a condition which, he believes, our ordinary understanding of the causal relation demands to be recognized. However, as far as what is to be found 'in the objects' is concerned, this, as indicated, makes for no more than a negative condition, a by-product of constant conjunction which is psychological only: on experiencing A we come, through custom and habit, to expect B; so readily, indeed, do we form this expectation, that we suppose B to be under some necessity to happen, given A. But such necessity is just a reflection of this propensity to pass in thought from the one happening to what invariably follows; it is not a reflection of any necessity in the things themselves (1902: 75–9).

Prima facie, it is possible to go along with Hume's dismissal of necessity, yet not agree that, for all its apparent inescapability, we have the materials for an adequate account of causation so long as we have no more than regularity of succession of spatio-temporally contiguous events to work with. Certainly, the rejection of necessary connection, conceived of as an extramental or extralinguistic relation, is the more secure feature of a Humean analysis—supposing the necessity to be prized off the distinct notions of *power, force, efficacy, agency, energy*, and, indeed, off *connection* more generally, all of which Hume runs together (1888: 157). We shall begin with this aspect of his account.

It is sometimes suggested that underlying Hume's rejection of necessity is the more general thesis that there are no logically necessary connections between distinct events, or events at different times. Norman Malcolm, linking this thesis to Russell as well as to Hume, objects: 'This is obviously false; keeping a promise logically implies a prior event, and so does changing one's mind or winning a bet' (1963: 202). Any number of other examples can be devised in illustration of this pattern, but their failure to advance the thesis can be seen as soon as we put the question: What are necessary connections connections *between*? Malcolm apparently takes it for granted that it is *events* that provides the answer, the event of keeping the promise entailing the prior event of its being made. Suppose, then, that the promise is a promise to return a book. When the person keeps his promise, we may say: Henry is putting a book on my desk, or Henry is at last keeping his promise. Use the latter form of words and you are, of course, committed to saying that Henry has already made a promise—a distinct event—though no such commitment arises with the other description. It is the words we use that commit us, not the activities which those words depict. Activities, events, and other worldly items are totally inappropriate terms of a relation of logical necessity, which is by way of a linguistic relation; in Hume's terms, a relation of ideas.

It is not being claimed that the example of promise-keeping presents us with a causal relation, but a simple syllogism makes it clear how the argument applies to causation: a logical relation is a species of linguistic relation; it holds only between things said or sayable, between propositions, descriptions, and the like. A causal relation, by contrast, holds between agents and events. Ergo, a causal relation is not a species of logical relation. *A fortiori*, causation is not a relation between propositions which is somehow opaque to reason where logical relations are transparent. If there is some sense in which causation can be described as an 'intelligible' relation, it will be in much the same way as one might speak of someone on the roof of a house as standing in an 'intelligible' relation to the roof, which would presumably mean no more than: in point of intelligibility, such relational propositions as 'Henry caused the tiles to move' and 'Henry is on the roof' are comparable.

The futility of seeking to milk anything of substance out of a logical relation becomes clear if we take a description for which correct application logically requires that whatever it is applied to be caused, or caused in a certain way. So, it has been suggested that calling a mark a scar commits one to saying that the mark was caused, and caused by a wound, that events are accordingly not always, as Hume avers, 'loose and separate' (Walsh 1963: 103). We may agree that if a given mark is a scar, then it must, logically, have been brought about in this way, but if the wound and the mark were separate, they remain so when the latter is redescribed as a scar. Plainly, the move tells us nothing about the causal relation, and it amounts to shifting, rather than resolving, the issue of substance, since we are required to settle the causal question before we can be sure that what we have to do with is, precisely, a scar.

Obvious though it may be, in view of our modest syllogism, it is worth stressing that the causal relation is to be characterized by having regard to the extralinguistic character of its *relata*, not by insisting that all causal *propositions* must be empirical rather than analytic. Consider the propositions, 'Stretching a strip of rubber causes it to lengthen' and 'Heating a piece of metal causes it to expand'. We do not have to wait to see if a piece of metal has expanded to be sure that it has been heated—touching it will suffice—so we are not concerned here with a logical truth, but while the rubber may snap when stretched, it would have to lengthen to some degree if we are to say that it has been stretched at all. Accordingly, while qualifying as causal, this constitutes a logical truth: 'stretching' just is a description of one way of causing something to lengthen.

As summed up in our syllogism, the argument against assimilating causal to logical relations appears evident enough, but the conception against which it is directed is one that has enjoyed enormous appeal. So, it is thought that, if we could somehow penetrate to the real essences of substances, it would become apparent how their observed character and behaviour flowed from their essences, where the 'flowing' would be a matter of something more than a brute-factual succession. Indeed, if Hume can be heard in Philo's voice, this is a position to which even he was drawn:

Chance has no place, on any hypothesis, sceptical or religious. Every thing is surely governed by steady, inviolable laws. And were the inmost essence of things laid open to us, we should then discover a scene, of which, at present, we can have no idea. Instead of admiring the order of natural beings, we should clearly see, that it was absolutely impossible for them, in the smallest article, ever to admit of any other disposition.

(1947: 174–5; cf. 191)

If the impossibility envisaged is logical or conceptual, we are, if I am right, dispensed from having to speculate about what this more advanced knowledge might bring to light, so our simple argument is one of some consequence. It is not that, if only we had access to the innermost natures of things, the logical relations between events would eventually be laid bare. Nothing will have been done with such an investigation to bridge the gulf between the terms of the two kinds of relation, but in this respect we, with our vastly increased scientific knowledge, are no better off than were Hume and his contemporaries. We are better placed to introduce and exploit more fruitful concepts, but, however more comprehensive and profound our explanations become, they will never culminate in a network of logical relations between events. The terms of the two relations, causal and logical, are destined to remain as far apart as ever. Nor is their failure to converge anything to lament, as one might lament a genuine possibility that fails, regrettably, to be realized. As something that makes no sense, such convergence is no more meaningful than the idealist's fear that reality might prove contradictory.

It is sometimes maintained that, while there may be no necessity in the domain of purely physical causal relations, when we pass to psychological events, the denial of necessity loses its plausibility (Blanshard 1974: 494–5). Suppose you are pleased at having won a game of bridge, or disappointed at having lost. These are not, surely, brute-factual relations, but there are conceptual connections: the responses *make sense* in the light of what has led to them (cf. Ewing 1932). That is indeed so, but is the relevant relation one of causation? How do you know that it is your loss at bridge that disappoints you? There may be feelings akin to those of disappointment at whose source you can only conjecture, but there is no room for conjecture as to what you are disappointed at, so that you might say: I think it is because I lost at bridge that I am disappointed, but it may be my failure to win the lottery that is having this effect. The inappropriateness of mere conjecture is not because we are infallible when it comes to identifying a cause in this connection, but because the very notions of cause and effect, as these are understood in the natural sciences, are out of place here.

Consider this in terms of reasons for action. You say that you are opening the door in order to let the cat out. If this is an explanation made in all sincerity, and with understanding of the words used, then the reason cited is indeed your reason for acting. Its being your reason just consists in its standing as an honestly made avowal, with no room for rival alternatives. It is not as with causal propositions, where one's honest say-so does not decide what caused what, but where it is always in principle possible that one's attribution of a cause will be overturned by further investigation. To say, for instance, 'I think I am opening the door to let the cat out', would be to relocate what would ordinarily be a matter of one's reason for acting in an altogether different domain. It would be to treat one's avowal as a matter for conjecture on one's own part, much as if the act were involuntary, as with 'I think I am sneezing because of the dust.' Just the standing appropriate to a causal hypothesis, but a distortion of our conception of a reason. The conclusion is not that causal relations are, after all, a species of logical relation, but that we are concerned here with reasons rather than causes (see Rundle 1997 for extended discussion). Compare reasons for a belief. Asked why I believe my neighbour is at home, I give the recent arrival of his car as my reason. It is again not a matter of conjecture that that is why I hold the belief, nor is my authority in this non-causal matter in any way remarkable if, as is likely, I am simply telling you how I reasoned, the course my thoughts took.

The general thesis we have been defending on Hume's behalf characterizes his opposition to a rationalist view, as advanced by, for instance, Spinoza in his *Ethics*, Book I, Axiom III: 'From a given determined cause an effect follows of necessity, and on the other hand, if no determined cause is granted, it is impossible that an effect should follow' (1910: 2). For the empiricist, it is as if any individual event could be plucked out of the world leaving everything else undisturbed. For the rationalist, by contrast, the removal of one event brings an indefinite succession of others in its wake: suppose the effect to have been wanting and we must suppose the same of its cause, and of the cause of the latter, and so on indefinitely. Hence, ultimately, the picture of reality as a seamless whole.

But the rationalist view is one of necessity as *logical* necessity. It is not clear that physical or natural necessity falls to the same considerations. Well, not immediately clear, perhaps, but a little reflection on the use of modal terms soon leads to a rebuttal of necessity of this species, if the aim is to identify something 'in the objects' as essential to the causal relation. Hume's argument against causal necessity does not take the form of the syllogism given above, but he proceeds by arguing that there is no contradiction in conjoining a description of a cause with the negation of a description of its customary effect (1902: 29). Rom Harré suggests that this argument at best shows that causal or natural necessity is not logical necessity; it does not show that such a statement as 'An unsuspended body in a gravitational field *must* fall if released, *ceteris paribus*' is incoherent (1986: 84). And, indeed, Hume might be expected to go along with this claim, given his insistence, when discussing liberty and necessity, that 'the operations of external bodies are necessary'. 'Every object', he writes, 'is determin'd by an absolute fate to a certain degree and direction of its motion, and can no more depart from that precise line, in which it moves, than it can convert itself into an angel, or spirit, or any superior substance' (1888: 400).

Certainly, we are unlikely to demur at Harré's modest claim. The question is: What is the force of the 'must' which supposedly expresses physical or natural necessity? Consider first the use of the verb in a non-causal context, as 'It must be raining.' What is the difference between this and 'It is raining'? The modal form is commonly thought to be somehow stronger than the indicative, but it is not clear how this can be. You cannot get more categorical, more uncompromising, than the simple 'is'. So how do they differ? On hearing 'It must be raining', we take it that the speaker has good grounds for a belief that it is raining, but that a degree of conjecture remains, a lack of finality being as much a condition for the propriety of the observation as is possession of suitable grounds. We may say 'It must be raining' on observing water seeping in under the door; we should not say this if standing outside with the rain beating down upon us, a situation where we have not merely signs or evidence of rain, but something better than that, viz. the rain itself. Is one who says 'It must be raining' committed to the plain 'It is raining'? He can hardly go along with the claim that it is not raining, but to the extent that 'must' remains appropriate, use of 'is' is presumptuous. There is a gap between the two in the sense that the correct use of each presupposes that the speaker finds himself, or takes himself to be, in quite different circumstances. As a modal verb, 'must' takes us to the *grounds* for affirming what follows, grounds which fall short of what is needed for direct verification, but which are ostensibly adequate for ascribing at least a high probability to the conclusion. More general considerations are in the background with the modal, considerations pertaining to, for instance, what is found in like circumstances.

When 'must' is stressed, something stronger than high probability may be at issue: this *must* be so; nothing else could explain what we have found. Here the possibility advanced is arrived at by eliminating alternatives, a negative basis which again falls short of the direct verification appropriate to use of the unmodalized form. Harré's example presents 'must' in a slightly different use, the proposition having a future rather than a present orientation, but this account would appear to apply here as well. Suppose our unsuspended body is a solid object such as a pen, not something as light as gossamer or a gas-filled balloon. Some things will rise if released, as with the balloon; others, featherlike, may or may not fall. With bodies which compare with the pen, however, there is one pattern and one pattern only: release is followed by a fall. The exclusion of any alternative may accordingly be marked by use of 'must'. Similarly with 'If you prick this balloon it is bound to burst.' Some things will not burst if you prick them, while others may or may not burst. With the balloon, however, it is supposed that there are no two ways about it: bursting, and bursting only, can be contemplated. Whether we think in terms of an outcome arrived at by eliminating alternatives, or of one for which there are reasons of a more positive character—as is appropriate with 'is bound to'—nothing 'in the objects' has been identified, via 'must' or 'is bound to', as a component in the causal relation. The modal term is in neither case the reflection in language of a metaphysical linkage between cause and effect, but its affinities are again more with relations whose terms are linguistic, as premise and conclusion. It serves to draw attention to the evidential basis for the pronouncement.

It may be felt that this analysis fails to do justice to, precisely, the element of compulsion which use of the modal conveys: put sugar in hot water and it *must* dissolve. It simply *has to*. What does the idea of compulsion add? What more do we have beyond an emphatic affirmation of the sufficiency of the cause? That is most easily answered when human beings are involved and where either the pressure is moral—'You *must* keep your word'—or where someone is physically constrained to do something, this latter being marked by the unavailing character of efforts to resist.

I suspect that, if it is felt that an element of compulsion is conveyed with 'it must fall' or 'it must dissolve', this is because a feature of the human contexts has been read into these. It is as if we were saying: an unsuspended body must fall; it has no choice. Or, if you put sugar into hot water, it must dissolve; all resistance is futile. Remove these inappropriate elements of personification, and all we are left with is the idea of the inescapability of the conclusion, where all it takes for this is the invariable character of the relevant behaviour in such circumstances, circumstances which leave no room for alternatives. Likewise with 'The sugar is bound to dissolve.' This belongs on a scale where we are calculating odds; not one specifying degrees of compulsion.

Explaining a necessity is often explaining why such and such will happen only in certain circumstances. The toaster must be plugged in if it is to work; only then will the element heat up. There could conceivably be other ways of making or enabling the toaster to work, but as yet none has been devised. It is of interest that uniformity or exclusivity of behaviour is what is central to the evidential basis which the modal proclaims; the contrast is not between a uniformity and something which, for the supporter of natural necessity, might have been felt metaphysically more satisfying, but it lies *within* uniformities—between those that are unvarying and those that are merely partial. The greater the range of potentially falsifying circumstances in which the underlying (open-ended) generalization has been confirmed, the greater the degree to which the use of 'must' is warranted. However, the uniformities may well be, as with the balloon, uniformities of causation, not of mere succession, and to this extent it could be said that causation has a role in explaining natural necessity.

It may be objected that, in looking to past happenings to justify 'must', we are turning away from the all-important present situation. Surely, it has to be something in the here and now that ensures the outcome, not mere past happenings; after all, the present situation could be unaltered in its power to necessitate the effect even if it were the very first of its kind. However, it is to be noted that, in saying that, if you put this sugar in hot water, it must dissolve, we are saying *before* the event that this must happen, and even if this is affirmed on the basis of present conditions, it is because of their past history that they can be seen to have the significance they have. If, when the event has taken place, it is said, 'That *had* to happen', the likely implication is that any attempt at preventing the occurrence would have been futile. Set aside this suggestion, and it is difficult to see how the remark can be anything more than an acknowledgement of the proven sufficiency of the cause or the invariability of the given consequence. The attempt to read more into these words, or into 'must', naturally invokes terms, like 'constrain' and 'compel', whose only contribution is, as just noted, an inappropriate personification.

There is nothing mysterious about the kind of necessity that can be secured for many empirical propositions, but the idea that it can be grounded in nothing more than a uniformity may still be resisted. To try to weaken this resistance, we might consider how a justification of inductive reasoning may proceed on the same basis. If, on examining a new species of animal, we find that the heart is situated at a certain point in the body, we may well conclude that this is the norm for the species, even if only a handful of specimens has been examined. Our reasoning could be an instance of the principle that being F is the kind of characteristic such that, if it is found to hold for even a few members of a species, it can be counted on to hold for the species at large. The high confirmation which the general principle has received may warrant an emphatic prediction that the next member of the species encountered is *bound* to have its heart in the place in question. And this stands even if we are quite unable to explain why no variation in location should be met with.

It is just such confirmation that we should invoke in seeking to provide a justification of inductive reasoning generally. The argument is not that, because the relevant principle has been confirmed so often in the past, its future confirmation is assured, but we can appeal to the record of past confirmations to back a claim that the use of this form of reasoning, or the conclusion which it yields on this occasion, is *justified*. Equivalently, we may speak in terms of a principle of inference of proven dependability, a principle that has seldom, if ever, let us down. What more could we ask for by way of justification? Not 'has been confirmed, so will be so on this occasion'—which requires a principle to the effect that the future will resemble the past—but 'has been confirmed, so is justified on this occasion', where what is being affirmed is a *grammatical* connection between the notions of having been confirmed and being justified, or between proven dependability and being justified, and where the latter notion is, as it were, backwards-looking: whether the assertion of P is justified is dependent only on what has happened to date; it does not await developments which will show P to be true or false. Compare the notion of reasonableness. A person who acts unreasonably—overtaking a car on the brow of a hill, say—cannot deflect criticism by pointing out that the risk to which he exposed himself was not in fact realized. Whether the motorist's action was reasonable is to be judged in the light of the circumstances as known to him when he acted, and without regard to what subsequently happened. The notion is thus backwards-looking in the way here claimed for justification.

But, surely, the necessity that falls to a natural law requires more than mere confirmation, however extensive, can furnish? Consider this objection in terms of an argument of Fred Dretske aimed at showing that natural laws are not simply what universally true propositions express: 'If diamonds have a refractive index of 2.419 (law) and "is a diamond" is coextensive with "is mined in kimberlite (a dark basic rock)" we cannot infer that *it is a law* that things mined in kimberlite have a refractive index of 2.419. Whether this is a law or not depends on whether the coextensiveness of "is a diamond" and "is mined in kimberlite" is *itself* law-like' (1977: 249). Replacing 'is a diamond' in this way appears to introduce an element of contingency into the proposition which destroys its lawlike standing. However, we must ask what is meant by saying that this phrase is coextensive with 'is mined in kimberlite'. Since the law will have an atemporal reading, it is not enough to suppose that the two phrases have converged in their application to date, but the supposition must be that this will continue into the indefinite future, and it is difficult to see how this could be maintained unless we had the kind of evidence which ruled out a mere chance agreement in application. That is, the supposition that 'is a diamond' and 'is mined in kimberlite' are coextensive is the supposition that, not only has their joint application been comprehensively confirmed, but we have no reason to suppose that circumstances not as yet encountered will find the one without the other, as knowledge of a breakdown among comparable uniformities would provide. We can thus go along with Dretske in his demand for a lawlike connection at this point, but it is misleading to say that mere coextensiveness is not good enough, since the only sense one can make of coextensiveness with respect to an open-ended proposition of the kind in question is coextensiveness as assured by a backing of this kind. I suggest that we are looking in the wrong place if we seek a notion of necessitation in the nexus between one property F and another G, the attribution of necessity demanding no more than is given with good inductive support.

It is not being claimed that every highly confirmed open-ended generalization can appropriately be reckoned a law. We are allowed some latitude in what we place in this category, but it would seem that the more difficult it is to specify realistic falsifying circumstances for P, the more lawlike P may be held to be. So, suppose that it is a general truth that the roots of a tree go as deep as the tree is high. To the extent that we are reluctant to call this a law of nature it will be, I surmise, because, appealing only to possibilities that are grounded on the way things actually are, we can envisage changes which would lead to a breakdown of the generalization. Whether, on this way of looking at the matter, there *are* any laws, remains an open question.

There is, it would appear, nothing in the notion of natural necessity, understood as indicated, to trouble the upholder of a regularity theory, though nothing that might usefully supplement such a theory either. What of the concept of *power*? This appears to be allied to the notion of natural necessity, and as relevant to a proper understanding of causality as it is foreign to an account which seeks to make do with regularity.

We have here not one, but two notions. First, 'power' may signify some energy source, as when we speak of turning the power on, or of a power failure. Clearly, this is too specific to apply generally; we make no reference to such power when we say that our blisters were caused by contact with a noxious weed. On the other hand, there is also power as capacity: a panacea has the power to cure all ills. How possession of a power in this sense is to be verified is plain enough: we check to see what the agent can do. But, by the same token, it does not take our analysis far: if x's ability or capacity to V suffices to show x to have the power to V, attribution of a power need be in no way a questionable step; not a leap into the unknown, but a redescription of something not in contention; certainly nothing to which a Humean need take exception. At best, reference to a power highlights the notion of a capacity or ability to *act*, something we shall turn to shortly. Note that, if we should speak of a power as 'hidden', that would have to be with respect to something more than a capacity, which is as evident as the activities which give proof of it. Aqua regia has the power to dissolve gold. The power is apparent in the action of the acid on the metal. It is the chemistry of the reaction that may be obscure or hidden.

3.2   NECESSARY AND SUFFICIENT CONDITIONS

In our discussion so far we have largely sided with the Humean tradition on the place of necessity in causation, but agreement here need not go with agreement as to the place of constant conjunction. We shall now touch on this topic before suggesting an alternative analysis to Hume's.

Investigations of causation often fasten on the statement form 'A causes B' as the object of analysis, and the frequentative 'causes' featured here makes talk of regular co-occurrence natural. However, such a statement as 'The damage was caused by a spillage' is ostensibly about an occurrence which took place over a limited period of time, so it is not clear how the wider reference—'Whenever such a spillage occurs . . .'—is to be read into these words. Repeated occurrences may give us grounds or evidence for supposing this to be the cause of that—if *C* is always around when *E* comes about, then it is clearly a candidate for cause. In particular, if our concern is to make a well-founded prediction that *C* will cause *E*, we can hardly dispense with some form of supporting generalization, a generalization which, as we have just seen, may license the introduction of 'must'. However, in so far as this is their role, we are not to say that an allusion to repeated occurrences is part of the *sense* of the singular causal proposition.

Before going further, it should be noted that the generalizations here at issue may be of a stronger or a weaker form. They are weaker if all they are required to codify is a constant conjunction experienced to date. In so far as Hume considers us warranted in affirming a causal proposition on an experiential basis, this is how, for him, they are to be construed. That this is his position appears clear from a number of passages (cf. Jacobson 1984: 75–91). Thus:

The idea of cause and effect is deriv'd from *experience*, which informs us, that such particular objects, in all past instances, have been constantly conjoin'd with each other.

(1888: 89–90)

. . . all kinds of reasoning from causes or effects are founded on two particulars, viz. the constant conjunction of any two objects in all past experience, and the resemblance of a present object to any one of them.

(1888: 142)

There are, it is true, passages which are suggestive of an association that extends into the future:

we may define a cause to be *an object, followed by another, and where all the objects similar to the first are followed by objects similar to the second.*

(1902: 76)

I should think that, natural though it would be for Hume to slip into this more general formulation, his explicitly restricted variants show that he thought experience to date could suffice for a causal judgement. However, whatever his position, it would appear that some of his successors, no doubt feeling that bare juxtaposition is too meagre a basis for a causal relation, have sought to make good its impoverished character by appealing to the more substantial notion of a law, or lawlike generalization. Philosophers who take this step will presumably exceed Hume in their caution when affirming a causal link; given that a falsifying instance may yet occur, the relevant generalizations can never be secured more than provisionally.

Regularity theories of causation are often expressed in terms of necessary and/or sufficient conditions. The appeal to necessary conditions may be made as a way of capturing the idea of a cause as something that makes a difference to the course of events. In Hume's words, 'if the first object had not been, the second never had existed' (1902: 76). However, it is not difficult to show that such necessity is far from mandatory. We can describe situations in which a cause C of E will, through its operation, prevent something else, C^*, from bringing about the same result, either because C actually inhibits the operation of C^*, or because it brings about E before C^* has had a chance to do so, whence neither can be regarded as necessary to the occurrence of E. Again, perhaps it is impossible to have a totally silent explosion, or an explosion which generates no heat, but although a degree of noise and heat will then be empirically necessary conditions for there being an explosion, they need not contribute to the causation of the damage which the explosion brings about. And not because they will perforce be temporally mislocated—occurring after rather than before the damage. The notion of the necessary condition as a condition necessary for the *production* of the effect is what eludes us, some means being needed of confining the relevant conditions to the right line in space as well as in time—the line of action of the cause, as it were.

It has to be granted that a given cause may not be necessary to the effect in question, but surely it must often be possible to say that C was a necessary condition for E *in the circumstances*, where the qualification, 'in the circumstances', is intended to rule out the possibility of events which had not happened taking place had C not occurred. And of course that is so, but it tells us nothing about what is involved in being a cause. It comes to saying simply that E could not have occurred without a cause, and that C was in fact responsible for its occurrence. After all, if $C_1, \ldots, C_n$ exhaust the possible causes of E-type events, then, given that some one of these must operate if E is not to occur uncaused, if you rule out all but C_i, C_i is what it has to be. The only alternative is that no other condition would have been followed by E, that occurrence of C_i was necessary in this stronger sense, and that is not in general possible to affirm. Certainly, it goes beyond what is involved in saying that C_i was a cause of E. This is not to deny that, in a vast number of cases, it will be possible to say that E would not have come about had C not taken place. It is just that such an inference is not assured simply by the fact that C caused E.

But could it not be said that C is necessary for E *as it came about*? Suppose that a neurone is made to fire by an electrical impulse. It could be that the last stages of this process were the same whether neurone C or neurone C^* originated the impulse further back, so to ensure that C is none the less necessary for the firing, E, as this came about, it has to be that, without the action of C, E would not count as having come about in the way it did. But this is now as with the earlier example of wound and scar. A condition which makes the way E came about logically dependent on the identity of its cause, C, presupposes that C was its cause; it does not tell us in any way what that causation involves, what it is for a cause to be necessary for the *production* of an effect.

It is worth noting that the appeal to necessary conditions is even less inviting if we are dealing with effects which we might predict rather than effects which have already come about. How, we wonder, might E be effected? How, say, might mosquitoes be eradicated from this area, how might this log be shifted, how might that stain be removed? In coming up with a possible cause we are clearly not in general fastening on something which, as against everything else, might serve to accomplish the job in hand; we may be able to think up numerous recipes for achieving our end, and if one somehow proves necessary in the circumstances of its operation, that is an adventitious fact about its history. Suppose we conclude that some condition is in fact necessary: the only way you can eradicate mosquitoes is by destroying the larvae. That is not to say that it will be possible to reckon the destruction of the larvae as the cause of the eradication of the mosquitoes only if, in the circumstances, it will not have been possible to eradicate the mosquitoes in any other fashion.

The formulation of the necessary condition as a simple future—'If C does not occur, then neither will E'—is, as such examples make understandable, not something that philosophers have rushed to defend, but past occurrences of causation are usually considered, occurrences which make the corresponding counterfactual conditional the appropriate form to invoke: if *C* had not occurred, then neither would *E*. So, if you had not shaken the branch, the apple would not have fallen. This would not be offered as a *ground* for a causal claim—something established independently of knowledge of what caused what—but at best as something one was obliged to accept through having accepted that *C* caused *E*. And if it can be said that the only way, in the circumstances, that *E* might have happened is if *C* had occurred, that, as just noted, is extra to *C*'s being the cause of *E*. The derivative standing of the counterfactual comes out more clearly if we take a more precise formulation, as with 'If you had not shaken the branch, the apple would not have fallen just when it did.' How could this be defended if not by invoking considerations pertaining to the actual history of what happened, a history in which the actual cause will figure prominently?

The form of generalization thought to be bound up with the causal relation, and the source of the relevant counterfactual proposition, will involve at least the proposition that *B* happens only if *A* does, but there is also the proposition more commonly entertained in this connection, and this is simply that *B* happens whenever *A* does. This notion, of a cause as a sufficient condition for the effect, looks more promising. When considering ways of bringing about some future happening, we do not in general look for conditions necessary for the occurrence, but we shall surely give thought to what might suffice. And how could it be disputed that if *C* caused *E*, then *C* was sufficient for *E*, and conversely?

If *C* caused *E*, then *C*'s sufficiency for *E* on that occasion can be granted, but if the converse relation looks obvious, that may be because 'sufficient' is being read as 'sufficient to *produce E*', and not merely as 'sufficient *condition*' demands, viz. a matter merely of an adequate ground from which the occurrence of *E* may be inferred. That is, it has to be that if *C* is a sufficient condition for *E*, then not only will occurrence of *C* provide a basis for inferring that *E* has taken or will take place; *C*'s character as a *cause* has also to follow from this sufficiency. However, the red glow of the poker implies that it is hot, so furnishes a sufficient condition for the heat, but it is not its cause. The position is as with necessity. Occurrence of *E* may be enough for an inference to *C*, but the necessity which *C* is thus shown to enjoy does not ensure a causal role. Nor does a further condition of temporal priority elevate mere sufficiency to causal sufficiency. *C* may provide an adequate ground for an inference to *E*, but as something which merely heralds or presages *E*, as the cows' behaviour in sitting down is a sign that rain is imminent. Note, too, that it takes more than a true counterfactual conditional to assure causal dependence. If the cows' behaviour warrants a claim that rain is imminent, then we can maintain 'If it hadn't rained, then the cows would not have sat down' without ascribing responsibility for the rain to the cows.

3.3 CAUSATION AND CONNECTION

Back to constant conjunction. This is frequently judged inadequate through failing to provide the foundation of a specifically *causal* relation. Consider the familiar counter-example of night following day—as regular a succession as one could wish for, but not causal. This association may be taken to illustrate a more general pattern which Hume is unable to distinguish from a causal sequence, namely, that in which we have two phenomena co-varying simply because they are effects of a common cause—in this case, the rotation of the earth about the sun. Mill sought to exclude such effects by arguing that they lacked the unconditionality of a causal sequence. Matters could, in principle, be so engineered that night occurred but the earth was destroyed before day could dawn. Since much the same strategy is no less of a possibility with respect to genuine causes, the suggestion fails, but there is in any event a more radical objection. The proffered solution apparently allows that it is at least a possibility that night should cause day, and this is to be queried. Why? A term signifying a period of time is not a term which may denominate a cause of *anything*; something more substantial is required than is afforded by a mere temporal period, which is powerless to induce a change, which cannot in any circumstances *act upon* anything. Instead, we must turn to agents which act, or events which take place, during such periods.

But is that how it invariably is with night and day? Is neither to be allowed *any* causal role? Does not the night bring terror to some? That, perhaps, is something that comes *with* the night, rather than an effect of it. But darkness can have an effect on plants, and is not 'night' just another name for darkness? Not at all; darkness may occur other than at night. But in any event, it is dark *at* night, during that *time*. It does seem right to say that 'night' signifies a temporal period marked by the absence of sunlight, and as such does not identify a possible causal agent, but if this is not accepted, or if there is more than one use to complicate the example, we can shift to terms whose purely temporal character is plainer: Monday does not cause Tuesday, nor June July. Compare beginnings of movement. The train begins to move only after having been at rest, but a state of rest is so clearly wanting in what it takes to engender movement, or indeed to bring about anything, its inescapability as a preceding state can do nothing towards endowing it with a causal role. Here we note that the necessity of night to day's dawning and of a state of rest to the beginning of movement is *logical* necessity.

There are further complications with other types of term, but I suggest that the reason offered for disqualifying temporal periods as causes takes us to our basic conception of a cause. The leading idea in this conception is that of one thing acting upon another, where such action involves actual physical contact. This is exemplified in a hundred-and-one familiar notions, as given with *bend, break, cut, shake, dissolve, scratch, twist, crush, trip, stir,* and a multitude of other transitive verbs (cf. Stebbing 1950: 260). It should surely be no more difficult to give an account of this conception of causality than to generalize on what is involved in such happenings. Or better, in such *agency*; it is this category, rather than the more general *event*, that must be given its due. With this host of everyday notions as our guide, it is clear that talk of mere constant conjunction is inadequate; this simply passes over the central feature of acting or impinging upon something. The extra imported with this condition satisfies the demand for some species of non-logical connection to supplement the bare pattern of constant conjunction, something intrinsic to the sequence of events involved in an individual causal transaction.

It is true that, in the *Treatise*, Hume places considerable emphasis on spatial contiguity as a component in the causal relation (1888: 75). However, the notion does not get elaborated into any form of action of the cause upon something to produce the effect, but the contiguity is between the cause and the effect itself: 'whatever objects are consider'd as causes or effects, are *contiguous*'. Moreover, far from being the key component, it is dropped altogether by the time of the *Enquiry*. Note too that, when the effect is represented as a change or a state of affairs, such as a power failure or a decrease in the bird population, it is not something with which a cause could be contiguous. The notion of cause which we have been expounding is, as just intimated, one which involves three items rather than the two which Hume envisages. It is a matter of *C* acting upon *B* to produce *E*, not just of *C*, or *C*'s action, together with the following *E*. Talk of a causal *relation* is perhaps more fittingly reserved for the relation between the cause and what it acts upon. *C*'s causing of *E* is not a case of *C* standing in a relation to something already in existence when C acts; it is not like A's heating, striking, or smothering of B. There are certain changes, to be considered shortly, as with a change in temperature, size or position, where we have successive phases of a continuous development, and where the former pattern may not be in evidence, though a Humean regularity is discernible—a further argument against Hume's account.

Constant conjunction leaves us with mere juxtaposition—A followed by B—and however much further we take our analyses of A and B, we remain confronted by nothing more than this brute-factual succession. However, we are not obliged to stop with A—a movement of the body, say—and make a fresh start with B—a wheelbarrow moving. You can decompose pushing a wheelbarrow into these two events, but what you then have is not simply two happenings that have been found associated with one another, where the association is by way of nothing more than spatio-temporal juxtaposition, but happenings which have entered into a more specific, more intimate relation of physical contact. Finding out in greater detail what then takes place, in a way that elaborates the significance of the contact, is finding out just what causation here *is*, whereas this all-important feature—a matter of imparting momentum, say—is bypassed if we simply address A and B in isolation, or take the relation between them to be nothing more specific than that of juxtaposition—a mere succession of events, or, even worse, one *object* followed by another *object*. Pushing a wheelbarrow is not reducible to gardener's body moving followed by wheelbarrow moving, let alone to the one object being followed by the other, but a more grammatically complex drama is being worked out. One of the 'objects', the gardener, is *doing* something, not to an 'object' which is the effect, but to the wheelbarrow, which he is pushing, and the effect—better: result—of this interaction is a happening or state of affairs—the wheelbarrow moves or is moving.

I spoke above of causation as a matter of C acting upon B to produce E. This serves to draw attention to the threefold character of the transaction, but 'produce' clearly repeats the causal notion. A description which avoids this might simply specify that an agent, A, acts in a way which, through the contact it makes with B, culminates in a state of affairs, E, further features of the action, together with its outcome, identifying it as one of pushing, pulling, cutting, twisting, and so forth. In many such cases, just what is causing what is easily established: by taking into account nothing more than considerations of spatio-temporal continuity, we are able to follow a process through to its eventual culmination. The notion of a regularity, let alone of a causal law, need not, we may note, have any place in our considerations, nor is there any call to invoke some form of natural necessity, though the concept of power is brought in—harmlessly—with such notions as those of pushing and pulling.

As remarked above, Hume locates 'connection' within a cluster of terms—'power', 'force', 'efficacy', 'agency', 'energy'—which he imagines to relate to a reality to which we can never penetrate. All we are asking is that he give us back our term 'connection' and let it continue to perform the innocent and useful role which it enjoyed prior to its misappropriation. Far from its being the case that the mind perceives no real connection between distinct existences, it is *only* between distinct existences that such a connection is to be perceived. Where Hume would find a real connection there is nothing beyond a relation of ideas, a species of relation which logically *cannot* embrace that of causation. Action at a distance is problematic, not because there is anything wanting on the side of constant conjunction, of some functional relationship, but because *connection*, as met with in our everyday instances of causation, is lacking.

Those who are dissatisfied with a regularity theory of causation may be drawn to postulate some causal mechanism which underlies and explains a regular succession, but they are then confronted with the Humean objection that such a mechanism would simply present us with yet another succession. But what is lacking in the kind of connection that may well have been apparent at the outset, the kind of connection which, when disclosed, may put an end to uncertainties about what is causing what? You find out how your key turns the lock by investigating the bolts and levers which it activates. What is it that still eludes you? What is a hypothetical, possibly metaphysical, mechanism required to do that a mechanism, normally understood, cannot do, and *how* is it to do it? A mere succession does not call for reinforcement by a logical connection. As a species of linguistic relation, that will fail to link the action of the cause with what it produces. What is required is an acknowledgement of a genuine connection in what was characterized as a mere succession.

Again, there is a connection between your over-eating and your weight gain. The latter is not just an inexplicable concomitant of the former. What more is wanted? An elaboration of a familiar kind of the process whereby excessive consumption has this outcome, but beyond that, nothing. Or, rather, nothing beyond an admission that this can be reckoned a *connection*. For Hume it is not, but his claim that it is not is put to us in the guise of an empirical proposition, or at least as having a comparable import: as though he had discovered that everything is 'loose and separate' where we had thought things were connected. What is being communicated to us is better construed as a matter of no more than Hume's determination to *call* things 'loose and separate' when by ordinary standards there is a connection. It is only as an empirical proposition that it could have a consequence which might trouble us—to wit, that something is in fact missing—yet it is only as a decision that it stands any chance of our endorsement—and that, surely, is not to be counted on.

There is more than one way in which we might speak here of a connection. Most obviously, we have the connection implicit in the action of one thing on another, as when we split or burn a piece of wood. This is not so much a connection between cause and effect as between cause and thing affected, the effect being a happening or state of affairs, as with the splitting of the wood, ensuant upon the action of the agent, though we extend the notion to the latter in speaking of a connection between the agent's splitting of the wood and the wood's splitting. Again, suppose you erase a pencil mark. Your act of erasing is connected with what it acts upon—the mark—in the sense that it is applied to it, and it can also be said to be connected to what it brings about—the removal of the mark. The latter connection is really nothing more than the causal relation itself, but by considering what is and is not connected in the former way we can eliminate and identify causes and their effects. Rule out a connection and you rule out causation, as we observed with temporal periods, and which we might illustrate further with abstract terms such as *polynomial, ambiguity, identity*, and so on, terms which do not even begin to qualify as possible designations of a cause. Without the requisite connection, occurrence in a regular succession will count for nothing; on the other hand, by tracing an appropriate connection we may be able to identify cause and effect in a way that eludes attempts to make do with necessary and sufficient conditions.

So, consider the problem of distinguishing the succession, A causes B causes C, where B is a genuine cause of C at the same time as A is a more remote cause of C via B, from the case where C is caused by A but not through the intermediary of B, both C and B being on a par as effects of the common cause, A. It may be suggested that the latter possibility can be eliminated if, on B's being suppressed, C is none the less found to continue as before. If, on the other hand, the pattern is one of A causing B causing C, where B remains cause of C even if that role also falls to the earlier A, then A followed by not-B followed by C will not now be possible. However, distinguishing the two possibilities remains problematic. One case may appear straightforward. If B is suppressed and C continues to occur, C's occurrence is not due to B. However, in saying that B cannot have been the cause of C, if C still comes about even when B fails to occur, we are treating B as a necessary condition for C, a status which we have already seen to be not in general mandatory. Suppressing B may involve activating another cause of C. More importantly, what if B is suppressed and C ceases? That might be a matter of suppressing the cause of C, but could it not equally be a matter of preventing or inhibiting A from yielding its joint effects, B and C?

Think of our suppressing cause X as (i) a switch on a line from A to B, and (ii) as a switch on a line from A which branches to B and C. Taking the suppressor as operating when the switch is off, we have two possible observable consequences. If we are dealing with a physical set-up, wires connecting A, B and C according to the two arrangements, we should also be able to observe which of the two possibilities is realized, but this is to introduce something—patterns of connection and disconnection—over and above the bare relations of succession which the current hypothesis allows. Note that it does not help to have X antedate A. Once more, if an occurrence of X is followed by A then C, but no B, B is shown to be superfluous for the causation of C, but if only A, and neither C nor B, occurs after X, we are still in the dark about X's role: is it somehow interfering with A's production of its joint effects, where these remain independent of one another, or is X inhibiting the production of B by A, and thereby putting paid to a further effect C of B? If we can follow the line of action of the causes, we may be in a position to discount various possibilities, but specifications of necessary and sufficient conditions do not appear adequate to pinning down the causal relations.

Further support for our analysis, as opposed to one in terms of such a specification, can be found in a consideration of 'backwards' causation. Michael Dummett notes that the 'thought that an effect might precede its cause appears at first nonsensical. If the table is laid, that can only be because someone *has* laid it', and he goes on to remark that whatever a person does to bring about the plates being there will, we want to say, be pointless (1978: 319). At first blush, it would appear to be 'nonsensical' that gives the right description. It is not so much that any table-laying activity will be pointless, as that it is *senseless* to speak of laying a table that is already laid. You can, of course, add to the place settings, but that is not to the point. Similarly, if we can paint something that is already painted, that is only in the sense of adding *another* coat of paint, and if we stretch something that is already stretched, that will be to extend it beyond the point to which it has already been taken. Again, it is not coherent to suppose that the filling of a glass should take place subsequent to its being full, since nothing that was done now would merit the description: filling an already full glass. Likewise with closing a door that is already shut, breaking a bottle that is already in pieces, melting ice that is already liquid, and so forth.

However, this is not the most pertinent objection. There can be no filling of an already full glass, thought of as doing something to the glass as it now is. The question is, rather, whether something done now could conceivably count as filling the glass when, as we may suppose, the glass was observed to fill, for no apparent reason, at an earlier time, and here we are confronted with the difficulty that the only acts we might now perform which would count as filling a glass are acts which would count as filling a glass that is *now* empty. Indeed, an act that is normally totally irrelevant to the production of the effect, as uttering an incantation or blowing one's nose would be in this instance, is just as appropriately invoked as a putative cause as is pouring water into a glass, given that the usual causal/explanatory powers of the latter count for nothing in this context, yet even if the glass filled *subsequent* to an incantation, it is doubtful whether the latter could be described as the filling of a glass. A happening which is both yet to take place and, when it does, has no title to the description, 'filling the glass', in any recognizable reading of these words, could hardly be less promising as a candidate for cause.

If, as we have suggested, causing is a matter of acting upon x to produce y, then the rejection of backwards causation has a clear rationale: there is no acting upon x to produce result y if x is not present to interact with, so nothing we might now do would count as setting fire to, dissolving, or shattering an object which no longer exists. Note that this is not begging the question. We are not saying that nothing we might do now would count as bringing about the earlier disintegration of a glass, say, but that nothing we might do now involves the necessary contact with the glass. It may be said that it hardly needs any analysis of causation to exclude the backwards variety, given its patent incoherence, but it is noteworthy that what stands in the way of this reversal is the feature of causation which distinguishes this relation from a mere Humean correlation. Given two non-simultaneous events—two flashes of light, say—such that the occurrence of the one is a sufficient condition for the occurrence of the other, we may have to do with cause and effect, or we may not: we could be witnessing a flashing object on its travels, each flash being caused, but neither being the cause of the other.

Once we have causation, the two flashes will stand in an asymmetrical generative relation, but think of them as totally discrete and symmetrical— as bare succession allows—and you can more readily imagine them inter-changeable as cause and effect.

This, indeed, is how some see the issue. Causation is thought of as a relic of a primitive way of viewing Nature—perhaps one centred on human action—which is to be replaced by the notion of functional dependence. It is then noted that formulations of functional relations, as with the equa-tions of dynamics, remain invariant under a change from t to $-t$. Not only, it is supposed, is backwards causation now given the seal of approval of physical law, but someone who refuses to call the later event the cause of the earlier will not be making a point of substance, since there will be *only* the temporal difference to distinguish the two; there will be nothing pertaining to different physical processes.

To enlarge upon this point, the claim that it is part of the meaning of 'cause' and 'effect' that a cause is never later than its effect is sometimes dismissed as an objection of little force against the possibility of backwards causation (cf. Earman 1976: 10–11). And it is true that, if successive events were denominated 'cause' and 'effect' respectively *just* on the strength of their temporal ordering, if this categorization did not reflect any further difference in the two happenings in relation to one another, then there would indeed be something to this dismissal. It would not be unreasonable to abandon the usage for one in which symmetry was preserved, the later event being allowed as a possible cause of the earlier. We want a physical constraint to give substance to the temporal ordering, and this we have in the notion of one thing acting upon another. The effect is not in general something *acting*; indeed, the asymmetry is particularly marked when the effect is a state of affairs, something specifiable with a noun clause, as 'that the wood was burned'. If we do not venture beyond the more general notion of functional dependence, such asymmetries will escape our scheme, but the availability of that scheme does nothing to support the possibility of backwards causation, or to make it a matter of surprise that this should not in fact occur. The notion of causation has given way to that of another kind of dependence, and one that differs precisely in the respect that matters to the issue.

The point might be made in the following way. If someone postulates backwards causation, our natural response is to decry it as an absurdity. However, it is perhaps more fruitful to enquire about the character of the concept of cause that would then apply. And now, if regularity of succession is all there is to causation, why not allow that a cause *should* act in reverse? We have one event—knives, forks and plates suddenly taking up their rightful places on the table—and a subsequent happening: someone, let us say, invokes a certain incantation. This happens with great regularity; and, indeed, the table is found laid in this way only when the incantation is subsequently invoked. If your conception of causation asks no more of the notion of *bringing about* than may be satisfied by some combination of necessary and sufficient conditions, what is there, in such a circumstance, for that conception to offend against? How could we as much as suppose there to be anything amiss? In speaking of causing the table to have been laid, any appeal to recognizable ways in which laying a table is realized, as with actions of grasping, lifting, placing, and so forth, has been relinquished. We might say that to invoke talk of causation is, accordingly, to take cover behind a term which has been voided of sense, but if we do choose to retain it, it will not be a notion of causation that poses a problem, precisely because we have stripped it of those features which were at odds with a reversal of the usual temporal relation. But, of course, this point is more critical than conciliatory, since, if I am right, it is only with genuine causality, rather than with necessary and sufficient conditions, that we achieve an explanation. If, as in a regularity theory, there is no connection between cause and thing affected, no relation between cause and effect beyond that of temporal succession, then we have to do with events and things which occur or exist in total independence of one another. Have the cause act after the effect, and it is difficult to see how the former can have anything whatsoever of relevance to do with the latter, let alone be what *makes* it happen.

Does the problematic character of action at a distance point to a defect in our account? The earth is held in the sun's orbit through gravity, but it may be wondered whether we are making a problem for ourselves in speaking of *action* at a distance, when, as here, the body 'acting' patently does not *do* anything, does not change in any way. Suppose we ask why unsupported bodies fall to the ground, and are given the answer: because of (the force of) gravity. Has a causal explanation been offered? I do not believe that 'gravity' denominates a cause, but what has been passed off as an explanation is little more than a redescription. It is not so much that the fall is *caused* by gravity, as that the fall is a *case* of gravity. We invoke gravity when bodies *merely* fall—when, that is, they fall, but are not acted upon in a literal sense, as when they are pulled or pushed. Indeed, the appeal to gravity imports only as much of an explanation as this observation would imply: when answering the why-question by citing gravity, we at least rule out these alternative explanations. Gravity may be considered a phenomenon which confirms rather than overturns the present characterization of causation. Indeed, by paying closer attention to our concept of causation we could have seen that an understanding of gravitation was called for that eschewed action at a distance. Far from it being a defect that it should cast doubt on the propriety of speaking of a cause in this connection, our account has the virtue of leaving room for the very different approach provided by the general theory of relativity. In the context of this theory, the notion of the earth as exerting a pull on bodies is seen for the figure of speech, the misleading redescription, that it really is.

But suppose that doing *x* proves to be an absolutely dependable means for ensuring that a spatially distant and disconnected event, *y*, takes place. Would it not in time become unreasonable to deny that *x* was a cause of *y*? So, throwing a certain switch is invariably followed by a light going on some miles away, yet there is no physical link between switch and light, and the light goes on only when the switch is thrown. In the usual case, throwing the switch would lead to a succession of changes along a path between switch and light, changes which culminated in the light's going on, but in this instance there is no such path, the only clear instance of cause and effect being given with the act of throwing the switch and its immediate effects. In place of something that acts upon the light, it seems we are left with a curious complex consisting of the local happenings subsequent upon throwing the switch and the distant illumination of the light. The causal episodes cease with the last local act so describable, any change which results from this joining with the distant event to form a composite 'whole' constitutive of the effect. Such a description does not, of course, remove the mystery from this sequence of events, but by incorporating the spatial disconnectedness into the event itself, we can legitimately avoid speaking of the cause as acting at a distance. Conceivably, quantum non-locality could be looked at in this way, though again with no real diminution of its paradoxical character.

It is useful to look further at relations with which causation can be contrasted, a task we may approach in the following way. It is not unnatural to suppose that the cause–effect scheme is one which we impose, somewhat arbitrarily, on any process; somewhat arbitrarily, in that there can be more than one point where we draw a line prior to which what occurs is deemed (the action of the) cause, and what succeeds is deemed effect. However, to be a phase of a change is not necessarily to have a role in instigating that change. Indeed, in giving a sketch of the Humean account, an account from which many have felt there is no escape, we could equally have been describing a succession of happenings which would provide no grip for the notion of cause. Let me explain.

With causation we have an interaction which results in things being so and so. This is to be distinguished from a movement or other change having a state or condition as its result or outcome, but where this is an end phase or upshot of preceding happenings which are not interactions. I am thinking here of successive stages in a uniform development, as when something gets brighter or smaller or cooler, when it fades, unwinds, hardens, or melts. When a colour fades there will no doubt be a cause of the fading, but the antecedent states characterizable in terms of the colour as it originally was and as it successively becomes do not have the role of causing the eventual fading. A drop in temperature does not interact with, or act upon, anything to bring about a subsequent drop. Likewise with changes in sound, volume, size, intensity, and so forth. Causation is not a 'relation of ideas', but a cause can explain *why* a colour or sound faded, whereas an earlier state of the colour or sound cannot.

Suppose that, to all appearances, C has given rise to E on a number of occasions, but then fails to do so. For instance, the destructive power of flames is apparent beyond any shadow of a doubt, but we may none the less find ourselves presented with an occasion when the familiar results are not met with. Such an eventuality would show, of course, that fire is not efficacious in this way in all circumstances, but it would cast no doubt on its established destructive capacity. It is not: we must verify that C continues to produce E in like circumstances if we are to maintain that C has been a cause of E. Rather, if we find circumstances in which E is not forthcoming, we have to acknowledge limits to the causal power of C. It is the failures that are explained by finding a difference, rather than that the successes are recognizable only once sameness of conditions is established. There are, after all, countless well-known causal truths, but this would not be so if ascertainment that C caused E waited upon establishing the truth of an open-ended generalization. I know that I felt a pain in my toe because you trod on it, and I know that I fell over because you pushed me. I do not have to wait to establish general truths about such correlations before demanding an apology—indeed, I should not know even how to formulate them. Again, it is frequently our knowledge of causation that grounds our belief that conditions were relevantly the same. Objects cannot be too damp if they are to burn, so since the leaves caught alight, they must have been of the requisite degree of dryness. As I say, there are countless cases where we know that C caused E, but have no idea what beyond this was relevantly true from occasion to occasion, except as follows from the fact of causation. As a result of being frozen, the pipes burst. It would doubtless be agreed that if the conditions which led to the bursting of the pipes are repeated with identical pipes, these too will burst, but such a consideration is of no help in telling us anything more about present circumstances than we know already, let alone anything we should need to know to be sure that the freezing caused the pipes to burst. The supposition that C will yield E whenever the right conditions are repeated is, of course, not a supposition we should be willing to relinquish, but I suggest that it is grounded in the thesis that differences in behaviour are explicable, rather than being a simple inference from purely causal considerations. We can and do make extensive use of this principle—the principle of sufficient reason—in determining what is causing what, but this reliance requires no more than the correctness of the principle, not that a particular instance of it should be deducible from the truth of 'C caused E', that this should itself imply that a further occurrence of C in like circumstances will have E as outcome.

We may seek to reinforce this stance in the following way. Suppose that any regular succession, actual or merely hypothetical, is independent of what is to be found on the particular occasion. That is, there may be this regularity, there may not. Neither way is there, on the regularity theory, a scrap of difference in what can be expected to turn up on the occasion in question. It is just that, depending on what happens—or is envisaged as happening—on other occasions, we shall or shall not be prepared to attach the description, 'cause'; our labelling as 'cause' is thus provisional, but not because there was something we failed to find but might have found. But then, in being irrelevant to what then happened—in respect of anything other than the matter of usage—the regularity seems irrelevant to what is of interest. To repeat, evidence for C's causing E is evidence for something's occurring at a particular point of time; it is surely more plausible to explain that something in terms of one thing's acting upon another than to follow a regularity analysis at this point—that is, to construe the evidence simply as evidence that C falls under the general truth that whenever it occurs, so too does E. Nor should we be moved by the Humean complaint that we never observe an agent *producing* an effect, that we are presented with no more than a *succession* of changes: in many cases, as when we stir our coffee, or when we cut, tear, fold, or crumple a piece of paper, it is not only crystal clear that one thing is acting upon another, there is literally no room for an alternative cause to operate.

Such examples as these make it plain that causation is something we can observe, a possibility that has often been denied. Thus, in a passage reminiscent of Descartes' rebuttal of the claim that it is the senses rather than the intellect that perceive, J. L. Mackie suggests that if he sees someone peeling a potato, he does not *see* the knife *making* the peel come up, since by using his eyes he does not learn the truth of the counterfactual proposition which the idea of a cause as necessary for its effect involves:

> I don't *see* the knife *making* the peel come up. And what I most obviously fail to *see*, though I do *judge*, is that each bit of the peel would not have come up if the knife had not moved in there.

(1974: 133)

Presumably Mackie also does not see the cook emptying a jug of water, slicing a loaf of bread, crushing a clove of garlic, or stirring the soup. Mackie's general position is that A's causing B involves, over and above the joint occurrence of A and B, no more than the condition that B would not have happened had A not occurred. Since we do not go along with this analysis, our failure to see this to be so would not, on our account, show causation to be unobservable, but, of course, unobservability might be argued on other grounds.

First, there is more than one sense which might be attached to 'observing a cause'. The reading which, in the first instance, concerns us, may be indicated as follows. Suppose we see someone unconscious being administered oxygen, whereupon the person immediately starts to come round. To the suggestion that we witnessed the causation, the bringing about of the recovery, it might be objected that significant assumptions are being made, notably (1) that the treatment was all that the person was undergoing of relevance at the time, and (2) that unconscious people do not just become conscious without some cause or other coming into play. We can accept this objection. What has been described is not what would qualify as a clear case of observing a cause in the right sense. We have not seen the cause *operating*, in the way we may see someone sharpening a pencil or cleaning a window. It is the causing rather than the cause that is central. And, indeed, Mackie's example is one of the more straightforward. We do not have to see that each bit of the peel would not have come up if the knife had not moved in there, but we do see the knife lifting the peel, separating it from the potato. True we are supposing that the knife is a solid object, that it is making genuine contact with the potato, and so forth, but these are presumptive truths, not uncertain hypotheses from which we should withhold assent until further evidence is in.

My main concern is to insist that it *makes sense* to speak of observing the operation of a cause, but it is also important not to exaggerate the difficulties that may confront us. Not all situations are observationally 'ambiguous', and we should not lose sight of our central point that facts about causes, as involved in cutting, breaking, twisting, and so forth, are among the most familiar facts of experience. You cut a piece of fabric with a pair of scissors. Hume would not allow that you are witnessing the operation of a cause, since that would require penetrating to secret powers not given to observation (1902: 42). However, all that further investigation may supply may simply be more detailed information about the already identified cause and its mode of operation. The cutting and what it gives rise to will be difficult to keep secret from all but the most unperceptive observer.

Granted, it is conceivable that the fabric is not dividing in response to the passage of the blades, that independent forces are drawing it apart. But if these are genuinely distinct possibilities, there has to be some further finding which would enable us to choose between them; we do not wish to have to do with no more than alternative modes of description for a single happening. And, indeed, in so far as nothing can be detected which might be the agent exercising the conjectured causation, and nothing providing the vehicle whereby the causation is being exercised, then we have no reason not to accept what we observe at its face value. Actually to engineer a situation in which the pattern of causation is plain, we may, of course, have to engage in experimentation to eliminate rival hypotheses, rather than simply leave it to events to oblige. Since, in clearing away the clutter which obscures the functioning of the cause, we shall be making use of our knowledge of causes, we should want there to be occasions when no such manipulation, no such presupposition, is called for, but then there is no shortage of more primitive cases of this kind; and indeed it is often these, with ourselves in the role of undoubted agents, that we exploit with our manipulations. Again we may note that the importance of repetition lies in the way it confirms a judgement made on a particular occasion— confirms a *causal* judgement, rather than supplies mere facts of succession which, *sub speciei aeternitatis*, somehow add up to such a claim.

4
Creation and Conservation

The concept of causation that we have been exploring is not the only one, but we also have what might be called a causal condition, as presented in such propositions as 'The weight of the bridge caused it to buckle', 'Incompatibility is a cause of marital breakdown', and 'Unemployment is one of the chief causes of crime.' It would be absurd to construe 'the weight of the bridge' as anything like the name of a cause in the sense so far considered—something which could act upon the structure—but phrases with such abstract nouns typically give way to verbal or adjectival phrases rather than to designations of potential agents: it was because the bridge weighed what it weighed that it buckled, is what we are saying. Similarly with 'The height of the tower cause it to topple.' The height of the tower will not have caused the tower to topple by acting upon it, but it can be said that it is because the tower was as high as it was that it toppled. This is the concept of cause that can accommodate negative conditions, such as a lack or a failure, as with 'Lack of vitamin C causes rickets'. Roughly speaking, causal conditions enable a dynamic cause to operate, or make for variations in its operation.

If, with respect to our central concept of causation, an analysis along the above lines is correct, the significance of constant conjunction is evidential only: the notion of *acting upon* takes over the substantive role; it does not supplement so much as *supplant* that of constant conjunction, regularities providing a pointer to what is to be found in this capacity. It is often felt that the reality of the causal relation has to be defended against impoverished reductive analyses of the Humean variety. We may claim to have offered such a defence, but success in this respect does not mean vindicating either a rationalist or a metaphysical account of causation. That is, there is no question of construing causation as a species of logical relation, and the causal relation is inseparable from the physical world. This latter point, the point to which our discussion has been largely directed, will now be elaborated for the sake of its theological implications.

4.1 DIVINE AGENCY

For Hume, the uniqueness of the universe was an obstacle to saying much about it as a whole, there being no precedent to which we might appeal in our reasonings: 'To ascertain this reasoning, it were requisite, that we had experience of the origin of worlds' (1947: 150). However, any wholesale exclusion of such reasonings on the grounds of uniqueness is surely unwarranted: the arguments advanced by cosmologists are not invariably suspect because we lack the knowledge of other universes which would furnish the basis for an induction about universes in general, and hence about this one in particular. It may be countered that, while the cosmologist can hardly make inductions on this basis, any generalizations that he enlists must at least have instances within the universe (cf. Gaskin 1988: 26). However, the major difficulty resides, not in finding a precedent among evidential or empirical relations, but in *making sense* of descriptions which we might hope to extend from part to whole, and here it is true that the special character of the universe is always in danger of frustrating such projections, as when we treat the universe as something *in* space: a displacement *within* the universe makes sense, but not a displacement *of* the universe. We are understandably wary of extending to God descriptions which we should explain by reference to features of known species of individual—notably human beings—but we tend not to be sensitive to the same degree when extrapolating to the universe itself. It is surely not because we lack experience of different universes and their causation that we have doubts about the causation of our universe, but it is whether we may intelligibly speak of a cause at all in this instance that is problematic.

For Aquinas, knowledge of God that does not come from revelation is derived solely from his effects, a conception that assigns a key role to divine causation. For those who espouse pantheism—the world being conceived of as identical with God, or at least as an aspect, modification, or extension of him—such causation is not to the fore as far as grounds for belief in him are concerned, but traditionally the causal dependence of the universe on God has been the supremely important relation to be defended, a relation which has been held to take two forms, that of an originating and that of a sustaining creative act. Our concern will be to determine just what needs causal explanation, divine or otherwise, and whether causation by God can ever be intelligibly invoked. The preceding discussion of miracles, together with our account of causation, presage a negative answer on the second issue, and we shall give greater attention, in this and following chapters, to the question of need, since this may carry over into a non-theistic framework.

The concept of causation plays a pivotal role in the cosmological argument for the existence of God. There is more than one argument that goes by this name, but most versions seek to introduce God as an originating cause, whether of particular causal series within the universe, or of the universe itself. One form having the latter focus is the pleasingly simple *kalām* cosmological argument:

> Everything that begins to exist has a cause of its existence.
> The universe began to exist.
> Therefore the universe has a cause of its existence.

If the cause thus arrived at is taken to be God, the agency exercised may be located in the sphere of the *intentional*, where an association with laws or generalizations is not called for, but where a key explanatory role falls to intentions and decisions. The considerations just advanced do something for the notion of divine causation, in the sense that we are not obliged to reject such causation for lack of knowledge of pertinent generalizations, as Hume would require (1902: 148), but it is not because intentions or decisions can be appealed to as causally efficacious that we can demote laws from a central position. With human action, instrumentality remains with the agent's body; not only can that not be dispensed with, but intentions and decisions, as also will and desire, are not simply one stage back in the causal chain. They are not to be found at all on that line, and are not to be invoked when, as with God, the bodily dimension is wanting.

The idea that an ultimate source of being and becoming is to be found in the purely mental and non-physical is at odds with the conception of mind espoused by most contemporary philosophers. It is commonly held that the mind can impinge upon the world, indeed that mental states are to be characterized in terms of their causal role, but since such states are thought to be states of the brain, there is no lessening of a dependence on the physical. This is not a position I wish to invoke. It is doubtless true that we could not believe, desire, or intend without a brain, but any attempt to construe belief and the rest as states of that organ involves a serious mismatch between the psychological concepts and physical reality. Beliefs can be obsessive, unwavering, irrational, or unfounded, but nothing inside anyone's head answers to such descriptions. Of course, even a more general dependence on a brain is at odds with the theist's appeal to the mind of God, but I propose to argue against the sufficiency of the mental by stressing the necessity of the physical, both as this is bound up with our conception of an action, and more generally. The question of mental causation will be touched upon in Chapter 7, but whatever is said here, it is doubtful that there is any entitlement to speak of causation when the supposed agent is outside space and time. Certainly, the account of causation that was developed above is not favourable to an extension of the concept to the supernatural.

Causal transactions are often plainly observable, not happenings to which, ignorant of the inner powers of things, we are unable to penetrate; and, of course, changes induced in these familiar ways are very much in the realm of the physical. Not only is causation not a metaphysical concept in its application to events in the natural world; it does not appear to be metaphysical in the sense that it might apply *beyond* that world. I can get no grip on the idea of an agent *doing* something where the doing, the bringing about, is not an episode in time, something involving a changing agent and a change induced through its action. What is there left of the notion of cause once it is stripped of these features? A pebble can have little effect on the ocean, and a speck of dust even less. Chaos theory may allow them some larger influence, however improbable, but replace pebble or speck with something not even in the world, and an effect is not ruled out as physically impossible; it does not even make sense to speak in this way.

It is sometimes suggested that, if God is the author of temporally separated events—miracles at different times, for instance—we are forced to acknowledge successive acts on his part, a succession which contradicts his timelessness. To this it is replied that the time at which an action is performed need not be related in this way to the time it takes effect: letters posted together may reach their destinations on different days. There is a problem in conceiving of a single act achieving everything that God has supposedly accomplished, but our present problem is not with the effects, nor with the singularity of the act, but with the difficulty in speaking of an act when the *acting* is not temporally extended, a difficulty which is no less acute when the 'acting' is purely mental.

It is also worth stressing that our objection does not rest on any form of verificationism. Consider one form that an objection thus based has often assumed:

Taking for our example the statement 'God created the world', we can put the difficulty in the form of a dilemma: either this assertion selects from among conceivable alternatives, and as such is a cosmological hypothesis subject to scientific refutation; or it does not select, and in that case it is impossible to say what it means.

(Crombie 1957: 46)

This criticism, not endorsed by Crombie, depends on supposing that 'God created the world' is thought of as having a quasi-empirical construal, and contending that the proposition does not live up to the demands of such a reading, whereas the point of the present objection is that the proposition lapses before the question of what, if anything, counts for or against it can even be raised.

Scepticism concerning our capacity to know of causes is not uncommon among empiricist writers. Thus Comte thought that we must give up the search for what are called causes, these being 'beyond our reach', 'an unattainable mystery' (1957: 51), and Duhem thought that scientific theories cannot get at the real causes of things (1954: 30). As we have seen, this is not where a problem lies, but it is the further extension of the concept, as found in arguments for the existence of God, that stands in need of justification. Suppose that, far from being a relation which may take us to a transcendent reality, causation is bound to the physical every bit as much as are length, breadth, and depth, that it is as much a relation between bodies as being above or behind, as much a physical phenomenon as the collisions and explosions in which it can be discerned. The concept of causation having then lost any metaphysical pretensions to which it might aspire, it is an illusion to think that supernatural agency can be behind the universe's existence, especially if we think of a divine agent not acting *upon* anything but creating out of nothing. A sculptor creates a statue by chipping away at a block of marble. When God supposedly created the universe, there was nothing that had the role of the marble, and no act analogous to the chipping. Given the complete absence of any transformation, modification, or reorganization in creation *ex nihilo*, our understanding of this notion can hardly profit from our understanding of causation. This is not to say that creation, as we understand it, is always creation *out of* something. Think of creating havoc, creating difficulties, or creating a false impression. There are these ways of speaking, but none appears to offer any help in understanding creation of a physical universe out of nothing.

Aquinas is clear that such creation, properly understood, is not an instance of change, 'for change means that the same thing should be different now from what it was previously' (*Summa Theologiae*, I, Q. 45, Art. 3, ad 2), whereas nothing is transformed in creation *ex nihilo*. But he still regards creating as an instance of causing, and this brings with it two outstanding difficulties. Not merely the difficulty that causing is a matter of doing something *to* something, but the more general consideration that, as an *act*, it will perforce occur in time. When the temporal dimension is removed, we are left with just a *relation* (ibid., Q. 45, Art. 3), but it is difficult to see how this could now qualify as causal, a difficulty further exacerbated by Aquinas's contention that, while the relation of creature to God is a real relation, the relation of God to creature is not (ibid., Q. 45, Art. 3, ad 1). Reading Aquinas, one has the impression that the notion of *act* is thought to be sufficiently clear simply through its contrast with *potency*, and that it is a short step from the notion of *act*, taken at its most general, to that of *acting* or *being active*. Compare:

God is pure act, absolutely and universally perfect, and completely without any imperfection. Whence it most fittingly belongs to Him to be an active principle, and in no way whatsoever to be passive. On the other hand, the nature of active principle belongs to active power. For active power is the principle of acting upon something else; whereas passive power is the principle of being acted upon by something else, as the Philosopher says. It remains, therefore, that in God there is active power in the highest degree.

(ibid., Q. 25, Art. 1)

I was earlier dismissive of the pretensions of 'Let there be light' to serve as an explanation of the origin of light, even when uttered by God, but it might be maintained that, on the contrary, it is through just such acts that creation *ex nihilo* could be channelled. It is not inconceivable that God should speak and that something should come into existence as ordained, so we cannot rule creation out as logically impossible. Very well, but to say that creation is logically possible is only to say that, if anything rules it out, it is not logic; there could still be other reasons for its exclusion. What would warrant us in speaking of *creation* when, on God's speaking, something came into existence? *How* is it that the divine act is efficacious, when uttering words does not normally have such consequences? It is no good saying that the difference resides in the fact that the utterance is an expression of God's will, and God is all-powerful. That leaves us none the wiser as to how it is that the divine word has this consequence. As it stands, the 'explanation' is surely no better than the supposition that something might spring into existence uncaused. But suppose that, whenever a certain person uttered certain words, a leaf, say, appeared, seemingly from nowhere. This would hardly be something we could ignore. True, but note that this is an event in *time*. An act is performed, and something then comes into existence. We have at least the beginnings of a framework in which we might hope to make sense of such happenings, but in the divine case that is totally lacking. To have as much as a relevant fantasy, we had to place God in time and have him decree that something be so; refuse such conditions, and we are left with nothing even to consider as a possible creative act. Again, we have just noted examples of creating which do not involve creating something out of anything, and there are many cases where an *F* comes into being though nothing becomes an *F*, as when we dig a hole, utter a cry or start a fire, but whether thought of as temporally extended, as with digging, or occurring at a point of time, as when a flame is caused to be, the causation has an essential temporal dimension.

4.2 GOD AND TIME

Does it help if we cease to require that God be outside time? Time is generally thought of, by theists, as having its beginnings with the creation of the universe, and physicists, too, consider time to be intimately bound up with matter and space. On this view, locating God in time would be as inappropriate as attributing spatial extension to him. However, if time's being bound up with matter means only that a material universe devoid of time is impossible, it remains open whether a non-physical being— a Cartesian thinker, say—might be subject to time. The question has recently been the subject of vigorous debate, with increasing sympathy being shown to the untraditional view of God as everlasting, rather than as timeless (see the essays in Ganssle 2001 and Ganssle and Woodruff 2002). Since our central problem persists whatever the stand here taken, we shall consider the issue only briefly, but it is worth some attention, given that it also leads onto questions about time of relevance to later concerns.

It may be argued that the very existence of a spatio-temporal world is sufficient to place God in time. Imagine a totally static universe. In so far as there is no change, there will be no call to regard that universe as having a temporal dimension, but so long as events have a place therein, it will be possible to give sense to the notion of the duration of an unchanging object. God without the universe could be both timeless and unchanging, we shall suppose, but if there should be a spatio-temporal universe, that will enable us to say both that God existed at some past point of time and that he exists now, which implies that he endures over time. He need not change for this to be so, any more than a physical object need change in order for it to have a duration. On the other hand, if there are difficulties in speaking of far-off events as taking place now, how much more difficult is it to make sense of the current existence of a being quite outside our spatio-temporal reference frame. Perhaps we should hold out for God's timelessness by parsing 'exists' in 'God exists' timelessly, and regarding 'God exists now' as affirming that 'God exists', so understood, is true now. The proposition would, if true, also have held at any earlier point of time, but since then, too, only timeless existence would have been affirmed, there would be no implication that God had endured over the intervening period.

As well as excluding existence *over* time, we shall have to ensure that God does nothing *at* a time. It is sometimes argued that if God experiences a past and a present event simultaneously, then, since each event is simultaneous with God's experience of it, each is simultaneous with the other, contrary to hypothesis. But if God exists timelessly, he does not have experiences that are states or events in time and which might accordingly occur at the same—or a different—time as the episodes of which they are experiences. This is not to say that there is nothing amiss with the idea that what we deem past, present, and future should all be equally present to God. While becoming aware and ceasing to be aware are episodic happenings, being aware is a temporally extended state. I am aware of the sunset; it is making an impression on me; I take in its features, entertain thoughts about it. Being aware may be described as a passive condition, but that is not to say that it is static, yet if God is outside time it is difficult to know what awareness for him could consist in.

For those who believe that nothing objective answers to our distinction between past, present, and future, a further step would be to align the universe itself with God, the static four-dimensional array constituting the 'block' universe being comparable with God in its timelessness. Just as there would be no real change, no real becoming, in the universe, so there would be no acts on God's part which were once present and subsequently past, but he would timelessly stand in the relation of creator and sustainer to the universe—see Craig 1998 for extensive discussion. However, there is still a difficulty. Upholders of this 'tenseless' theory of time believe that we can dispense with the notions of past, present, and future in favour of the relations of *earlier than, later than,* and *simultaneous with,* and the temporal features of an action will be retained in the applicability of these notions, an action having an earlier and a later phase, for instance. We may not be troubled by the notion of God acting now, say, and so of his standing in a real but transient relation to his creation, but the notion of a divine action, both as having the residual temporal characteristics and as bearing *upon* something, would continue to be problematic.

And, of course, the tenseless theory itself can hardly count upon our ready assent. How, after all, can *x* be earlier than *y* without being past when *y* occurs? It is claimed that there is no need to enlist tenses when stating the truth conditions of tensed sentences, but only unchanging relations of simultaneity and the rest need be invoked. We need to ask ourselves what this means. Consider a proposition which might seek to associate a tensed sentence with a tenselessly given truth condition; say, ' "Vesuvius erupted" is true if and only if the time of Vesuvius's eruption is before the utterance of these words.' The concern here may be to lay down truth conditions appropriate to 'Vesuvius erupted' as a sentence *type*: we wish to accommodate utterances of these words at any time, past, present, or future, in which case a suitably general, timeless, reading of 'is' is called for—though it is somewhat misleading to say that the truth conditions are tenseless, since they are not so individually; it is a matter of covering all the tensed possibilities indifferently, rather than introducing a possibility of a different variety. Suppose, now, we consider a particular past utterance of 'Vesuvius erupted'. The proposed specification of truth conditions remains correct, but we could now replace 'is true' by 'was true' and 'is before' by 'was before', as indeed would be more natural. If it is insisted that the truth condition can still, should we wish, be expressed timelessly, we may observe that to have recourse to such a formulation in no way affects the correctness of '*was* before'. It is simply: a verbal form might be enlisted which *fails* to convey what 'was' conveys. With the first possibility, a timeless 'is' was appropriate, since we wished to do equal justice to the three possibilities—past, present, and future; in the case now being considered, one of these only is at issue, and persistence with the timeless use represents not a necessity of even-handedness, but an omission, a failure to indicate the temporal relation in question. It is of no great interest to claim to have dispensed with considerations of tense when all this amounts to is *ignoring* them.

Supposing that 'knowledge' of tensed facts is genuine knowledge, can God's omniscience be maintained so long as he remains outside time? For such a being there is no *now*, so no question of a belief on God's part that a certain event is currently under way. God can know of temporal relations as specified tenselessly, so can know that the Treaty of Versailles antedates my writing of these words, but he cannot know that my action has a present rather than a past or future reality. But I know that my writing is taking place now, so is there something I know that God does not and cannot? On the one hand, to say that he is ignorant of such matters suggests that there is something which it makes sense to speak of him as knowing to be so, but which somehow escapes his knowledge, whereas no conceivable perspective for an atemporal being is conveyed with 'has happened', 'is happening', or 'will happen'. The words lack application for God, rather than have an application which eludes him. On the other hand, given that they do have application for us, and given the vast number of tensed facts of which we, but not God, have knowledge, perhaps there is a damaging conflict between God's timelessness and his omniscience.

Before considering what conclusion should be drawn from the possibility of such conflict, let us look at the analogous problem posed by divine omnipotence. A theist, whilst holding that God is all-powerful, might well not wish to regard God's omnipotence as an ability to do anything without qualification. When the putative deeds prove to harbour a contradiction, he is surely right. God could not prove that 2 cubed is less than 2 squared. However, such inability is in no sense a limitation on God. It is, rather, that whatever God might do, *we* would not allow the description, 'God proved that 2 cubed is less than 2 squared.' There is also a question as to the scope of 'do'. Is 'God can do anything' to cover involuntary acts? Presumably not, if this puts them beyond his control, and presumably, too, acts which are failings or defects are not to fall within his competence. So no acts of deception, no changes of mind, no making a mistake, no ceasing to exist.

That such acts are to be denied to God does not appear to detract from his power, but consideration of the notion of perfection brings to light more troublesome possibilities. Aquinas claims that, since God's being contains in itself the perfections of all beings, the divine goodness must contain in its way all the virtues. However, because bodily delights are foreign to God, such virtues as sobriety, chastity, temperance, and continence are not attributable to him, though they will have their exemplars in the divine nature (*Summa contra Gentiles*, I, 92). Since certain actions, as acting temperately, are accordingly not possible for God, it would seem that what we are seeking to characterize is specifically *God's* omnipotence—something more circum-scribed than might originally have been supposed. That is, there are acts which, whilst not of themselves contradictory, cannot be reconciled with other attributes of God, thus opening up the possibility that omnipotence for another being might not be subject to the same constraints. Perhaps the most telling challenge to God's omnipotence is of this character. It is no limitation on God that he cannot do what is logically impossible, and it could be that the virtuous acts which he cannot perform are possible for us only because of imperfections in our nature, as Aquinas suggests (ibid., I, 93). This suggestion is not altogether persuasive. Courageous action is possible only if something is perceived as a threat, and since nothing can be a threat to God, such action by him is ruled out. That we can act courageously reflects a limitation on our powers, but it is not clear that this is a matter of a failing on our part. Indeed, if a being's nature logically precludes a departure from the straight and narrow, the scope for praiseworthiness is surely greatly diminished for that being. More importantly, while our capacity for certain virtuous acts may presuppose character as bodily agents, such character is not itself to be seen as a limitation or imperfection, since it is precisely what makes action possible. Our understanding of 'do', 'act', and other more specific verbs imposes a restriction which we have been constantly stressing: what would *count* as an action by an immaterial agent? If, as we have argued, the answer is 'nothing', then, while God may be supreme among those of his kind, his power may none the less fall far short of ours.

Faced with possible restrictions on God's omniscience or omnipotence, a question the theist might ask is: What does it matter? So, on the one hand, we may rest content with the idea that God possesses the maximal degree of power and knowledge consistent with his nature, any apparent shortfall being seen, not as a failing, but as an inescapable consequence of the demand for consistency. Thus, since God is everywhere, he cannot, unlike us, be nearer to Rome than to Paris, but that inability is outweighed by the virtues of ubiquity. On the other hand, if the nature that provides these constraints means that God cannot be or do what for other reasons he is required to be or to do, then the shortfall may be held to be a defect. God's ignorance of tensed facts could be thought tolerable as reflecting the superior position of one not subject to the restrictive perspective of beings whose awareness is confined to the present (cf. Helm 1989: 76–7). Or again, it has been suggested that, as not caught up in time, God is not subject to the irretrievable loss that time may bring and that militates against perfect happiness (see Leftow 1991: 278–9). However, a failure to be an agent of change surely cannot be tolerated, and this remains a major problem even if God is to be regarded as in time. If he is to act on or in his creation, physical attributes proper to spatio-temporal, and not merely temporal, character would appear necessary, and if it is a matter of acting so as to produce the universe, not acting *upon* anything, we still have the problem of making sense of such an accomplishment.

As with miracles, it needs more than a failure to come up with a naturalistic explanation to confer sense on the notion of supernatural agency. None the less, the position we have reached is not satisfactory as a resting place. Suppose we are right in refusing to allow that God, or indeed any other non-physical being, could have caused the universe to be, that the universe is closed under the causal relation. Does this resolve the queries that prompted the cosmological argument? A cause of the universe was apparently needed to explain why it exists, yet if there can be no cause external to the universe, and if the universe cannot be *causa sui*, then we have seemingly blocked all avenues that might lead to an explanation, and are forced to conclude that the universe exists as no more than a brute, causally inexplicable, fact. However, we can move a stage on from this bleak conclusion if we can reject the claim that the universe *came* into existence. A universe whose existence had a beginning, but for which any cause of that beginning is to be excluded, is a universe that remains puzzling, but if that exclusion can be joined by an exclusion of what it is called upon to explain, the puzzlement will have lifted significantly. True, if the denial that the universe had a beginning means that it has existed for an infinite time, we have another formidable problem on our hands, and, whether the universe is temporally finite or infinite, we still do not have an answer to our question as to why it exists. The universe may neither have, nor be susceptible of, a causal explanation, but the why-question seemingly remains. Not 'Why does it exist?' where a cause of becoming is sought, but 'Why does it exist?' where the query is motivated by considerations of modality: the universe need not have existed, surely, so the fact that it does is a fact that calls for explanation.

4.3 SUSTAINING CAUSES AND PERSISTENCE

This is where we shall leave our why-question for the present, turning now to the question of the supposed need for a causal explanation if we are to account for the *continued* existence of the universe. When something comes into existence, the question of why or how this came about is always in place. Without some indication of what made the particular circumstances exceptional, it would be arbitrary to rule it out of order, and it is of interest to consider whether the contention that continued existence requires a cause is likewise one whose rejection would fly in the face of what would be regarded as eminently reasonable outside the present context.

Defenders of the cosmological argument have commonly contended that, even if every event in this world has a causal antecedent, the series of events as a whole remains in need of a cause to sustain its existence. This move may strike us as curious. No dissatisfaction is shown with the explanations so long as they can be taken to terminate in a self-sufficient originating cause, but if an infinity of causes and effects is proposed, it is claimed that the whole series requires an explanation of its continuing existence. If that is so, then, despite their apparent representations to the contrary, those who shift tack in this way were not really explaining the existence of the things which *were* traceable back to an initial generating cause. However, if a common interpretation of Aquinas is correct, in neither the First nor the Second Way is he concerned with sequences of changes which go back into the past, but he is from the outset envisaging sources of movement and existence contemporaneous with what they explain (see Kenny 1969: ch. 2, 3; Coplestone 1955: 117–18). This so-called 'vertical' reading is thought necessary in the light of Aquinas's admission that it is not impossible to go on for ever in a series of efficient causes. However, it has been argued, in Fogelin (1990: 308–9), that not only does the text not appear to warrant this reading, but it also takes into account the possibility of such series by distinguishing between efficient causes *per accidens*, for which the possibility is allowed, and efficient causes *per se*, for which it is not (*Summa Theologiae*, I, Q. 46, Art. 3, ad 7). In an essentially ordered series of causes, a given member is dependent on its predecessor in its very act of causation, as with Aquinas's example, following Aristotle, of a stone being moved by a stick which is in turn moved by a hand. The contrast is with such series as those of men begetting men begetting men . . . A man is dependent for his existence on his father, who is in turn dependent for his existence on his father, but grandfather does not cause father to cause a son to be born, whereas the movement of the hand does cause that of the stick. It is when the series is one of C_n's causing C_{n+1}'s causing C_{n+2}'s causing . . . that we can conclude that n must have had the value 1.

The vertical interpretation can be sustained if the only examples of essentially ordered causal series involve the requisite simultaneity of causes and effects, as indeed Aquinas held to be so for ordered series of movers and things moved (*Summa contra Gentiles*, I, 13). Motion transmitted through a succession of gear-wheels comes close to satisfying this demand, and we shall take up this example in the final chapter. However, whether or not the 'horizontal' reading is to be preferred, there is no doubt of the centrality of the notion of divine conservation in Aquinas's thought: 'the being of every creature depends on God, so that not for a moment could it subsist, but would fall into nothingness, were it not kept in being by the operation of the divine power' (*Summa Theologiae*, I, Q. 104, Art. 1), 'The conservation of things by God is not by a new action, but by a continuation of that action whereby he gives being, which action is without either motion or time' (ibid., I, Q. 104, Art. 1, ad 4). Not only every being, but every act, every thought, every choice is thus dependent—something of an embarrassment, surely, if the bad as much as the good owes what persistence it has to God. Even if evil is a privation, that which is evil is not. Later philosophers, including Descartes, Leibniz, and Berkeley, agree that divine creation is a continuing action. One would expect this from Berkeley, given the demands of his idealism, but on this point he is, as he appreciates, in step with those who do not go along with his immaterialism: 'Those who have all along contended for a material world have yet acknowledged that *natura naturans* (to use the language of the Schoolmen) is God; and that the divine creation of things is equipollent to, and in fact the same thing with, a continued repeated creation: in a word, that conservation and creation differ only in the *terminus a quo*' (1975: 345–6). More recently, John Polkinghorne has written: 'the assertion that God is Creator is not a statement that at a particular time he did something, but rather that at all times he keeps the world in being' (1990: 54).

This conception of a sustaining cause is theologically important. Not only does it have repercussions for the character of an originating act of creation—that is not something that is now over and done with—but it may lead to a revision of the theist's way of thinking about acts of divine intervention, as with miracles. Thus, the notion of God acting from time to time on or in the world may be resisted even by a theist, since it would appear to require that the world be sufficiently independent of God for it to be appropriate to speak of him revisiting a reality with which he is customarily out of contact. If his sustaining act is one of immanence, then a miracle would be not so much an intervention, more by way of a perturbation in the ever-continuing *creatio continuans*. Pursuing this line of reasoning, it might be suggested that if the theist wishes to insist on a role for God in keeping the universe in being, he would do better to argue that we cannot meaningfully distinguish between a continuing sustaining act and an initial creative act subsequent to which God withdraws his influence, since this distinction would require that the initial act be temporally bounded, thus placing God in time. However, while the difficulties noted with respect to a divine *act* are still with us, it would not appear that the distinction inevitably collapses in this way, since we can think of the difference as one in the sphere of influence of God's act, this being confined either to the bare origination of the universe, or extending, in addition, to its further continuation. Compare Aquinas: 'Nor is it necessary to say that a creature is being created during its entire existence; for creation imports a relation of the creature to the Creator *with a certain newness or beginning*' (I, Q. 45, Art. 3, ad 3). Accordingly, the claim that the universe is in need of a cause of its continuation is one that we may call upon the theist to defend. The question is of particular interest in that, if no such cause is needed, and if the universe did not *come* into existence, there is no call to posit a cause of its existence at any point, neither a cause *in fieri* nor a cause *in esse*.

When, we may ask, is a sustaining cause needed? Most obviously, when there is a disintegrating factor to be countered or inhibited, as when a structure will collapse unless it is supported. However, if there is no such threat there is no such need. What is being claimed when a causal explanation is none the less demanded for a persisting state, as with the continued existence, shape, or colour of a rock? It is not so much that waiting in the wings is something which will act upon the rock to alter or destroy it, as that there must be something to keep it going—as though things and their states have a natural tendency to cease to be, and will do so unless this is countered. And, of course, there is such a tendency, found with unstable elements, but it is not a condition met with quite generally. If objects tended to disintegrate more readily than at present, we should ask, as we now do, why something had not shown this behaviour at the expected time; we still should not consider that persistence up to that point needed explaining. This would be called for only if something extremely unstable, something which disintegrated as soon as it was formed, exceptionally endured. Note that if a body remains intact because of cohesive forces binding its parts, whether at a macro or a micro level, we shall be talking about the operation of forces internal to the body. Moreover, there is no general demand that the parts themselves will require a sustaining cause of their existence.

A further possibility is that there should be changes within the persisting state. Contrast continuing in a state of rest or motion with continuing to vibrate or oscillate, the kind of phenomenon where we are happy to apply the scholastic dictum, *cessante causa, cessat effectus*. A cause may have brought something to a certain point, or got motion under way, but, unless we have a repetition of the first case, no further cause is needed to sustain the states brought about, whereas with a vibration or oscillation a sustaining cause may be called for. However, we note that when a cause is required, it will be as much an initiating as a sustaining cause. Think in terms of a single state—a prolonged vibration—and it will be appropriate to speak of a sustaining cause; focus on the discontinuities within that state—changes requiring a renewed input of energy, a repetition of a cause—and talk of a series of initiating causes is in place.

It has been suggested that the proposition 'God made the world' is more like 'The musician made music' than 'The blacksmith made a horseshoe.' This is an appealing analogy. The world is represented as the upshot of a divine act without being a transformation of pre-existing material, a conception which may again be continued into the acts thought of as (miraculous) interventions: a novel variation in the music is no more the result of the musician acting upon the music than is the music which follows the score. Likewise, whether God is maintaining the world in existence, or inducing within it episodes which do not follow laws of Nature, the world is not to be taken as some given on which he acts. However, while sounds have the kind of dynamic quality which requires sustained production, the universe at large appears to have more the character of the horseshoe. Certainly, many of the causal questions posed by the existence of things within it may be answered by appeal to agents which no longer exist. More importantly, the analogy of the musician keeps us within the familiar framework of causation, a framework which appears difficult to extend to God's creative act, in that the musician, when blowing his trumpet or wielding his violin bow, acts upon something to produce the sounds he makes.

A cause which accounts for the coming to be of an object, or the beginning of some state, will not provide what is sought by those who demand a sustaining cause. We already have such generative causes, but the supposition is that they have done what they can do with the bringing into being of the object or state, x, that something further is needed to account for continuing existence. But if anything which ceases its operation while x continues in being is disqualified, our sustaining cause will have to be in existence for as long as x continues in being. However, the demand for a sustaining cause is surely repeatable, to the detriment of this conception: if y is what maintains x in being, then there must be something, z, which performs the same service for y, and so on ad infinitum. But, surely, a continuing change, process or activity—as burning, vibrating, or resounding—does require a cause, and if this takes us to a further change as a cause, and so on and so on, do we not have here too a demand for a cause that is repeatable? So why, when it is a matter of a generative cause, is this not a problem? The difficulty with the sustaining causes is that they are required to be in existence so long as the state endures, and this requires that the infinitely many causes—agents for whose existence we have no evidence—exist simultaneously.

However, the considerations which would have us posit a series of simultaneous causes result in reasoning which the theist will endorse, reasoning which would have it that the series must terminate in a first cause. Accordingly, we can hardly take the resultant proliferation of causes as a reductio of his position. Moreover, it is still perhaps not evident that a sustaining cause is not to be found in preceding conditions, as Mackie has suggested: 'The earlier phase of a self-maintaining process surely brings about, or helps to bring about, the later phase. If the concept of cause and effect does not yet cover them, it should: we can recognize immanent as well as transeunt causation' (1974: 156). Furthermore, 'Is not any physical object a self-maintaining process or a cluster of such processes . . .?' (ibid., 156; cf. 221-1). It is true that, unless there are expectations to the contrary, we do not usually consider continuing in existence as calling for explanation, so do not turn to an earlier phase to explain the phase that follows, but Mackie considers this to be a superficial reason for withholding talk of causation. The common pattern is as much there 'in the objects' as it is in cases where we are happy to invoke causation (ibid., 158). Mackie looks to preceding conditions to find a cause, not to causes simultaneous with their effects, but a conservationist may still take heart from his contention that we are right to seek a cause of persistence.

There are two issues here: whether a continuing state requires a sustaining cause, and whether, if it does, a preceding phase of that state is a suitable candidate. First, it is difficult to see how such a phase can be fitted into a sequence of causes. Consider the example of a spinning top. According to Mackie, if a top is spinning from t_1 through t_2 to t_3, then the rotation from t_1 to t_2 causes the rotation during the ensuing interval from t_2 to t_3. However, the spinning cannot be said to cause its subsequent spinning in anything like the way the initial action exerted upon the top caused it to spin. Causing a rotation is causing the top to rotate, and one rotation does not act upon the top to cause its successor. Again, if the initial impetus can cause the spinning for some part of its duration, why not for the whole of its duration? How can it be anything but arbitrary to reckon the action which got the spinning under way as causing the movement of the top only up to t_n, rather than to t_{n+1} or t_{n+2}? Or, if the causal role of these rotations does not pre-empt that of the action, for what are they needed? It is not as if some period of rotation represented a renewal of the force which set the top in motion, so *how* is it imagined that it operates? The likeness to a cause is thought by Mackie to be given with relevant necessary and sufficient conditions: 'the rotation between t_1 and t_2 was necessary and sufficient for the rotation between t_2 and t_3' (ibid., 156). However, this appeal is misplaced: a first rotation is necessary if something is to *count* as the second rotation, but that is not causal necessity, and sufficiency has to mean sufficiency for the *production* of the rotation, which is just what is at issue.

It is, I suggest, by revealing certain conditions as not changes in the relevant sense that we rebut the need for a sustaining cause. The examples discussed indicate that, as a change, the *cessation* of a state requires a cause, and this in two possible ways: a cause acts so as to terminate a state, or a sustaining cause ceases its activity. With the continuation of a state, a cause is needed if the state is of the latter kind, involving certain kinds of change within it, or if a cause which would terminate the state needs to be inhibited. This leaves persisting states, as with simply existing, or being oblong, seemingly without need, in general, of any causes of their persistence, the most obvious reason being that persistence does not involve *change*. If something is still around after many years, this may well be remarkable, but that will be because it has somehow, against the odds, survived threats to its integrity. If there are no such threats, there is nothing to explain.

The opposing view may well go with a wrong picture of time. For an unchanging object or state, temporal duration has meaning only thanks to the possibility of bringing the object or state into a relation with a series of changes, as might be given with a clock. To explain getting older, and indeed to explain why something gets older, where this means no more than 'continues in being', is not to give a causal explanation, but to explain what conditions have to be satisfied for a description in these terms to be warranted: you can talk of 'continuing in being' because the changes necessary to make sense of the passage of time have been taking place.

We are not to read real changes into the object on the strength of these relations—as if we might take away all change and our static objects would none the less continue to beat out their internal rhythm, of themselves marking out periods of time. There is not, merely by dint of having endured, any feature of the object that needs accounting for; that need arises only with the real changes which might give the measure of its persistence. The object itself is merely co-present with certain of these. Not a change in it, but a mere change in a relation. The claim is not, we may note, that no cause is necessary because an object which continues in existence remains in the *same* state. It is the absence of change in the object that matters; the same state, as one of pulsating, could none the less involve changes which called for a cause.

This resolution of the issue is of a piece with our explanation of why it is that the laws of Nature continue to hold. This took us immediately to the question of why the things whose behaviour is codified by the relevant laws continue to be as they are in relevant respects, and that poses no problem so long as nothing has happened to alter their behaviour. Of course, if alterations had occurred, that need not mean that the given laws would have been falsified rather than merely rendered inapplicable. Once more, there is no call to invoke the deity as the sustainer of laws. Nor is there any call to ascribe a sustaining role to the laws themselves, as maintained by Norman Kretzmann, who suggests that, if we consider the succession of conditions required for continuing existence, as an atmosphere is necessary for living things, and gravity for an atmosphere, we shall find natural laws at the top of the hierarchy: 'And, naturally, part of any generally correct answer to the question of what keeps the world going, what explains the producing of things over time, will have to be that natural laws continue to obtain' (1999: 62). Laws can indeed have the standing of necessary conditions for continuing existence. That is to say, something like the current laws may have to be in force if, for instance, life is to continue, but what that means is that things must continue to behave much as they currently do for that to be so; it is not a matter of the 'persisting efficacy of natural laws' (ibid.). Altered behaviour may result in altered laws. It is the laws that are sustained by the constancies in behaviour; they do not *keep* the world going. Note too that, if there were certain changes, if, say, the earth lost its atmosphere, then while many things might well go out of existence, they would not necessarily be annihilated; their constituents could persist after their disintegration. Likewise, too, if the laws should change.

The theist's position has not profited from our discussion of causation. In laying emphasis on the relation given with *x* acting upon *y*, we introduced into our account of causation a factor which, in the present context, is more demanding than mere regularity. On a Humean view, whereby anything can cause anything, there should be no problem in conceiving of psychophysical interaction. If constant conjunction is all there is to such 'interaction', then the notion of a thought causing a bodily movement is no worse and no better than that of one movement causing another. Likewise with divine acts and their tangible effects. There is, for the regularity theorist, the problem of bringing act and effect under a suitable generalization, but if the temporal difficulties associated with the notion of such an act could be resolved, we should not need to ask for more than the fulfilment of suitably austere necessary and sufficient conditions in order to speak of divine causation. However, not only is it not possible to discharge that *if*, but, given that our concept of causation makes the more specific demands of interaction, we do even further violence to that notion in extending it beyond the natural order. The mediaevals regarded causation as a relation that transcends particular categories of being, much as number can be applied across diverse categories. However, its roots in the physical are such that nothing is left of the relation when the state of affairs ostensibly brought about is in the domain of the physical and the supposed agency is 'wholly other'.

Moreover, no form of causation, divine or otherwise, is in general required to ensure persistence in being. That is not to say that explaining how it is that certain things continue to exist may not be a matter of some importance—as with Darwin's theory of evolution by natural selection, which gives us a recipe for explaining the existence of species in the sense of their continuing existence, rather than how they came to exist in the first place. However, many things in the universe, as indeed the universe itself, do not have to fight for their survival, but, in the absence of forces which would bring them to an end, their continuation from moment to moment is in no need of explanation.

With material things, what we describe as bringing into existence is no more than the inducing of a change in some persisting substratum; old matter is simply endowed with a new form, a point which leads Aquinas to say that finite agents are causes merely of becoming, not of being (*Summa Theologiae*, I, Q. 104, Art. 1). Why the substratum continues to be is not explained by alluding to the changes which account for its present character, any more than explaining what made the ripples in the water explains the presence of the water. What this highlights as in need of explanation is the underlying substratum, but since to explain how something came to exist is to explain its existence subsequent to, as well as at that point, an explanation of how this came to be would be an explanation of its existence at this later time. Explaining how the room came to be in such a mess is explaining why it *is* in such a mess, and the same point holds even in more cosmic cases, the difference with the latter residing in the problem of explaining how what is *came* to be. Our next task is to try to reach a better understanding of this challenge.

5

Essence and Existence

Current discussions of why the universe exists, or, more generally, why there is anything at all, tend to look either to physics or to theology for an answer. That there might be a distinctively philosophical resolution of the question is not a possibility that is commonly raised. True, it is difficult to see how *any* discipline could provide a satisfactory answer to such recalcitrant why-questions. Scientific theories appear to have something to say only once their subject-matter, the physical universe, is supposed in being, in however minimal a form, while theological answers introduce a being, God, who is even more problematic than the universe which he is called upon to explain; and how philosophical considerations might succeed in accounting for substantive matters of existence is far from clear. However, whether there is in fact a substantive existential issue is a philosophical question, and given the way such concepts as those of causation and coming into existence are pushed to the limits when, discussing the origins of the universe, we move so far from the domain where these concepts have their home, there is unquestionably a role for the kind of conceptual investigation which might reveal that these seemingly unfathomable issues rest on misconceptions.

5.1 COSMOLOGICAL AND ONTOLOGICAL ARGUMENTS

To the best of my knowledge, anyone who has ventured a positive answer to the question why there is something rather than nothing has thought it necessary to posit a *being* of a certain kind: the mere fact that something exists is held to point to a being that exists of necessity. The arguments to this end fall roughly into two categories, those in the tradition of Aquinas, and those in the tradition of Leibniz. First, Aquinas.

In his Third Way, Aquinas argues that, while the familiar processes of generation and corruption establish that some things have the possibility of being and of not being, not everything can be of this nature, since what has the possibility of not being, at some time is not. If, then, the possibility of not being arose for everything, then at one time there would have been nothing, and hence nothing even now. That is, what exists does not begin to be except through something which is, so a time when there was nothing could not be followed by a time when there was something. Given that not everything can allow both of existing and not existing, there must be something which is necessary. For any such being, the cause of its necessity will lie outside it, or it will not. It is not possible to go on for ever in a series of necessary beings having a cause of their necessity, so we must assume something that is necessary of itself. Such a being will not have its necessity caused by another, but will be the cause of necessity in other things, 'and this all men call God' (*Summa Theologiae*, I, Q. 2, Art. 3).

Aquinas has been represented as seeking to establish the existence of a being whose existence is logically necessary. His claim that in God, and in God alone, existence and essence are identical, may be interchangeable with the claim that, for God, existence is a logical necessity, but the necessity at issue in the Third Way extends to beings other than God—to celestial bodies, prime matter, human souls, and angels, beings which might not have existed (ibid., I, Q. 10, Art. 5; Q. 104, Art. 4; Q. 75, Art. 6; Q. 50, Art. 5). However, while Aquinas's argument may not have to be defended against the common charge that the conception of a logically necessary being is incoherent, there are still features of the argument which have been a matter of some puzzlement to his commentators. It is claimed that not everything can be subject to decay and corruption, that there must be at least one being which does not have the possibility both of existing and of not existing. To speak of a necessary being in this sense, a being which does not go the way of the transient occupants of the physical universe, is not obviously incoherent, but the argument which would establish its existence is questionable. Aquinas, following Aristotle, appeared to think that if everything were perishable, then at some time everything would actually have perished, with the consequence that there would not now be anything at all in existence. However, when something decays or dies, the matter which constituted it is re-formed rather than annihilated, so generation and corruption, however pervasive, are hardly features of the material world which make its continued existence in any way more precarious—as the characterization of prime matter as necessary would appear to acknowledge.

It is of interest to note that in his attempt, in the *Summa contra Gentiles*, to demonstrate that God is eternal, Aquinas presents what is essentially the Third Way but without any reliance on this questionable step. The argument, which in effect takes up the above reasoning from the point where matter is acknowledged as necessary, runs as follows:

We find in the world, furthermore, certain beings which can be and not-be. But what can be has a cause because, since it is equally related to two contraries, namely, being and non-being, it must be owing to some cause that being accrues to it. Now, as we have proved by the reasoning of Aristotle, one cannot proceed to infinity among causes. We must therefore posit something that is a necessary being. Every necessary being, however, either has the cause of its necessity in an outside source or, if it does not, it is necessary through itself. But one cannot proceed to infinity among necessary beings the cause of whose necessity lies in an outside source. We must therefore posit a first necessary being, which is necessary through itself. This is God, since, as we have shown, He is the first cause. God, therefore, is eternal, since whatever is necessary through itself is eternal.

(*Summa contra Gentiles*, I, 15)

It is not just being necessary, but being necessary through itself that is the distinctive mark of God. We might take this to mean that, while some things owe their imperishable constitution to another, God has such a constitution through his own nature. However, that cannot be quite right, since even if it depended for its existence on another, a being could none the less have an imperishable nature. The difference would reside in no more than the matter of causal dependence: one imperishable being is also the first cause, God, others owe their existence to that being. Only being necessary through oneself, it would appear, offers protection against eventual non-existence. Matter, say, may be naturally indestructible, but not indestructible absolutely, since God can put an end to it. Think of the 'everlasting' motion allowed by Newton's First Law. A body in uniform motion will continue indefinitely in that state unless and until some force should put an end to it, a state which can be reckoned 'natural' to the body, in need of no further explanation. So, too, with a necessary existent such as matter—there for the duration unless God should see fit to destroy it. Note that necessity of this variety is quite clearly not logical necessity. Logical necessity is not something which one being could somehow *have* from another, however powerful, but the source of such necessity is to be found in relations between concepts.

Does the fact of God's existence furnish an answer to the question why there is something rather than nothing, given that he is necessary through himself? If he is imperishable, then future existence is taken care of, but can we ask how it is that he exists in the first place? We cannot ask how he *came* to exist if his existence had no beginning, but the question, how is it that there is such a being, appears to make sense, and to be in need of an answer, yet it is not easy to see how an answer can be given in terms of God's nature or essence. A given nature may confer indestructibility, may ensure the unending existence of a being, but how could it explain why there had to be something of that nature in the first place, why *something* had to answer to the description, 'indestructible'? Surely, the nature of a being can ground truths which hold of that being only *once* it exists. Any idea of self-necessitation, of being *causa sui*—the kind of bootstrap operation which being necessary 'through itself' does indeed suggest—appears incoherent. On the other hand, we have to bear in mind the exceptional character of the subject-matter: if the being in question did not come into existence, did not begin to exist, then the question why it exists surely takes on a different force from that question raised of the things of which we have knowledge, things having a beginning of existence in time.

Norman Malcolm has attempted to defend a form of the ontological argument which centres on the notion of a necessary being defined in this way—as eternal and indestructible—but his defence is not, I believe, successful. Before considering the argument, a brief word about the ontological argument in one of its more familiar forms. God being understood as a being a greater than which cannot be conceived, it is claimed that such a being must exist in reality, since if it existed in the imagination only, it would fall short of being the greatest conceivable, existence in reality clearly being superior to a purely mental existence. Since this pattern of reasoning would allow us to establish the existence of an unsurpassably dangerous or unpleasant being, along with the perfect island, we can be confident of its invalidity, but identifying the precise error is not straightforward.

Following Kant, it is customary to fault the argument on the grounds that extra-mental existence is not to be regarded as a superior attribute, a perfection—the verb 'exists' is not a real predicate. However, is there not a sense in which a being which exists in reality enjoys a superior standing to a being having no more than a mental existence? Existence as a substance, say, might be deemed superior to the existence enjoyed by a property or quality; again, existence as a cartoon figure could be reckoned superior to existence in one man's imaginings—as, perhaps, an imaginary cartoon figure—and existence in the animal kingdom could be reckoned superior to both, the measure being, say, the degree of independence enjoyed, or the impact that occupants of the different domains might have on things generally. True, there is a question whether the same thing can be said to exist both in the mind and in reality: if, when the fool of the Psalm says there is no God, what is in his mind is an idea, then that is where it stays. Compare a human being and a fictional counterpart. Sherlock Holmes may have been based on a real-life person, but there is no question of the two being literally the same individual. None the less, whether or not we can speak of the *same* being enjoying the two modes of existence, a being which exists in reality can be deemed greater than a being endowed with no more than a mental existence. It may be objected that this is more a matter of kinds of thing rather than kinds of existence, but even with the latter way of speaking it would not appear that the argument can be rescued. If God is to be the greatest conceivable, then he has to be placed in the highest of the categories which an extension of this list delivers, but the only constraint imposed by that demand relates to how we are to conceive of him. 'I can conceive of God only as existing in the highest possible way' is not 'I can conceive of God only if he exists in the highest possible way', but 'A being would not count as God unless it existed in the highest possible way—not, for instance, merely on paper, in the mind, or whatever.' And this does not entail actual existence.

Of course, it has to be argued that something could answer to the description, 'the greatest conceivable'. Perhaps, as with numbers, there is no greatest, but any specification of a being endowed with certain attributes can be bettered by a specification of something superior. Indeed, our argument in the preceding chapter amounted to the claim that in this connection 'x is superior to y' does not define an asymmetric relation, x being superior to y in some respects, but y possibly proving superior in others. Still, let us grant that a characterization as the greatest conceivable is coherent. God has then to be thought of as a being such that, if he exists, he exists as something more than a character in fiction, folklore or legend, but whatever category is deemed highest, we can again insist that God's defining characteristics be drawn from that category without having to acknowledge his actual existence.

The rejection of the ontological argument may rest on the idea that existence cannot belong to the nature or essence of a being, and the reasoning that leads to this rejection is sometimes held to show that no existential proposition can be analytic or necessary: if existence is not to be reckoned a property, then a fortiori it cannot be a necessary property, an integral component of the essence of a being. There is accordingly no way in which the status of necessarily existing can be conferred: 'existence cannot be held to be a quality which a perfect being would have to have, since it is not a quality at all. So it further follows that no existential assertion *can* be analytic' (Penelhum 1960: 184). As well as the particular issue of necessary existence, there are other questions relating to essence which arise here and which merit our attention. We shall begin by considering more generally the links between essence and necessity.

The most important shift in thinking about essence—indeed, one of the most important shifts in modern philosophy—lay in the relocation which it underwent with the 'linguistic turn' in the subject, essence moving from the world into language; in Wittgenstein's formulation, '*Essence* is expressed by grammar' (1958: §371). This relocation is a consequence of considerations relating to our understanding of logical necessity. There need be nothing amiss with the idea that the essence or nature of carbon is a matter for scientific investigation, but once the notion of necessity is introduced, empirical enquiry has to give way to logical or linguistic considerations. We may discover fundamental features of a substance, but however fundamental they may be, we do not *discover* that they form part of the substance's essence, in the relevant sense. That is for us to lay down, to stipulate, a stipulation which grounds a claim that, to be a specimen of the substance in question, those features must of necessity be present.

If essence thus lies in 'grammar', then it is something we can know about; if, as Wittgenstein claimed, there are no surprises in grammar, it is something we actually *do* know about, but we can more plausibly settle for knowability. In considering what is implicit in the meaning of a term we are confronting a source of necessity, but we are not now in the realm of the unknowable; we are dealing with what anyone who as much as grasps that part of the language thereby appreciates, at least implicitly. And that is as true when we are speaking of God as when our subject is more familiar. However much one holds to the mysteriousness of God, there is a presumption of *some* knowledge of what is being spoken of when 'God' is invoked, since the title would otherwise be without meaning, and in so far as 'what is essential to being *w*' is taken to paraphrase 'what is comprised in an account of the meaning of *"w"* ', it cannot be the essence of God that is unknowable.

As an application of this point, consider Aquinas's claim that, while the proposition that God exists is not self-evident to us, it is inherently self-evident—*per se notum secundum se*—to God, who has a knowledge of his essence far beyond anything to which we can aspire. It is true that God, or indeed some other conceivable being, could have an advantage over us in being able to conduct reasoning of a degree of complexity which defeated our limited powers. This might be so with respect to mathematics, for instance. However, with respect to truths which are grounded in the divine essence, we are on a par with God. Or, we are on a par if what goes to make up his essence is determined by the meaning of 'God'. As with any other word, the meaning of 'God' is the meaning that our usage has conferred upon it, so what is true of God of necessity—that is, by dint of being required for the applicability of the term—is in principle something of which we can know. The basis for such knowledge is there, in our usage, even if articulating that usage is less than straightforward. Accordingly, if 'God exists' can be appreciated as a necessary truth by God, but not by us, this will be so because of God's superior powers of reasoning, not because he has a knowledge of the divine essence that is not shared by us. In passing, it was argued earlier that the title of *possible explanation* has to be earned. So, too, does that of being *mysterious*. To say that there is a reality of which we can know next to nothing is to make a claim of substance, a claim which raises questions of intelligibility as much as of fact.

Not only can God not be totally beyond our comprehension—supposing talk about him to be intelligible—but we can have God's essence comprise anything we wish so long as it is possessed by him. Essence is not, if the above observations are correct, imposed upon us by reality, but it is enough that God should be *F* for being *F* to be a characteristic which, given his immutability, we may reckon to his essence. This being the only requirement, the insistence that it is of God's essence that he should be *F* does not mean that *F*-ness is somehow more securely lodged in his nature than characteristics not accorded this standing. God is of necessity infinitely just. This attribute flows from his essence. What is such necessity worth? Not much, it would seem, if this reduces to the claim that we should not deem a being to be divine were he not supposed to be infinitely just.

Or is this to take too short a way with the notion of essence? One possible objection relates to the conception of meaning, and its relation to our knowledge, on which I have been drawing. Suppose two people use the term 'water' of two different substances, but in ignorance of their respective chemical constitutions. According to Hilary Putnam, even if there is agreement on the criteria for the term's application, these unknown differences make for a difference in the meaning that each person attaches to the term (1975: 224). The meaning of a word is thus not necessarily known to its users in the way I contend. There is a use of the verb 'mean' in which it compares with 'refer to' and for which something like this point certainly does hold. If, say, you use the phrase 'that metal' with respect to gold and I use it with respect to silver, there will be a difference in what is meant, where 'what is meant' (German *meinen*) picks out the two substances. However, this is not a difference in what each of us means by the phrase, where that is a matter of the meaning (German *Bedeutung*) it has for each of us. To allege such a difference is surely to sever the links between meaning and understanding: if what you go by in judging something to be a metal is the same as what I go by, if you would explain the term in the same way as I, then we have the same understanding of the term; it has the same meaning for each of us.

As already indicated, this is not to say that explaining how a word is understood is a trivial matter. To pursue this point, consider the question whether the account of essence just outlined may be thought of as 'conventionalist'. That label can be in place, but it is not always the case that we *stipulate* that a property is to be essential to something. The alternative is not a view of essence which locates logical necessity *in rerum natura*. It could be that the relevant connections are buried in the language, that it takes some reflection to tease them out, but it is still to the language that we are to look. *Pace* Wittgenstein, grammar may not be without its surprises. Note that, whether or not it is a matter of stipulation, the necessities which emerge here do not oblige us to go beyond the scheme suggested: we may not have to do with an explicit stipulation, but the necessity is founded on linguistic considerations. This puts us at odds with those who show greater sympathy with past ways of thinking to the extent of rejecting any such foundation, at least when matters of identity are at issue. Thus, Saul Kripke has argued that the actual constitution of an object is necessary to that object: a lectern made of wood could not have been made of ice and still be the same lectern; indeed, had it been made of wood, but wood from some other tree, it would not have been the lectern that it is (1980: 141f.). This we can accept, but it is a mistake to suppose that it presents us with a notion of necessity which can dispense with the relevant linguistic considerations. It is a question of what counts as *this*, or the *same*, lectern;

we have to do with a connection—between identity and constitution—that is as much within language as is one between the concepts of *God* and *infinite justice*. Of course, while what makes for essence is linguistically determined, that does not leave empirical investigation without a role. We may reckon atomic number to the essence of a substance, but what that number is in a given case is an empirical question.

Grammar, I suggested, may have its surprises. To explain, there is room for surprise in that, while having a practical mastery of a word or phrase, we may none the less not be aware in any articulate fashion of the network of conceptual connections into which it enters. Think here of the task involved in giving a comprehensive account of the use of the definite article in English or of the subjunctive in French. Think, too, of the difficulty in explaining the occurrence of tenses in conditional statements or in giving an analysis of modal terms, such as 'must' and 'probably'. Even with such familiar concepts there may be interrelations which become apparent to native speakers only, if at all, on reflection. Indeed, were that not so, were conceptual connections one and all immediately obvious, there would be no need for philosophy, but we could unhesitatingly map the 'logical geography' of even such philosophically troublesome terms as 'meaning', 'truth', and 'mind'.

However, if our concern is with the term 'God', it is not clear that there is much comfort to be gained from these observations. With many philosophically problematic words we have at least a basis of assured judgements to build upon. Take the example of 'mind'. We can agree that Mary has a sharp mind, that she hasn't got her mind on her work, that she has changed her mind, and so forth, judgements which need not be in doubt, even if an illuminating analysis of 'mind' proves elusive. Contrast 'soul'. There are contexts where we can be confident both of meaningfulness and truth—'Mary was the life and soul of the party', 'She went in for much soul-searching'—but this confidence does not extend to the metaphysical uses: 'We are blessed with an immortal soul', 'The soul can exist without the body.' With respect to 'God', likewise, there is not the agreement in judgements which testifies to a coherent concept. Given the uncertainty in its usage, it is questionable whether there is a well-defined network of conceptual relationships which further reflection might bring to light and which might provide a firm basis for a conception of the divine essence or nature. However, the main point remains that, even if the coherence of 'God' is not in dispute, God's essence cannot, on the present conception, be forever beyond our comprehension.

But is this how essence is best understood? Is there not a conception that is more robust than anything mere considerations of usage can afford? What belongs in essence, it may be said, is what *explains* why something is the way it is. Not now a matter of looking to the meaning of a name to determine essence, but to, say, the atomic structure of the individual or substance. However, while we may think in terms of a constitution which assures the existence of certain features, as the behaviour of a given compound may be traceable to its chemical constitution, there is a difficulty in transferring this model to God: not having any parts, in what sense does he have a constitution, or a structure? As an immaterial being, he is surely not *made up* of anything at all. However general we seek to make our characterizations of God, it appears that we continue to run up against the difficulty that our words have been pre-empted for a use solely within our world.

To return to our main concern, if existence is not a property, then it is not a property having a place in the essence of something. However, it has been held that the denial that existence is a property, or predicate, is not true without exception (see Geach 1969: 54). Consider the following sentences:

> These buildings existed as long ago as the twelfth century,
> The bridge still exists, but it is not in use,
> The original manuscript no longer exists.

Some may wish to say that there cannot be any question of reference being made here to individuals, since this would be to make a predicate out of 'exists'. That is, if 'exists' is not a predicate, the grammatical subject of an existential statement cannot be the logical subject. In greater detail, contemporary arguments designed to show that 'exists' is not a predicate generally allege an incoherence in the claim to be referring to something and at the same time to be asserting or denying existence of that to which reference is made. Thus the assimilation of existential statements to statements of the subject–predicate form is thought to result in tautology or pleonasm in the case of affirmative existentials, and in self-contradiction or some kindred form of absurdity with negative existentials. To take an example, in stating 'The Loch Ness monster does not exist', we cannot be using 'the Loch Ness monster' to refer to a particular creature, for the whole force of our statement is to deny that there is any such thing to which we might refer. If, then, 'the Loch Ness monster' is not functioning here as a logical subject, then 'does not exist' is not, a fortiori, a predicate signifying a property of an individual named by the subject.

However, it is not true that 'exists' never enjoys a predicative role, but the belief that it never does results from an uncritical acceptance of the claim that to refer to something is necessarily to refer to something that exists. The ambiguity of this claim, and its consequent breakdown, may be seen by considering two possible interpretations which we might attach to the sentence, 'The Garden of Eden does not exist.' Leaving aside the question whether the only gardens that can be referred to are real gardens, somebody who believes that there never has been such a place as the Garden of Eden certainly does not intend to refer to a once real garden when he denies its existence in these words, and if what he says is true it is indeed difficult to see how he could be making such a reference. The situation is altered, however, if we suppose that the Garden of Eden did exist at some time in the past. If that is so, we can quite sensibly say 'The Garden of Eden does not exist', in the sense of 'does not now exist', and at the same time be referring to the very thing whose present existence we are denying. Using a term as a referring expression only presupposes existence at some time or other, not necessarily existence at the time of speaking, and it is only when an existential statement constitutes an affirmation or denial of the former condition that there is any need to distinguish it from ordinary subject–predicate statements. Similarly, if I say 'This room will exist long after you are dead', I can naturally and coherently be taken to be referring to the very same thing as if I were to say 'This room is lined with books.'

The claim that 'exists' can function as a genuine predicate is best taken in a fairly austere sense, as implying no more than the possibility that the grammatical subject of an existential statement should be a genuine logical subject. To state that existence is a property may be to state in the 'material' mode what '"exists" is a predicate' says in the 'formal' mode, but there is some reason not to draw the two ways of speaking so closely together. 'This building would not have existed but for the generosity of our benefactor' features a predicative use of 'would not have existed', but we should surely not wish to say that this is a matter of a claim that, had the benefactor not been so generous, the building would not have had a certain property. Note too that, as this example shows, it is not necessarily a matter of the *tensed* use of 'exists' which our initial examples featured.

It is not clear that the preceding considerations tell us anything about 'exists' as this occurs with a plural subject, as in G. E. Moore's example, 'Tame tigers exist.' The notion of a logical subject is ill-suited to this context, as also to such elaborations as 'Tame tigers exist in some zoos' and

'Tame tigers do not exist in large numbers.' More generally, it does not appear helpful to look to a different use of 'tame tigers' as it occurs here and as it is found in the other member of Moore's pair, 'Tame tigers growl', so let us leave aside the status of the grammatical subject and ask how, whether used predicatively or not, 'exists' is distinctive as a verb. In marking the contrast between the two contexts for 'tame tigers', it is natural to say that 'exist', unlike 'growl', is not something that tame tigers *do*. Just as no real change is involved in persisting in being, so no real act is involved in merely existing, whether it be a matter of contexts such as this, or of those in which the verb can be reckoned a logical predicate, as with 'The hut in the garden has existed ever since I can remember.' When change is explained as simply a matter of contradictory attributes' holding good of individuals at different times, Geach has spoken of a 'Cambridge' change (1969: 71). Such a change may be purely relational, as when I become less wealthy than you through your becoming richer than me, or when a child becomes an orphan through losing its parents. These are states of affairs which can come about without there being any change whatsoever in me or child, considered in isolation. Indeed, in many such cases it would seem hardly in place to speak of a change at all, at least as regards the subject of the 'change'. We argued that continuing in existence did not require a cause, since it was not a change in a relevant sense, but was, we might say, merely a Cambridge 'change'. Similarly, if we are to speak of an act of existing, it will be no more than what we might call a Cambridge 'act'.

In passing, we may note that the sense of 'bring about' may be correspondingly attenuated in respect of what is responsible for a Cambridge change. This is apparent in the unproblematic character of action at a distance in this connection, as when a child is made an orphan by the death of its parents many miles away. Action at a distance of a more familiar variety is also of interest here. It has been suggested that God's creation of the world compares with one body's exerting a gravitational force on another. Both the universe and the body affected undergo a real change, but the agents— God and the attracting body—are subjects of no more than a Cambridge change, a change which does not put God's immutability at risk (Ross 1980: 626). We may join Aquinas in rejecting the claim that God's creation of the universe involves a change in the latter, so the analogy falters on this point, but an equally important consideration is whether a body which is said to exert a gravitational influence is really to be described as an 'agent'. It was noted above that, precisely because the body does not *do* anything, does not change in any way, it is inappropriate to speak of *action* at a distance.

If, while not signifying a property, 'exists' may none the less be a predicate, is that enough to allow of its incorporation, suitably qualified, in a specification of the divine essence? Such predicates as 'has existed from all eternity' and 'will never cease to exist' surely could be enlisted to this end, but while we could then say that a being would not count as God unless it had existed from all eternity, there is no question of inferring God's existence from his essence, so understood. Or so it would seem. If Malcolm is right, the more sophisticated argument which he finds in Anselm allows just such a conclusion to be drawn (Malcolm 1960).

While rejecting existence as a perfection, Malcolm holds, with Anselm, that the logical impossibility of non-existence is a perfection, which he then further characterizes as unlimited, independent, indestructible, and eternal existence. These latter can be reckoned genuine predicates, and predicates which could be invoked in defining God's essence. Moreover, we have the indisputable premise that any given proposition is either contingent, impossible, or necessary. Indisputable, since we have that if a proposition P and its negation not-P are possible, then P is by definition contingent, and this yields: either P is impossible or not-P is impossible or P is contingent, whence either P is impossible or P is necessary or P is contingent. But contingency is ruled out by God's character as a necessary being, so since it would seem that his existence is at least a possibility, it follows that he exists of necessity. This looks to be an improvement on the more familiar version of the ontological argument, in so far as necessity is explained as indestructible and eternal existence, a mode of existence which a being could conceivably enjoy. However, the explanation is to be queried. Since we can meaningfully ask whether there is a being that is indestructible, that did not come into existence, the logical impossibility of non-existence is surely not to be elucidated in these terms. There is not the appropriate opposition to contingency that is required for the argument to go through; being necessary in this sense does not prejudge the matter of actual existence, but 'A necessary being exists' could be a contingent truth, or indeed falsehood. Malcolm argues that, since God cannot be conceived to come into existence, if he does not exist it is impossible that he should exist (1960: 48). This conclusion features a crucial ambiguity. It is, we may agree, not logically possible that he should *come* into existence, but this does not mean that it is logically impossible that he should *have* existed.

Suppose, now, that necessity is understood as the logical impossibility of non-existence—the condition which Malcolm mistakenly elaborates in terms of indestructible and unlimited existence. To say that it is logically impossible that God should not have existed is to say that it is logically impossible that nothing should have been divine. This is not a proposition about an individual, God, but one about whatever 'nothing' ranges over, that is, about whatever exists. Reality had to include a deity. It is thus inappropriate to speak of necessary existence as a perfection attributable to an individual, and indeed the point we are making is in effect just the point that is appropriately made when it is said that existence is not a predicate. Malcolm claims that, if merely contingent existence can be ruled out, then, if God's existence is not impossible, 'Anselm is right to deduce God's necessary existence from his characterization of Him as a being a greater than which cannot be conceived' (1960: 49). What Anselm is right about is surely only a hypothetical proposition. Not 'God necessarily exists', but 'If God is a being a greater than which cannot be conceived, then his existence is necessary', and so long as the necessary existence is of the indestructible and eternal variety, this is acceptable. It is not 'If God is a being a greater than which cannot be conceived, then he necessarily exists', where this means 'If God is a being a greater than which cannot be conceived, then there necessarily is such a being.' If this is true, then God does indeed exist, but no argument has been advanced for its truth.

5.2   WHETHER THERE MIGHT HAVE BEEN NOTHING

We shall return to the notion of a beginning of existence, but first let us consider the rationalist's approach to the argument from contingency. When, as with Leibniz, the problem is formulated with the question, 'Why is there something rather than nothing?', the being in which the consequent enquiry may terminate is thought to be such that its non-existence is logically inconceivable, the conception which has often been considered empty. However, it is not evident that existential statements are invariably non-necessary, as Hume and subsequent philosophers have insisted, Hume doing little more than declare this to be so: 'Whatever we conceive as existent, we can also conceive as non-existent. There is no Being, therefore, whose non-existence implies a contradiction' (1947: 189; cf. 1902: 164). In the context in which it occurs, the declaration is particularly lame. As D. C. Stove has pointed out, to argue in this way against someone who believes that there is something 'which cannot be supposed to exist without contradiction' is simply question-begging (1978: 304). Contemporary writers have often concurred with J. J. C. Smart's view that an existential proposition does not say that one concept is involved in another, as is the case with logically necessary propositions, but that a concept applies to something (1955: 38–9). Very well, but why should there not be a concept that applies of necessity? Why can it not be necessary that *some* concept or other should apply? Nor does the consideration that the necessity in question reflects the arbitrary conventions of our language appear to preclude these possibilities. If the meaning of some term is such that it is assured of application, this assurance is not diminished by the fact that the usage might have been different. Our concern is only with the implications of the given usage. And, of course, the arbitrariness of the convention in no way tells against the necessity of the proposition, here or elsewhere. The word 'prime' could well have borne a different meaning, but while its usage may be reckoned arbitrary, this arbitrariness does not extend to the *truth* of '17 is prime' or of other propositions in which the predicate figures. Admittedly, given that a necessary proposition is consistent with all states of affairs whatsoever, there might appear to be a presumption against the necessity of any existential proposition, but this general category is broader than that comprising propositions about specifiable individuals: it could be that no being can be held to exist of necessity, and yet it was a necessary truth that something existed. Nor is it clear where mass terms such as 'matter'—not the name of an individual— fit in. We might argue: there has to be something, and if anything exists, matter does; therefore, matter exists. If, as seems plausible, the two premises are necessary, then so, too, is this conclusion.

There are several important points to develop here. We note that Aquinas and Leibniz are in agreement in so far as each supposes that the problem posed by contingency is to be resolved by positing a kind of *being*. What, indeed, might there be by way of an alternative? It was mentioned above that the source of logical necessity is not provided by some being, but is to be found in relations between concepts. Now, there is clearly a difference between the claim that there has to be something or other, and the claim that there is some particular being which has to be. The latter, of course, posits a being, but the former rests content with a more abstract *principle*, and it is of interest to note a way in which a very different, and seemingly more economical hypothesis might be invoked in line with this latter alternative. That is, the conclusion, that there exists a necessary being, has, in this principle, a weaker consequence which would itself serve to answer the original question why there is anything at all, and, if the principle has the standing of a conceptual truth, is certainly to be preferred to the theistic hypothesis.

To elaborate, there is clearly a difference between maintaining that there has to be something or other, and claiming that there is some particular being that has to be. We might insist that it is not possible that there should be, or have been, nothing at all; whether animate or inanimate, material or immaterial, there had to be *something*. On the other hand, it may well be that of no particular thing can one say that it is inconceivable that it should not have existed; our galaxy did not have to exist, nor did galaxies quite generally. Now, it is clear that if the existence of a particular being were necessary, then the more general statement that there was something or other would have the same standing. If, accordingly, God's existence is necessary, then we can say that there must be something, so the theist for one believes this latter, more general, proposition. This is, however, a supposition which is both weaker than the theistic hypothesis from which it is derivable, yet strong enough to enable us to answer the original query, why is there anything at all? If there just has to be something, the inescapability of this fact suffices to lay that query to rest. Since it is sufficient, and since it is accepted by the theist anyhow, we may wonder where the pressure might come from to affirm the stronger, more problematic, thesis. Of course, there is an answer open to the theist: he can hold that the only grounds for affirming the weaker proposition could be grounds we might have for affirming God's existence. In that he may be right, but at the present stage of enquiry this is not the most plausible of the alternatives: given the lack of transparency in the notion of an individual whose existence is logically necessary, or of a being which somehow has its existence through itself, it is prima facie more likely that we could sustain an argument for the claim that there has to be something without having to demonstrate that there is something that has to be.

How might this weaker claim be supported? Our first thought may well be that it, too, is unsustainable: there is an essential contingency about affirmations of existence, both particular and general, which means that there might indeed have been nothing whatsoever. However, I suspect that our attempts at conceiving of total non-existence are irredeemably partial. We are always left with something, if only a setting from which we envisage everything having departed, a void which we confront and find empty, but something which it makes sense to speak of as having once been home to bodies, radiation, or whatever.

'There might have been nothing' need not, of course, be the same as 'Nothing might have existed', an evident falsehood contradicted by the many things which could—indeed do—exist. Likewise, imagining (conceiving, supposing) nothing is not what we are being called upon to do. That is not imagining anything, which is simply failing to imagine, not imagining at all. None the less, talk of imagining there was nothing—which is what is called for—does run the risk of being treated as if a matter of imagining nothing, and that is refraining from imagining anything. Either that, or, I suggest, it is to imagine things lacking where there might have been something: we suppose we can imagine the stars ceasing to exist one by one—like so many lights going out—but we still look to where they were. It makes sense to suppose a reversal of the development described—objects now start reappearing before us in the space which had been vacated. We have not discarded the setting; something we might search in vain, but something—a previously occupied region—none the less. Envisaging an empty terrain, sky, chasm, or even space does not give us what we want. To imagine, conceive, or postulate space is not to imagine, etc., nothing; as I say, that is not to imagine or postulate anything. Space is not *nothing*, it is something you can stare into or travel through, something of which there can be volumes; objects can be separated by, or take up, space and we can make space for them. Moreover, while we may think of space in terms of absence of body where there might have been such, body is still not out of the picture. A determinate volume of space requires something to define its limits; there is nothing on offer from space itself, but a physical marker or boundary has to be introduced. Indeed, while it appears to make sense to imagine things going out of existence to such a point that our hypothetical observer is left contemplating a totally empty space, if the observer then goes, so too does any space. But that is not: we are left with nothing—as if this could be the state of affairs that *succeeded*. Note that a substantivalist conception of space does not result in a different conclusion—just that the minimal state of affairs possible on this conception is a totally empty, rather than a sparsely populated, space—though the conception itself, like that of an empty world, is surely itself empty.

In his Third Way, Aquinas argued that if at one time there was nothing, there would be nothing even now. This is correct, but not in the way he presumably thought, both antecedent and consequent expressing an impossibility. Clearly, 'There might have been nothing now' and 'There might have been nothing then' contradict themselves through the presuppositions behind the use of 'now' and 'then'. However, the theist might argue that we can make sense of the coming to be of the universe without having to rely on a misconceived contrast with a state of nothingness, since before all things were, God was. This will not do. It is not just anything that can be called upon to furnish the required contrast, but an antecedent condition appropriate to a spatio-temporal system of bodies is demanded. This could be given by a region of space which was devoid of a given object up to the point of time when the object came into being, but a being outside space and time, as is God, is no part of such a backdrop. The only thing which would provide a setting into which our universe might make an *entrée* would be another universe.

To have literally nothing, rather than a domain we might meaningfully speak of as becoming progressively re- or de-populated, seems not to make sense. Consider 'There was nothing, and then the universe spontaneously sprang into being.' Here it is as though 'There was nothing' sets the scene for this cosmic event: there was nothing *where* the universe came to be; 'There might have been nothing' is a matter of: 'There might have been nothing *there.*' We can envisage all manner of things *in place* of what we have, but 'There might have been nothing' is not a truth about anywhere, is not about the way things might have been, does not describe anything at all. Is the supposition that there should have been nothing shown to be incoherent through its implication that it would have then been a fact that this was so, whence the existence of at least one thing— that fact—would have to be acknowledged? Some may not wish to rest anything on there being a fact, but it is true that it is hard to get away from this and related ways of speaking, as, when faced with the suggestion that there might have been nothing at all, we respond by saying that that is no way things might have been. There is just no alternative to being. When we say 'Nothing is . . .', far from talking about nothing, we are talking about everything. Nothing is immortal; that is, everything is mortal. Nothing might have been here—neither you nor I, the cat, the dog, and so on indefinitely. Again, it is suggested that there being nothing is the 'normal' state of affairs, one that would not call for any explanation, but do we even have to do here with a state of affairs? Not, it would seem, if that is a matter of how things might be.

Someone might object: 'When you dismiss the claim that there might have been nothing in this way, all you are saying is: that is not a describable *scene.*' No. What I am suggesting is, rather, that in trying to give sense to the claim, this is the best we can do. We are not talking, as we should wish, about how things might have been; we are not talking about anything at all. We cannot conceive of there being nothing, but only of nothing being this or that, and this is a use of 'nothing' that presupposes there being something. Intelligible contrasts are within *ways of being*—near or far, long or short, young or old. Existing and not existing fit into the scheme—existing now, not existing then, and, more radically, there being a so and so and there being no so and so—but the contrast is still within how things are: at least one thing's being a dragon, say, and the failure of every single thing to be a dragon. This is as far as it goes, there being something and there being nothing not being contrasting poles with respect to the way things might be.

It is of interest to note that the interpretation of 'There is an *F*' given with the existential quantifier harmonizes with the view that we cannot discard existential presuppositions to the point of allowing that there should have been nothing whatsoever. The quantificational rendering treats 'There is an *F*' or 'An *F* exists' as equivalent to 'Something is an *F*', propositions detailing what there is becoming propositions concerning the character of objects in a given domain. So, 'There is a comet in our solar system' is rendered 'Something is a comet in our solar system', or 'Something in our solar system is a comet', the pronoun 'something' ranging over the universe at large, or over some more restricted region thereof. Likewise when existence is denied. 'There is no photograph of me as a child' can be taken as 'Nothing is a photograph of me as a child', where 'nothing' has the same range as would be appropriate to 'something'. That we have to do with some non-empty domain is taken for granted, the question being just how its occupants are to be characterized.

The supposition of a non-empty domain is, of course, one that can be relaxed, but it may be thought that when certain distinctions of tense or modality become important, we must go further: the supposition *has* to be abandoned. Consider 'A unicorn might have existed.' This can be represented as 'Something might have been a unicorn', but only in the sense of 'There might have been something that was a unicorn', not in the sense of 'One of the things there is might have been a unicorn.' The phrase 'something that was' is redundant in 'There might have been something that was a unicorn.' Likewise with 'There might not have been a horse.' It is not merely that it might have been that none of the things that are horses were horses. It is simply that there might not have been anything that was a horse. Again, redundancy creeps in here with 'anything that was'. Compare, too, 'Matter might not have existed.' We do not want to interpret this in terms of a quantifier which ranges over a given totality—the present universe—since it is not clear that anything thus picked out could have failed to be matter. It is again: there might not have existed anything that was matter, rather than: all this might have failed to be matter.

However, the sentence 'There might not have been a horse' could be read as 'It might have been that nothing was a horse', where 'nothing' is thought of as having, not its current range, but whatever some conjectural universe might have offered, thus enabling us to retain an equivalence between 'There are no *F*s' and 'Nothing is an *F*.' Similarly, 'There might have been a unicorn' can be rendered as 'It might have been that something was a unicorn.' No assumption is made as to the persistence of the *actual* domain into the state of affairs envisaged, but we are still thinking of the existential forms as enunciating possible truths about some conceivable domain.

The quantificational rendering of existence gives expression to the view that questions as to what exists are questions as to how things are, how reality is to be described, the presupposition of a reality to be characterized being made equally with 'Something is an *F*' and 'Nothing is an *F*.' If that presupposition carries on into 'Something exists' and 'Nothing exists', then we should expect these to be logically true and logically false respectively. Take 'It might have been true that nothing existed'; so, nothing material, nothing immaterial. That is, it might have been that nothing was anything, a supposition that contradicts the evident truth that everything is something. It is sometimes wondered why, if there can be logically impossible existential propositions, there should not also be logically necessary existential propositions. Symmetry here would not necessarily mean that there was some species of thing that had to be but, just as there could be nothing that was both breakable and unbreakable, so there has to be something that is either breakable or unbreakable. If there has to be something, then the latter is thereby assured.

It is worth pointing out that the use of 'exists' as a genuine predicate does not pose a special problem for a reading in terms of the existential quantifier. If we are happy with a parsing of 'A black hole exists' as 'Something is a black hole', there appears to be no reason why we should not rewrite 'My first overcoat no longer exists', say, as 'It is no longer the case that something is my first overcoat'. The quantificational treatment of existential statements does, however, have limitations, being unsuited to the case where there is no nameable individual, nothing that may be identified as subject of a property (cf. Rundle 1979: 198–9). So, the rendering of 'There is a chance that she will succeed' as 'Something is a chance that she will succeed' prompts the query, 'What is this chance?'—in the sense of 'What is thus describable?'—a query whose inappositeness reflects adversely on the proposed rendering. Likewise with 'There is a risk of failure', 'There is no hope of success', and so forth. On the other hand, a richer setting is presupposed by such forms, if only indirectly. It may be inappropriate to speak of something being a hope of success, but it can be said that no one can hope for success, and there is a risk of failure or a need for care only if someone risks failing or needs to be careful.

Are there any alternatives to this analysis of existential propositions? The customary approach, just discussed, takes as its starting point predications of the form 'A is F', as 'This is a whelk' or 'Roger is a soldier', replacing the name or pronoun to give us 'Something is an F', or the logician's '∃xFx'. More generally, a distinctive feature of predicate logic is to be found in the restricted way in which general terms, such as 'house' or 'mouse', may occur. In English we have such contexts as 'my house' and 'these houses', but in predicate logic we have to make do with the single context, '. . . is a house'. Often some form of paraphrase using the latter can be invoked, but we shall then be operating in accordance with different semantic rules from those governing the vernacular, and even then the central case of phrases with plural nouns, as 'the mice' or 'these mice', cannot be accommodated in the standard formalization—an extraordinary deficiency. A logic which acknowledged as referential units such phrases as 'my cousins' and 'every seat' would take us a step nearer to natural language. Present purposes do not require that we argue the point, but there is no compelling reason to insist, as is customary, on construing the predicate in, say, 'Every seat is taken' as 'Every . . . is taken' rather than, in line with the surface grammar, simply regarding '. . . is taken' as predicate and 'every seat' as subject.

Suppose that, rather than make do with replacements for our usual existential propositions, we seek an account of the latter which stays closer to their actual forms and underlying principles. Where might we turn? It is evident that the behaviour of 'is a mouse' in 'There is a mouse', understood as a statement of existence, is just as in the same sentence when 'there' features as an adverb of place. Indeed, it could have been that phrases such as 'is a mouse' never occurred linked to names, but only in conjunction with adverbs such as 'there' and 'here'. We should not then have had predicative uses of the noun phrase, yet the existential form could be as now. 'Here is a mouse' is not like 'Minnie is a mouse': 'a mouse' is a predicate of something named 'Minnie', but not of something named 'here'. The affinities of existential 'There is an F' are quite evidently with this same form, but where 'there' is no longer given its full force as an adverb of place. In neither case, certainly, is there any question of a predicative use of 'an F', but the comparison is with 'Somewhere is an F' rather than with 'Something is an F.' Even more clearly with plural nouns: in 'There are several solutions', 'are several solutions' is not being affirmed of anything for which 'there' stands in. Here we may note that, if 'a black hole' is not a predicate in 'There is a black hole', then 'there is' is not, *a fortiori*, a predicate of a predicate.

The difficulty in getting away from *something* is matched by the difficulty in getting away from *somewhere*, but, just as there are limitations to the applicability of the former, so too with the latter, as again with much the same range of examples. However, it is perhaps not too fanciful to regard existential 'there' as directing us to *some* sort of setting, in however stretched a sense. Not a matter of 'There, in that place, is an F', nor even of 'Somewhere is an F'. 'In reality is an F' is nearer the mark, but will not do for 'There are many mythical monsters.' 'There' has to be as accommodating as the character of F requires, but some kind of a domain seems always to be implied, even with this last kind of example. It may be felt that no amount of stretching will find room for 'There is some chance of success', 'There is no possibility of error' or 'There is no telling what might happen', but even here a non-empty domain could be said to be in the background, soon to come to the fore when we elaborate upon such propositions and what they involve. There is no question of pressing a spatial reading of 'there' in the existential idiom, given the wealth of abstract, non-spatial characterizations which may complete 'There is . . .', but since abstractions make sense only against the supposition of a more substantive physical reality, there is no eluding the spatial setting which is inseparable from the physical world. If such a reality is inescapable, there is nothing restrictive about the claim that 'There might have been nothing' prompts the questions as to where and when this might be so, questions harbouring a presupposition that is damaging to this supposed possibility. We shall argue shortly that such a reality is indeed inescapable.

Two strands of argument have been interwoven in our investigation of the claim that there might have been nothing. First, we have suggested that attempts to think away everything amount to envisaging a region of space which has been evacuated of its every occupant, an exercise which gives no more substance to the possibility of there being nothing than does envisaging an empty cupboard. Second, we attack the question more generally by arguing, not that, specifically, a setting is a *sine qua non* of the states of affairs envisaged, but simply that *something* is always presupposed when existence is affirmed or denied. These two considerations link up with two ways in which existence may be expressed. On the one hand, and corresponding to the latter, more general possibility, we have the rendering of 'There is an *F*' as 'Something is an *F*', or, in symbols, '∃xFx'. On the other hand, and staying closer to natural language, we have the reading as, roughly, 'Somewhere is an *F*.' Both analyses have limitations, the first being strained when there is no identifiable subject of being *F*, the second when locatability is lacking, but in neither case do the problematic contexts appear to be any less demanding than those that are straightforward in what they require by way of relevant presuppositions. Moreover, the proposition that nothing exists comes out as questionable on both accounts, being incoherent when formulated as 'Nothing is anything', and at least highly dubious when taken as positing some kind of domain, as with 'Nowhere is (there) anything' or 'Nothing is anywhere.' We have focused on the difficulty of excluding a spatial framework, but could equally have pointed to comparable difficulties posed by time. If 'There might have been nothing' comes to grief through its natural expansion to 'There might have been nothing anywhere', so a similar fate awaits the expansion to 'There might have been nothing at any time.' Difficulties peculiar to temporal considerations will be our next concern.

5.3 BEGINNING AND CEASING TO BE

Our general query as to why anything at all exists has a simple answer if there is no coherent alternative to something's existing, but this solution would appear to be at odds with the view, strongly supported by cosmological theories, that there was a beginning to the universe. Supposing that this universe was not somehow begotten by another universe, or indeed by anything else, it can only be consequent upon a state of there being nothing. If, then, such a state is to be rejected, it would appear that we are committed to accepting that the universe must have existed for an infinite time, a conclusion which we might well not wish to have thrust upon us without considerable weight of argument. There are several issues intertwined in this dilemma, and we shall begin with the propriety of speaking of the universe as *beginning* to exist.

To say that the universe came out of nothing is to say that it did not come out of anything, but accounts of physical reality as 'coming out of nothing' risk not taking 'nothing' seriously, perhaps replacing it by 'nothingness' to make, as it were, something out of nothing. Understandably, given not only the peculiarities of 'nothing', but also the way 'coming' signifies a movement having its origins *somewhere*, in *something*. Thus:

On the far side of the Big Bang is a mystery so profound that physicists lack the words even to think about it. Those willing to go out on a limb guess that whatever might have been before the Big Bang was, like a vacuum, unstable. Just as there is a tiny chance that virtual particles will pop into existence in the midst of sub-atomic space, so there may have been a tiny chance that nothingness would suddenly be convulsed by the presence of a something.

(Crease and Mann 1986: 405)

The authors do not speak of a tiny chance that nothing would suddenly be convulsed by the presence of something, since that would not have led to the presence of anything. Talk of nothingness seemingly avoids this negative reading, but it requires that 'nothingness' be interpreted as something like 'the void', retaining the existential implications which, we have argued, are so difficult to evade.

We are spared from having to fathom a mystery on the far side of the Big Bang, since there is no far side. Nothing stable, and nothing unstable. Again, any speculation about the origins of the universe which talks in terms of the *chances* of an initial event occurring is surely committed to positing something by way of a domain or setting which antedates that event and is of such a character that certain developments are somehow favoured over others. There have to be things, circumstances, with a propensity to develop one way or another. There have been a number of cosmologists who represent their theories as explaining how the universe came from nothing, but what they reckon nothing turns out to have some reality, however simple or primitive it may be. As Richard Swinburne observes, 'under close examination "nothing" never really turns out to be nothing; it is some sort of empty space in a quiescent state' (1990: 178). Perhaps we all come from stardust, but even the tiniest speck of dust is infinitely far from being nothing at all.

An attempt has been made to explain the emergence of something from nothing by exploiting the cancellation of opposites:

If the cancellation is thought of as reversed, then opposites separate from nothing. The world can be pictured as being constructed in such a distillation. At the creation, in some sense nothing has to separate into exceedingly simple opposites. If the separation generates a sufficiently complex pattern, the opposites acquire stability, and then richly persist.

A mundane example of this behaviour is the existence of matter and antimatter. A particle and its anti-particle on collision collapse into essentially nothing, a blob of energy; a particle and its anti-particle can be generated out of essentially nothing.

(Atkins 1994: 139)

To be relevant, it has to be, surely, *simply* nothing out of which a particle and its anti-particle can be generated, talk of 'essentially nothing' being another way of leaving room for there being something, however nugatory. And to say that 'opposites separate from nothing' is to say that opposites do not separate from anything, in which case, can we speak of them as separating at all? Again, in 'nothing has to separate into exceedingly simple opposites', no separation at all is envisaged unless 'nothing' is being treated as if it were the name of something, something in which opposites are somehow held in equilibrium, awaiting their separate existences. However, while the case for something coming from nothing has not been made out, there is a point here of some interest.

Can sense be made of the idea of two particles colliding and leaving nothing—not even the 'blob of energy' which Atkins allows? There is such a thing as failing to find any remnants of a body, but is there such a thing as finding that there are none? Perhaps the situation compares with uncaused happenings in quantum physics, where the move from failing to find a cause to the conclusion that there is no cause becomes more warranted as the failures mount up and the theory that rules out a cause becomes more and more well-confirmed. Again, it may be held that we could never be in a position to say that a body had come into existence out of nothing, since there would always be the possibility that, before materializing before us, the body had been elsewhere. This suggestion too could, with time, appear gratuitous: no comparable being is ever found to have been elsewhere, and the most sensitive instruments for tracking movement from place to place invariably fail to detect anything approaching the location where the body appears. Certainly, the suggested alternative is not shaping up well as an *empirical* proposition.

If a process which led to the annihilation of two particles were reversed, then we should have two particles coming into existence from nothing. Furthermore, it does not seem implausible to claim that a universe which is like ours but where the temporal direction of changes is reversed is logically possible, in which case the same could be said for the generation envisaged. This would simply be a particular instance of the many causally inexplicable happenings which such a world would harbour. True, we are speaking of a possibility *within* the universe, but a possibility that remains significant none the less, and one that would take on even greater significance if it could be argued that there is no intrinsic temporal order. So, consider the view that the directedness of time is not an objective feature of Nature, but something that somehow reflects our human perspective. With this standpoint, initial conditions of the universe do not prompt causal demands which might be met by a being outside the universe any more than do terminal conditions. That is, if there is no intrinsic temporal order, then no special significance is to be attached to what we denominate the end and what the beginning of the universe—supposing there to be such termini—yet many are driven to postulate events antecedent to the beginning while having no inclination to enquire about possible happenings subsequent to its end.

However, it is the supposition of such termini that we are querying. We have to rid our thinking of the conception of the universe as having the kinds of spatial and temporal limits which would allow us to make sense of 'beyond the physical universe . . .' or 'before the universe came into being . . .'. If the universe were like an agglomeration of bodies which one might encounter when progressing through space and time, only to leave behind when venturing on into a spatio-temporal void, one could make sense of a beginning and end in both spatial and temporal terms, but with nothing outside the universe in the way this requires, no pre-existent setting into which everything was placed, we have to make sense of the relevant propositions in a purely *internal* way. The expansion of the universe following the Big Bang was an expansion *of* space rather than an expansion *into* space. We are concerned with intrinsic features of the universe, features which can be determined without having to go outside it, as with H. P. Robertson's approach to the geometry of space: '. . . we propose ultimately to deal exclusively with properties intrinsic to the space under consideration—properties which in the later physical applications can be measured within the space itself—and are not dependent upon some extrinsic construction, such as its relation to an hypothesized higher dimensional embedding space' (1959: 317).

It will doubtless be agreed that you cannot have 'Before the universe existed, there was nothing'; there is no 'before'—a point appreciated by Augustine, who held that 'the world was not created *in* time but *with* time' (1972: 436). For the same reason, you cannot interpret 'The universe had a beginning' as meaning that at one time there was nothing, and then the universe came into being. The notion of something's having had a beginning concerns a state of affairs which is intelligible only as occurring within the universe. Compare movement. An antecedent period of rest is a necessary condition for starting to move; not, of course, causally necessary, but necessary for us to be able to speak of a beginning of movement. We cannot regard coming into existence as presupposing some analogous condition, but one that was external to the universe, yet if any necessary condition would perforce be a *prior* condition, there can be no beginning to exist for the universe as a whole, any more than there can be a beginning of movement for something that was never stationary. There is a real dividing line between a sunless period and the birth of a sun, and so on with other bodies within the universe, but not between no universe and universe. That is just a vain call upon an inapplicable condition to give substance to the contrast; it is like envisaging a spatio-temporal void into which the Big Bang explodes, the first event being one we can approach from two sides, before and after. We cannot think of the coming to be of the universe as the culmination of some development, nor even as an event. The former would obviously require a time antedating the universe, and the latter, in implying a change in the way things were, would make no less of a demand in this respect. If the notion of an event, a coming to be, is inapplicable here, to ask *why* the universe began to exist will be to compound the error.

If we cannot have 'Before the universe existed, there was nothing', or cannot ask how things were before the universe existed, a symmetrical observation should allow us to rule out 'When the universe has ceased to exist there will be nothing.' It is, on this hypothesis, as if we might say: first we have all this, and then, gazing into the void, absolutely nothing. If a body ceases to exist there may be nothing where the body had been. The point of time at which something ceases to exist is not only the end point of its existence but the initial point of the ensuing bodiless state, just as the point at which a body ceases to be in motion is also the point at which it begins to be at rest. If we say that something *will* cease to exist, we look forward to a time when it will *have* ceased to exist, and there is no such time with respect to the universe.

But surely it is possible to imagine everything gradually ceasing to be until we are left with nothing—cf. the 'subtraction' argument in Baldwin (1996). This would not be ceasing to exist as we know it. In that, transformations are undergone in which mass/energy remains constant, with no progress towards a terminal state in which there is nothing. Still, we can suppose that a cessation of existence means one thing less to be counted, and in envisaging all bodies as having finally departed, it may seem that we are simply carrying this development through to the limit. However, since we are excluded from saying 'and then there would be nothing' when the universe itself is in question, talk of the universe as ceasing to be is not to be compared with talk of the ceasing to be of any of the things that go to make it up. Compare a universe in which all bodies, while in fact at rest, might none the less begin to move. This possibility will continue to hold as successive bodies are removed, but not to the point at which only one remains, yet there need be nothing special about this body, nothing that makes motion for it impossible prior to its being the only body left in the universe. Here we glimpse grounds for invoking a notion of necessity. The universe did not come into existence, nor will it cease to exist. And this is not just a matter of empirical fact: there is nothing we could intelligibly describe as the universe's coming into existence or its ceasing to exist. Beginnings and endings join causation in being concepts which, while having innumerable instances within our world, resist extrapolation to the universe itself.

So, if the universe cannot have come into existence and cannot cease to exist, is it temporally infinite in both directions? When the question was raised (as in Locke 1975: 175–6) whether the universe was limited, it was supposed that a limit would have to be a physical boundary, in the sense of something one might come up against, like a wall. Finding this unacceptable, it seemed reasonable to conclude that there can be no bounds to space. However, this is not the most fruitful way of understanding the notion of a spatial limit, of the universe as being bounded, but this is more usefully given the now familiar geometrical interpretation, a matter of the path that might be taken on a journey out into the furthermost regions of space. If, however far and in whatever direction we travel, we eventually find ourselves revisiting known regions, rather than forever encountering new territory, then there is a sense in which our universe is not limitless. Of course, I am not supposing that that is how we might in practice find the universe to be. It would have to be that we had general grounds for believing our universe to have a spatio-temporal structure from which this inevitable return could be deduced. And, while the notion of beginning to exist is suspect in application to the universe as a whole, we have an allowable approximation to this notion in terms of the universe's having been in existence for only a finite time. This is not: there was a time at which the universe did not exist; the universe will have existed at all times. Nor will there be a future time when it does not exist. But, for all that, there could be a finite limit to its duration to date as well as to its future history.

Similar caveats apply when speaking of an initial event, as the Big Bang may be thought to provide. Consider the kinds of physical process required to make sense of temporal notions, and in particular that of an instant. An instant, a point of time, can be annexed to the end-point of a change, as with starting or ceasing to move. However, if there is no preceding state of rest, there is no starting to move, so no possibility of marking a point of time by reference to such a happening. With respect to an initial physical happening, we cannot invoke the model of an event to which an instant of time might be assigned which is in any sense a temporal boundary, a point of division between the start of the event and an eventless period which preceded. We must always remain temporally within the universe, never somehow break the barrier and find ourselves on the other side, but if there were an initial instant there would be another side—just as, for a body to have a surface requires there to be a contiguous space. None of this is to deny anything involved in a Big Bang cosmology. It is just that any talk about the universe as coming into existence is to be replaced by talk of its finite duration—a matter of a more apposite redescription. We want something more by way of a *limit*: we can get ever nearer, approximate to it as closely as you wish, but never reach it. This possibility can be modelled mathematically—for instance, by mapping the series of temporal instants onto the open interval (0, 1) on the real line. That is, t, our variable for temporal instants, takes on the values $0 < t < 1$, giving us a series without a first or a last term. In Hawking's cosmology, 'Space-time would be like the surface of the earth, only with two more dimensions. The surface of the earth is finite in extent but it doesn't have a boundary or edge: if you sail off into the sunset, you don't fall off the edge or run into a singularity' (1988: 135–6). Again, 'So long as the universe had a beginning, we could suppose it had a creator. But if the universe is really completely self-contained, having no boundary or edge, it would have neither beginning nor end: it would simply be. What place, then, for a creator?' (1988: 140–1). Big Bang or no Big Bang, there has never been a time when there was nothing, and our conception of the Big Bang has to be accommodated to that consideration.

The notion of a finite duration has been offered as an approximation to that of a beginning of existence for the universe, but someone who wished to speak of the universe as having begun to exist might reasonably protest that they had not meant anything more than what is captured by the former: to say that the universe came into existence so many years ago is simply to say that it is so many years old. There need be no implication that some event took place at a first moment of time. What is important is that we should avoid conceptions of a temporal boundary that carry over conditions applicable only to happenings within the universe; likewise with the notion of the universe as ceasing to exist. It is not as if, were this to happen, there would *then* be nothing *there*. States, more generally, may be handled in this way. If a body has at no time been stationary, then it will have been in motion at every moment of its existence, in which case we cannot say that it began to move, but we could still, it would seem, speak of it as having been in motion for only a finite time. What is important is that a beginning, whether of change or of existence, rather than a merely finite duration, appears to be needed if we are to have an event, a happening in time, which raises a question of causation.

On one interpretation, we have ruled out the possibility of any explanation in answer to the question, 'Why does the universe exist?' When, namely, this has the force of 'What brought the universe into being?' The universe may initially be supposed in the category of those things for which we can expect an explanation to be forthcoming, so something for which its absence is troubling. However, the universe is not to be aligned with the things within it, things which, like planets and stars, pose answerable why-questions. It is not to be aligned with these in so far as it did not come into existence, was not preceded by a time in which there was no universe, a condition necessary to make sense of a causal account of its existence. When existence is at issue, is there any alternative to a causal interpretation of a why-question? In explaining Aquinas's claim that, in God, essence and existence are identical, Geach (1955) has made use of the notion of a thing's being or *esse*, understood as that in virtue of which a thing can be said to be, or to continue in existence, just as a creature's intelligence is that by which it is intelligent. There is a non-causal sense of 'makes', as found in 'He is my sister's child. That makes him my nephew', or 'The desk was produced over a hundred years ago. That makes it an antique', and the *esse* of something could be said to be what makes it exist in this non-causal sense. However, to identify God with that by which he is, confronts us with the difficulties already noted in saying that God is identical with his wisdom, with that by which he is wise; and while we can ask what it is in virtue of which the universe exists, the answer will tell us no more than what it is that makes for character as a universe. It does not seem that an answer to our why-question is to be sought in this direction, any more than by finding a cause. How, then, can it be answered?

6
Matter and Abstractions

We have reason to think that the question why there is something rather than nothing can be answered, but the answer ventured—that there simply has to be something or other—is in no way enlightening as to why there is what there is. Why has reality taken the form it has? If its particular character cannot be seen as the realization of a divine plan, is it to be accepted as just a brute, inexplicable fact?

6.1 THE NECESSITY OF THE PHYSICAL

Here is an approach which seeks to avoid both these problematic alternatives. Although it is difficult to maintain that the way things are is the only way things could be, perhaps the proliferation of different kinds of thing, the variety which encourages the belief that things could so easily have been otherwise, conceals an essential simplicity which knows no real alternative—just as, superficially, the conservation of energy may appear belied by the more evident fact of unceasing change. Thus, while the immense variety of material beings seemingly emphasizes the contingency of our world, we can presume a lessening of diversity, a reversion to more basic and uniform properties, as we go back into the history of the universe. Look at many of the individual things that have evolved and we readily conclude that their existence is due to special conditions, not conditions so general that any universe would have to satisfy them; hence the overwhelming sense of contingency. But as we go back in time the picture perhaps changes, a progressively more simple pattern taking shape. After all, it is not implausible to think in terms of contingency creeping into the system through the operation of indeterministic or chaotic factors. This mirrors the argument, based on the second law of thermodynamics, which affirms that the entropy of the universe diminishes as we go back into the past, eventually reaching a state of maximum order, a 'beginning' in which all the mass in the universe is compressed into a state of infinite density. Again, if we go back far enough, the four fundamental forces appear to be unified, interactions between elementary particles becoming weaker and simpler as temperatures and energies rise, to such a point that the particles would not have reacted at all.

However, it is not clear just what we are hoping to lay bare with this imaginative exercise. The present and the distant past are on a par in the sense that 'There has to be something' is as much a necessity for the one as for the other, if it is a necessity at all, and if we are in search of a truth of the form, 'Things have to be this way', then this, too, will not know differing truth values at different times. Is it none the less possible that not so much is open here than we may suppose? Consider the question why the universe is the age that it is. Might it not have come into existence earlier? That, surely, does not make sense as it stands—there were no earlier times, times before $t = 0$. But can we not conceive of an earlier starting point in the sense that the universe might have been older *now*—say 20 billion years rather than the 13.7 billion currently estimated? We could then have gone back further, in thought. But this is still problematic. If the identities as happenings of what is taking place now are bound up with the date of their occurrence, where this is determined by the time elapsed since the beginning, then these happenings could not have occurred later. Consider a flash of lightning, something individuated by the time and place of its occurrence. A flash just like it could occur at another time and/or place, but no such flash would be *this* flash. Likewise for any other episode, at whatever time. The universe could not accordingly have begun sooner, in the sense that it might by now have been in existence longer. We have to be thinking, not of *this* universe, but of a quite different one, and even this is problematic. It might be said that we—or, rather, beings like us—could have been living in a universe which had been in existence for a longer time before a certain event—say, the first flash of lightning—took place, but we cannot say 'could have *now* been living'; and, as we shall shortly see, even the use of 'longer' can be queried.

The proposition 'Things might have been otherwise' raises questions of identity. This glass could have been otherwise; it could, for instance, have been chipped—had it been chipped, it could still have been the same glass, the one produced at such and such a place and time, so the possibility is genuine. Now take 'things' more broadly, as relating to this planet, let us say. The issue still seems the same, in that we can suppose that the planet might have been cooler provided that this supposition contains no threat to the identity of the planet. What of 'Our planet might have been different' in the sense of 'We might have lived on a different planet'? The question of identity now shifts to *us*. What grounds could we have for saying it might have been us located elsewhere, given that our identity is bound up with our origins, into the specification of which our planet enters? And 'The universe could have been different'? If the differences envisaged fall outside matters of identity, what we are envisaging may still be reckoned this universe, but 'It could have been that a different universe existed' is not to be granted so readily.

To take this a step further, the supposition that there might have been a universe other than this cannot mean that there might have been another universe literally in *place* of this. Nor can we ask *where* this universe might have been. You cannot say that it would have to have been somewhere; somewhere is always somewhere *in* the universe, never somewhere where the universe might be. Could this conjectured universe differ from ours through being of a different age? Being of a different age *when*, we may ask, and it is no use saying *now*. What point of time is to be designated *now* in this other universe? Given the impossibility of setting up any correspondence between our universe and this other, none imposes itself more than any other. Suppose we envisage a universe that is temporally bounded, so that we might assess its duration from beginning to end, and suppose we have a figure giving the measure of ours. Where can this imaginative exercise take us, given that we cannot possibly compare the units of the two measures? Each universe's space and time is its own; there is no common frame of reference in which lapses of time in the two can be compared. We cannot say that at this very moment there may be, or there could have been, beings in another universe puzzling about the same problems as we are. Such ways of speaking purport to affirm temporal links between the two universes, to place them in a common reference frame that breaks down the barriers which warranted us in speaking of two universes. There is no justification for distinguishing the suppositions that there has been a different universe from ours aeons in the past, that there is one now as you read these words, or that there will be one at some future time. The claim is not that the supposition that another universe exists at the present time is unverifiable, hence nonsense. Rather, what it is to exist now—or in our past or future—has not been defined for this case.

It was suggested above that we have no reason to suppose that there are or have been any other universes, but that, according to the present argument, is strictly a nonsense. Still, suppose that the supposition of another universe retains some sense once the inapposite distinctions of tense are discarded. What is important is whether the only alternative to the universe as we know it is another *universe*. Whether we envisage changes in our world or, at the extreme, a universe distinct from this one, the variations are in *physical* reality, and while that may appear not to make for any constraint, the common framework is very relevant to our general concerns.

What is there, if anything, that is somehow necessary, part of whose nature it may be, none the less, to be chaotic, capable of unlawlike change? If what is sought is a condition which is to hold whatever universe, or whatever phase of this universe, is in question, it would seem that something like 'There has to be matter' or 'There has to be a physical reality' would need to be established, or perhaps some more specific proposition pertaining to the way matter has to be. More specific, but such that it applies to the or a universe in any of its possible states. Here the concept of a *dimension* may prove fruitful. So, a one-dimensional universe need not detain us for long. There are perhaps such things as points of no size in reality—think of a point formed by the intersection of three differently coloured planes—but these are definable only against a background of at least two dimensions. A two-dimensional universe is sometimes ruled out on the grounds of the limited scope that it offers for the development of things with any degree of complexity: 'It is impossible to have a complicated network without the wires crossing; nor can an object have a channel through it (a digestive tract, for instance) without dividing into two' (Rees 1999: 136). It is not a question of lacking insufficient complexity for survival (Atkins 1994: 135), but these objections already concede too much in dignifying the relevant constructs with the title of 'objects' or 'clusters'. At all events, a two-dimensional surface has to be a surface of something, and this immediately takes us to a third dimension. To have *just* a surface is no more possible than to have the grin of the Cheshire Cat without the Cat.

Note that the existence of matter could emerge as inescapable without our having to equate existence with physical or material existence. Matter may be variable in its states—solid, liquid, gaseous—and much of what there is cannot be described as material at all—distances, dates, doubts, epidemics, consciousness, intelligence—but it could still be that a physical universe is a prerequisite, not only, of course, for states of matter, but for anything else that might be said to exist. The model may be as with mind and body. A crude form of materialism identifies thoughts, feelings, and the rest, with states of the body, an identification which will not stand up in the face of the vastly different things that can be said of the mental and the physical: one's thoughts may be muddled, innovative, inspired, illogical or obsessional, but none of this can be said of anything that is literally taking place in one's head. We have to broaden the terms of our identity: to be fantasizing, for instance, is perhaps to have such-and-such a process taking place in one's brain, even if the fantasy one is having is not locatable in this way. Even this may be too circumscribed, some psychological states requiring reference to conditions external to the mind for their characterization. 'I believe', for instance, is often like 'I gather' in implying an external source of ostensible information. All we may eventually end up with is the unremarkable conclusion that our mental lives would be impossible without a brain, a physical organ. There is this existential dependence, despite the failure of the cruder identities. Certainly, it does not seem that we could have some very general category such that something in this category could be either physical or in some other form, so there is no rival alternative to the physical at this point.

When it was argued that we cannot think away everything, what persisted so obdurately was the domain of the physical, the constraints upon our imaginings having to do with the apparent inescapability of a spatio-temporal setting. So, we can happily suppose that no abstractions should have existed—or so we shall argue—and we can suppose that matter should have taken on different forms, but we seemingly do not have the same latitude with respect to a spatio-temporal universe, broadly conceived. However, we should surely like to have more compelling grounds for identifying matter—better, perhaps, the physical—in this cosmically indispensable role. Consider, then, the following. You could not have a world in which there were just events, or just energy, let us say. Nor, in a sense soon to be explained, could there be just forces. Take events. A fall, a split, a quarrel, and so forth, are always the fall, etc., of or in something or someone. Something undergoes, is subject of, a change. Energy is often singled out as the ultimate reality, but again the grammar of the term makes demands that stand in the way of that status. We are not dealing with some kind of stuff, but 'energy' has the logic of a term such as 'ability', 'propensity', or 'capacity'; energy is a capacity for *work*, and capacities, as much as events, are capacities attributable to some subject. The requisite notion of a subject is more robust than is given with a purely formal characterization, but it interchanges with that of a *substance*. Thus, it is not good enough to say we have a suitable subject whenever we have a term enjoying nounlike behaviour coupled with a suitable predicate, since that would have us re-admitting events and energy in the role which we have denied them, sentences like 'The collapse of the star was unexpected' and 'Its energy diminished' clearly conforming to the less demanding characterization.

Admittedly, the term 'substance' is not entirely satisfactory, being tainted by various of its historical connotations, as when Locke would in the same breath speak of 'something I know not what'. However, it does serve to convey the key feature of independence given in the contrast with *events, surfaces, propensities*, and other such existentially challenged items. So, we have come as far as requiring some such term as 'substance', and we can take the final further step to our conclusion if we can equate substance to material substance. And this, it seems to me, would be correct, the more formal characterization being the only one available as an alternative to physical or material substance. True, the explanatory power of mind appears initially to be infinitely superior. How could ultimate reality rest with blind, unthinking matter? To many, the whole idea seems absurd. But the explanatory power of mind is the explanatory power of a physical being which can act in such a way that its words and deeds are describable as manifestations of thought. It is not the explanatory power of a purely mental substance conceivable in total detachment from the physical, an immaterial being lodged in the body but capable of being liberated from its physical shackles. There is no mental or spiritual substance, but these are notions founded on a misconceived comparison with material things. Indeed, any attempt to play down the centrality of the physical is likely to reflect adversely on the non-physical, since if the latter is thought of in more substantial terms than is given with abstract entities, it will be based on our familiar conception of physical agents, beings which can act on other things. The sense in which materialism or physicalism is wrong does nothing to help those who would assign to the non-physical a creative, constructive, active role.

To repeat, however, it is absurd to say that everything that is is material. When we say there are times when nothing goes right, there are ways of making you talk, there are possibilities undreamed of, we are not talking of material entities, but while times, ways and possibilities may be joined by any number of other intangible items, this does not mean that matter can in any sense be dispensed with. Take away the physical backdrop and all else departs. True, there is, as intimated, some question as to whether *matter* is the right term to focus on for this cosmic role. It is sometimes said that matter was a *product* of the Big Bang, so not there from the outset, when, for an infinitesimal period, more esoteric entities held sway— ten-dimensional superstrings whose breakdown gave rise to matter, perhaps. What is important is that there must have been something falling within a general category of the physical if we are to speak of it as having given rise to matter; whatever can be reckoned there without a predecessor, it has to be, logically if not literally, sufficiently in the same space as the ensuing matter for us to make sense of its generation of the latter. The constraints here are grammatical rather than empirical. You cannot make one phase of the universe too different from the phase into which it supposedly developed without putting the intelligibility of '*x* developed into *y*' at risk in this application.

6.2   ABSTRACTIONS AND NUMBER

A comprehensive inventory of all that there is, so of what might furnish a rival to matter, looks to be a tall order, but the non-physical is not an over-whelmingly extensive category. The major rival is provided by mind. So important is this category, if theology is denied its use, its subject matter would appear to vanish altogether. Leaving aside mind, which will be discussed in the next chapter, much of what falls outside the physical is in the realm of abstractions, as given with *consciousness, beauty, intelligence, being,* and *evil,* along with multitudes of less philosophically celebrated concepts, as those of *prurience, patience,* and *punctuality.* Our concern is, once more, not to deny the existence of abstractions, but to see them for what they are. Take the term 'evil'. There are some who, in asserting that evil exists, take themselves to be advancing a contentious claim. But of course there is evil. That just means there are evil men and their evil deeds. If—moral subjectivism aside—the claim is thought disputable, that is, I suspect, because evil has been mislocated in a more substantive category— as if the existence of evil meant the existence of a force that went by that name, or even a spirit that roamed the world. A spirit could be evil (adjective), but not evil (noun).

Terms which compare with 'evil' can be readily brought down to earth in a similar fashion, as we shall soon see, but more interesting are what might be called abstract *objects,* as introduced by such phrases as 'the equator'—Frege's well-chosen example of the genre—'lines of force' and 'centre of gravity'; and, of course, the objects that have been most favoured in this connection, namely numbers. True, whatever we fasten on in the general category, it is wildly implausible to regard it as a potential rival to matter, but, as with mind, there are those who have thought otherwise. Again, I have indicated that one who claims that there might have been nothing appears obliged to respond to the queries 'Where?' and 'When?', and the only items which appear not to prompt these unsatisfiable queries fall in the category of the abstract. Compare, too, laws of Nature, which are not uncommonly thought of as enjoying such a fundamental reality as both to antedate and to determine physical existence. And the topic is of some interest if we seek a better understanding of the diversity of what there is, as well as bearing upon questions having to do with necessary existence.

Abstract objects are sometimes characterized in terms of their causal impotence. They are incapable of inducing changes in anything. This characterization risks likening them too much to (impoverished) physical objects, or perhaps to some form of *stuff*, and a more fitting approach is to investigate the grammar of the relevant vocabulary, which is often the grammar of a clause. Take the term 'consciousness'. As with other nouns ending in '-ness', this customarily provides a variant on a phrase in which an adjective is coupled with some part of the verb 'to be'. So, 'Her kindness is overwhelming' means 'She is overwhelmingly kind' and 'His forgetfulness was irritating' means 'He was irritatingly forgetful' or 'It was irritating how forgetful he was.' The same holds of other abstract nouns, as 'life', 'indignation', 'existence', 'promiscuity', 'equality', and so forth. Life exists on other planets if and only if there are living things on other planets. 'Promiscuity is rife in rural Wales'; that is, 'A lot of people are promiscuous in rural Wales'. To say that consciousness is a human prerogative is just to say that to be conscious is a human prerogative; similarly, for consciousness to develop in creatures is just for them to become conscious, whereas to lose consciousness is simply to cease to be conscious.

The materialist's claim that all reality is physical is sometimes understood as a claim that there is just physical stuff. And no doubt that is so; certainly, given that stuff is something of which there can be a *volume*, we have yet to learn what immaterial 'stuff' might be. But then not everything is stuff. A contemporary writer tells us that he sees 'nothing wrong, metaphysically, with recognising that consciousness *is* a kind of stuff'

(McGinn 1991: 60)—an interesting thought, that the qualification 'metaphysically' might undergo a role-reversal to such a point that it could somehow turn nonsense into sense. Some such conception, we may note, is needed to give the appearance of sense to the question of *where* consciousness is to be found. But appearance is all there is. We make use of the notion of consciousness without having to give a meaning to the question of its location. Clearly, it is a person that is conscious, not a brain—unless perhaps in some transferred sense—and there is no more difficulty in identifying a human being as conscious than there is in ascertaining that someone is awake, responsive, watchful, or attentive. The question 'What is consciousness?' is sometimes held to present the last great scientific challenge. If its answer requires finding the right stuff in the right place, then it is a challenge that will never be met. Note, too, that it is not that the lack of an answer to the question of location is in some way peculiar to consciousness; it is the general rule for terms in this grammatical category, as is apparent with such fellow abstractions as *intelligence, duration, existence,* and others of the kind mentioned above. In so far as location is defined for F-ness, it will be a matter of the location of what is *F*, as weightlessness in space is a matter of something in space being weightless, and carelessness in the home a matter of someone being careless in the home.

To continue with the grammar, consider the term 'length'. Estimating, calculating, or measuring the length of a bridge is a matter of ascertaining *how long* the bridge is; calculations are performed with a view to determining the 'longness' of the bridge, the extent or degree to which it is long. Here we note that what such calculations determine is the answer to a *question,* and if the length of the bridge is uncertain, what is uncertain is again the answer to a question. Despite its character as a noun, the behaviour of 'length' is akin to that of a clause—often an interrogative clause. Again, 'His laziness surprised me' may be paraphrased as 'That he was lazy surprised me', or 'It surprised me how lazy he was.' The single noun may do duty for more than one type of clause, depending on whether, for example, it is the fact or the degree of the person's laziness that is at issue. Compare 'existence'. Discussing the existence of God is discussing *whether* he exists, proving the existence of God is proving *that* he exists. Perhaps the most notorious example of a word which has been misconstrued through a failure to appreciate its clausal value is that of 'meaning': to know the meaning of 'quark' is not to be acquainted with some entity, but to know what 'quark' means, where the 'what' is an interrogative, not a relative pronoun.

While, in the use under consideration, 'length' compares with 'laziness', in such a phrase as 'a length of rope', where 'length' has a material reference, there is, by contrast, no question of function as a clause. The same duality arises with other forms of measurement, and with counting generally. If you count the number of eggs in a basket, then you count how many eggs there are. What merits the title, 'the objects counted', is *the eggs*, not *how many eggs there are*. This latter phrase does not denote something to which the numbers 1, 2, 3, . . . are successively applied. It can, of course, be said that what you count is the number, but not in the same sense as that given with 'what you count are the eggs'. You may, it is true, count numbers, as when you count the prime numbers less than 100, but here numbers *are* the 'objects' counted. Again, contrast 'Sue learned a poem' with 'Sue learned how her mother felt.' A poem may be reckoned an object learned, but it is not the role of the clause to introduce an object of any kind (see Rundle 2001 for further argument).

Our understanding of *time* can profit from these distinctions. If I use a yardstick to measure 2 feet, in the sense of measure *off*, or lay off, 2 feet, then I do not measure 2 feet in the same sense as I measure a piece of cloth. I do not measure 2 feet to find out how long they are. And, just as 2 feet is not the object measured, so, too, time is not the 'object' which clocks measure. If you use a clock to time two hours, you will not be seeking a temporal measure of two hours, in the sense of timing the period to see how long it lasts, but you will be letting your clock run for a time which might measure some contemporaneous process. 'I timed two hours' is not like 'I timed the race'—as though two hours took a certain time which was to be ascertained—not a specification of what was timed. In saying that clocks give a measure *of* time, we are saying what *kind* of measure is at issue—namely, a measure of duration, of how long in temporal terms; we are not specifying the object measured, as though there were a quantity or volume of time recognizable as, say, two hours. Two hours is what is measured in the sense that 'two hours' *gives* the measure. Just as the number of eggs counted is the number in which the counting *issues*, so when time is measured, this is a matter of a form of measuring issuing in a (specification of a) time.

The idea of time as a quantity waiting there to be measured, as one might weigh a volume of water, is perhaps due in part to a misconstrual of such locutions as 'we measure time with clocks', an assimilation of this to 'we time races with clocks', or 'we measure bodies with rulers'—as though a period of time were, in its own way, like a stretch of water or a length of fabric. What we measure temporally is, roughly speaking, items in the category of events—speeches, races, journeys, quarrels, meetings, and so forth. It is to these, not to some questionable quantity, that we put a figure. The most notorious expression of this misconception is to be found in the absolutist conception of time, according to which the notions of temporal position and duration can be understood by having regard to no more than what time itself can provide; it is not required that we appeal to any happenings in time to provide markers in terms of which temporal points and periods can be fixed. Time itself is supposedly self-sufficient in this respect: a minute, an hour, or any other temporal interval is simply there for us to come across much as we may come across an event which goes on for a minute or an hour. Talk of the unreality of time may reflect an awareness that time is not something there to be measured alongside events in time, but 'unreal' does not do justice to the more positive way in which time figures in our discourse, nor to the truth of propositions in which the contribution of temporal qualifications is crucial.

Consciousness and time provide interesting examples where the superficial grammar would have us acknowledge substances or objects possibly of a character so basic as to compare with matter in point of independence. How do things stand with number? The pretensions of the kinds of abstraction so far considered are soon pricked, but the power, elegance, and objectivity of mathematics have led some to ascribe a reality to mathematical constructions which would give them the standing of serious rivals to matter.

One extreme is to regard mathematical constructions as the true reality, with the physical world downgraded to illusory status. This position is perhaps never fully endorsed nowadays, but a robustly Platonic conception of mathematics is certainly to be met with, as in this passage from Roger Penrose:

Since each [mathematician] can make contact with Plato's world directly, they can more readily communicate with each other than one might have expected. The mental images that each one has, when making this Platonic contact, might be rather different in each case, but communication is possible because each is directly in contact with the *same* externally existing Platonic world!

(1990: 554)

Again, 'To speak of "Plato's world" at all, one is assigning some kind of reality to it which is in some way comparable to the reality of the physical world' (ibid., 557), so if the physical world is somehow not as concrete as we have supposed, perhaps the very distinction between the two realms becomes blurred:

> On the other hand, the reality of the physical world itself seems more nebulous than it had seemed to be before the advent of the SUPERB theories of relativity and quantum mechanics . . . The very precision of these theories has provided an almost abstract mathematical existence for actual physical reality.
>
> (ibid., 557)

The identification here hinted at is openly affirmed by Atkins: 'physical reality is mathematics and mathematics is physical reality' (1994: 109). In whatever sense physical reality might be said to be 'nebulous', it would not help the claim that tables and chairs are mathematical entities. Perhaps the importance of mathematics can be dramatized by means of such an identification, but this is not to be taken as anything more than a figure of speech. Let us now consider what can be said in literal terms.

A seemingly uncontentious starting point is given with the observation that the signs and symbols with which the mathematician deals are indisputably meaningful. The question, or *a* question, is whether this might not also be a stopping point. Does mathematics require anything more than that such configurations as 4^3 and $\sqrt{-1}$ should have a use or meaning? Is it in some way lacking at its foundations if nothing can be exhibited as what is *referred* to by, say, '$\sqrt{-1}$'? The Platonist holds that there is indeed some such thing, and that it exists independently of us: even if there had never been a sign or word with the meaning of 'the square root of minus one', that number would have existed. And even non-Platonists may consider that we must give content to our symbolism by postulating numbers as referents of our number words and numerals. How this need might be felt, how the mere meaningfulness of the words or notation may be insufficient unless bolstered by such a backing, real or postulated, is not clear, but there are arguments against the non-Platonist alternatives. We shall consider one attack that still has its advocates, namely, that advanced by Gottlob Frege. Further details may be found in Rundle (1979: §31).

Frege's Platonism is summed up in his contention that numbers are self-subsistent objects, a view arrived at by eliminating the possibility that numbers are *properties* of objects. What we ascribe numbers to is a concept, never an object. To say 'The King's carriage is drawn by four horses' is to assign the number four to the concept, 'horse that draws the King's carriage' (Frege 1980: §46). It is not clear how this ascription is to be explained, given that such elucidations as 'The concept "horse that draws the King's carriage" has four instances', or 'Four things fall under the concept "horse that draws the King's carriage"', feature 'four' in just the kind of grammatical role which Frege considers secondary, being more akin here to an adjective than to the name which he takes it to be. Be that as it may, what is extraordinary is the idea that, when we count actual objects or groups of objects—individual playing cards or packs of cards, platoons or battalions—our ascriptions of number are to anything less than the objects or groups counted. So, having counted the books on the shelf you declare that they total, number, or add up to fifteen, or that they are fifteen in number. Of what is 'are fifteen in number' held to be true? Of the books just counted, obviously—taken collectively, not individually. And that remains the right answer even though we have first to make clear, by specifying a concept, just *what* we are counting—books, pages, dust-jackets, or whatever.

The qualification given with *collectively* is crucial, as is Frege's argument at this point with respect to the tree with a thousand leaves. So, being a thousand in number is clearly not a property of an individual leaf, but it is not difficult to think of properties which may hold of a plurality of leaves, as when we say that they form a pattern or weigh a stone, so why not say that it is the leaves that are a thousand in number? Frege, however, will have nothing of this: 'The green colour we ascribe to each single leaf, but not the number 1,000. If we call all the leaves of a tree taken together its foliage, then the foliage too is green, but it is not 1,000' (ibid., §22). Why, one wonders, does he consider it necessary to introduce the term 'foliage' (*Laub*), rather than simply stay with 'leaves', as a possible subject? It is hard to avoid the suspicion that he saw what was coming with this turn in the argument, and sought to circumvent the move by substituting for 'leaves' a term that refuses the numerical predicate. But, evidently, the inapposite-ness of the singular noun 'foliage' in place of 'leaves' no more rules out 'The leaves are 1,000 in number' than it does 'Count the leaves'. Nor is it necessary to regard the leaves as an aggregate in any sense that would be defeated by their random dispersal; all that matters is that we should know which leaves are to be reckoned to the totality in question. Much of Frege's argument is directed at Mill's use of the term 'agglomeration' to charac-terize the subjects of number ascriptions; there is no call for the objects numbered to cohere or be organized in a way that would make some such characterization appropriate.

Frege's position is not helped by the consideration, touched upon above, that we have to specify a concept to make clear just what we are counting. He writes:

If I give someone a stone with the words: Find the weight of this, I have given him precisely the object he is to investigate. But if I place a pile of playing cards in his hands with the words: Find the Number of these, this does not tell him whether I wish to know the number of cards, or of complete packs of cards, or even say of points in the game of skat. To have given him the pile in his hands is not yet to have given him completely the object he is to investigate; I must add some further word—cards, or packs, or points.

(ibid., §22)

The possible variations that arise with weight are not brought to light with the context which Frege envisages, viz. giving someone a *single* object with the words 'Find the weight of this.' Suppose instead that, pointing to a pile of cutlery, someone gives us the instruction, 'Find how much these weigh.' We can think of the pile as comprising knives and forks, or knife and fork sets, just the kind of variability relevant to ascriptions of number: are we to find the weights of the individual knives and forks, or of the sets? The former is, of course, the more natural interpretation, but so too is the interpretation of 'Find the number of these' as 'Find the number of these cards.' Whether counting or weighing is at issue, it is misleading to say that it is the same things that are assigned different numbers or weights, depending on the concept under which they are being considered; different things, in the sense of different *groupings* of things, are being weighed or counted. Thus, while we call upon a concept to make clear what we are counting, assigning a number to a concept is not the only alternative to assigning it to a given totality of individuals; subdivisions of the individuals also provide possible subjects. So, when a battalion comprises three companies, each of which consists of two platoons, we have not only groupings of men but groupings of groupings of men as what may be counted.

So what is the property that the leaves are said to have, when we declare them to be a thousand in number? Simply that of being pairable off with the numbers from 1 to 1,000. This might well be held to be an odd sense of 'property', but it is the sense that is relevant: in '*A* is *F*', '*F*' affirms a property of an object or objects, *A*, provided merely that '*A*' genuinely picks out an object or objects—the logician's sense of the term according to which to say that the jewel has been found or the thief has been pursued is to affirm a 'property' of jewel or thief. The contrast is with sentences in which apparent referential terms enjoy no such role, the traditional examples being, relevantly enough, those of statements of existence. Relevantly, because this is in fact what Frege has fastened upon, and wrongly generalized. Clearly, no reference is made to a moon of Venus with 'There are no moons of Venus', and *a fortiori* no property is affirmed of a moon referred to. Likewise with 'There are four horses driving the king's carriage.' But what holds for existential propositions does not carry over to propositions generally.

Frege is right to question the assimilation of number words to the category of adjectives. Words for particular numbers are like 'many' and 'several' in having only rarely the predicative use found in 'Her virtues are many.' Compare 'many angry old Scottish pensioners' and 'seven angry old Scottish pensioners'. We tend to order adjectives in accordance with the way in which the class defined by the noun is progressively contracted, so would prefer the ordering just given to, say, 'seven angry Scottish old pensioners'. The number term holds the outermost position—'angry seven Scottish old pensioners' is clearly impossible—not introducing any differentia into the class of pensioners, not being like adjectives which signify a *kind* (cf. Benacerraf 1965: 60). However, while it is right to draw a contrast with typical adjectival function, there is nothing at all unusual in the use of a number word in qualifying a general term, as with 'the twelve apostles' or 'my two children'. Indeed, it is this use that we invoke in our reading of arithmetical equations, such as '$3 \times 7 = 21$'. This is a matter of three times seven being equal to twenty-one, which is a matter of seven *things* being taken three *times*. There is an asymmetry between the 3 and the 7 in what they implicitly qualify. Or, again, we may say 'Three sevens are twenty-one.' What is a seven? In this context, a group of seven things, surely; that is why there can be more than one of them. It is not 'three number 7s'. Wittgenstein placed great emphasis on the *application* of mathematical concepts, their occurrence in pure mathematics being thought derivative. Addition, clearly, can also be readily thought of in terms that keep us close to actual applications. '$3 + 7 = 10$' is a matter of three things plus seven things being equal to ten things. No need to keep repeating 'things', but when this is dropped we are left with a form which, it is thought, tells us the result of adding one abstract entity named '3' to another named '7'. The error in the philosophical rendering—and you don't get philosophy much more primitive than this—is further compounded by the reading of '$=$' as 'is identical'. An aggregate of 13 things plus 19 things is equal in number to one of 32 things. We are not obliged to find a way of making sense of the notion that '13 + 19 = 32' informs us that an operation on abstract entities named '13' and '19' is identical with an abstract entity called '32', yet according to Quine, not only are our number words names of 'intangible objects', but these objects enjoy a standing comparable to that of the unobservable entities which the physicist postulates for the sake of their value in making observational predictions (Quine 1981: 149). Here we see the misplaced comparison with physical objects at its crudest.

I do not maintain that a namelike grammar is never appropriate to the use of number terms. On the contrary. Numerical expressions are not designations of abstract entities, but there are many names of numbers— 'Planck's constant', 'zero', h, e, i, and so forth. However, while 'zero' may be said to designate 0, this latter is not itself the name of anything, but the number figures here *in propria persona*. We have just written it down. Compare letters of the alphabet. 'Alpha' is the name of α, but the naming function stops there. In writing 'α' we give you not a name of the first letter of the Greek alphabet, but that very letter. As just observed, we have various ways of reading '3 × 7 = 21'—'Three times seven is twenty-one', 'Three by seven equals twenty-one' 'Three sevens are twenty-one'—and it is noticeable that we tend to shift to the word 'seven' rather than the numeral '7' in giving these written renderings. Indeed, 'three 7s' might well be used with respect to the array '7 7 7'. Likewise, asked to write down a number we should more readily opt for 7 rather than 'seven', whereas it is more naturally the word that is said to have a meaning, or to have a synonym in *sieben*, and it is the word rather than the sign that goes in the context 'x' plus noun—'the three bears' rather than 'the 3 bears', '3' being more suited to behaviour as itself an 'object'.

Is there not a clear enough sense in which, alongside the reading in which the application is brought to the surface, we have a use in which the subject matter is plainly, indeed literally, exhibited in the equations? But what could possibly be meant by saying of a number, as a notational object, that it is prime, or even? Clearly, such properties are not properties of the objects in the way being cursive or being italicized are, but we transfer to the numbers predicates that are explained, ultimately, in terms of operations in whose descriptions 'adjectival'—that is, *applied*—uses of number words figure. So, 1,000,000 is greater than 1,000, not because the former is physically larger, but because a million of anything is more than a thousand. Again, '10 is even' may be explained as 'Ten things is equal to twice some number of things.' You can add an apple to a pile, or take one away. That is addition and subtraction as operations on concrete things, and addition and subtraction of numbers is parasitic on this procedure, on adding or taking away numbers of apples, and so forth. Though they are not far in the background, we soon lose sight of such applications, and the rules which develop for manipulating the notational objects are very much geared to the notation in which they are carried out, being different if the number is given in the binary or in the decimal notation. There is not, over and above such rules, rules which would specify how abstract entities, numbers not given in a notation, are to be manipulated.

Compare the question: is there such a number as $\frac{0}{0}$? Or, is $\frac{1}{0}$ a number? If either of these concatenations of symbols is well defined, there is no question of a failure of existence, or a need merely to postulate the number. The sense in which we might go deeper, go beyond the 'mere signs', is given with the transition to the 'applied' reading, where the connection with counting and other operations is made explicit. For the rest—when we abstract or prescind from these uses—we are left with just the symbolism itself as the subject matter. A crude formalism is transcended by the former reading; there is not another direction in which depth is to be sought, namely, that in which we identify a *further* reference for the symbols. Here we may note that the construal of numbers as purely abstract entities has to confront the consideration that we can *write down* a number, that we can erase a column of numbers just as readily as we can add them up. We *can* say such things as that 0110 comes before 0111 in the binary notation; that we are speaking directly about the notation is not to be dismissed with the familiar jibes—so mathematics is just about marks on paper? But these are *numerals*, not true numbers, it will be protested. If they are numerals, then that gives a sense of 'number', but in fact you take the policeman's number, not his numeral, and you dial a number, not a numeral or series of numerals. And when there is no such reference, there is not, to repeat, reference to an abstract entity. In 'a number of (the) Fs', for instance, 'a number' is not a place-holder for a designation of an abstract entity, but for a numerical term enjoying the 'adjectival' use. So, 'A number of children—thirteen, as it happens—left early.'

Consider the question of providing a criterion of identity for numbers, a question whose difficulty to answer has frequently been thought to cast doubt on the acceptability of abstract entities more generally, and which would commonly be construed as a question of determining whether and when various numerical expressions have the same reference. There is more than one case to consider here, but to take an instance close to our present concerns, suppose we are dealing with different number systems, and we wish to know whether the hexadecimal number 3F8A has the number 0011 1111 1000 1010 as its binary equivalent. This is a question as to whether the relevant transformations will generate the latter from the former, a simple enough matter. Hexadecimal 0 to 9 and A to F are paired off with the binary representations of 0 to 15, and each of the hexadecimal digits in 3F8A is translated onto its 4-bit binary equivalent. Less concrete entities play no part in such transformations. And are these numbers products of the divine will, having existed in God's mind from all eternity? Possibly, but a more conservative estimate would date the hexadecimal system from the latter half of the nineteenth century.

It is clear that the numbers which we may exhibit must be associated with a broad criterion of identity if we are to accommodate such truths as that Arabic 7 is the same number as Roman vii, but that is no problem. Compare greetings. French *bonjour* is the same greeting as English 'good day', and that can be said despite the evident typographical and phonetic differences between the two, sameness of meaning or use being what counts—sameness as given with an equivalence relation rather than with strict identity. It is not that the two expressions *stand for* the same greeting. Likewise with 7 and vii. Someone might still balk at saying that 'is prime', say, can be a predicate of a notational object: we can write down *a* 7, but the 7 written down—and possibly smudged—is surely not the 7 that is prime. What is important is not to hold out for a common subject, but to insist that the ultimate explanations of statements of number are given with the applied forms, as when we say that '10 is even' may be explained as 'Ten things are equal to twice some number of things.' That, and the recognition that arithmetical operations can be performed on numbers as notational objects, as when we add a column of numbers, that the numbers or figures that we add up are not stand-ins for purely abstract items, items which alone constitute the true arithmetical reality.

6.3 MATHEMATICS AND NECESSITY

Is the fact that mathematics can be applied to the world a matter of mystery? Why certain physical constants should have the values they have may not be understood, and there are conditions that have to be satisfied before mathematics can be fruitfully used, but in general it is no more surprising that mathematics can be applied to the world than that language generally can be so employed. And, just as an application cannot always be counted upon for language, so too with some branches of mathematics—the theory of transfinite cardinals, for instance—but whether a given branch does or does not, explaining why is surely not an insuperable task. We should have no use for counting if things continually coalesced, and no use for measuring if bodies constantly changed their size, weight, and so forth, for no assignable reason; but they don't, so we do.

And what of necessity? Is that a feature of mathematical existence? On the one hand, the various number systems might never have been devised—no transfinite cardinals, no quaternions, no binary or hexadecimal numbers, and so forth. On the other hand, a proposition such as 'There might have been no number 8' is nonsense if it envisages a gap in the series of natural numbers, since a number at that point is provided for by the rules generating the series which is supposed otherwise given. The existence of a number is not further to the existence of coherent rules which define it, but these are rules which may evolve or be extended. The proposition about 8 will not pass muster, but 'There might have been no zero' is different in the way it involves not an arbitrary gap between numbers but a different starting point for their generation. Zero was, indeed, a relatively late arrival, and it is of interest that, for instance, the Babylonians' zero was not quite the same as our own, being used to signify an empty space in the accounting register, but not to express an endpoint of an arithmetic operation where nothing remains, as with subtraction (Barrow 2000: 29).

It has been argued by E. J. Lowe that, mathematical truths being true of necessity, there can be no possible world in which numbers do not exist; that would be a world in which, for instance, it was not true that 2 plus 2 equals 4 (1996: 118). However, on Lowe's account, the existence of the natural numbers requires the existence of concrete objects as well, so we may conclude that a world of concrete objects exists of necessity. But is it correct to say that, in the absence of the natural numbers, it would not be true that 2 plus 2 equals 4? If there had been no colour words, grass would still have been green, the sky still blue, though we might desist from saying that it would have been *true* that grass was green, given the closeness of this to 'It would have been true to *say* that grass was green'— the possibility being excluded. Numerical truths, whether contingent or necessary, are surely no different.

It is difficult to see how the mathematician's world, the world of numbers and the other exotica of which the mathematician treats, could be more fundamental than the world of the physicist, which delivers us *agents*, sources of being and becoming. We have no reason to revise this view, but we are also interested in the possibility that numbers might provide a model for understanding God, that some notion of necessity might apply to him as readily as it does to numbers. Consider 'There is a prime number between 10 and 20.' This qualifies as a necessarily true existential statement, but what is necessary is that at least one of the numbers between 10 and 20 should answer to a certain description, viz. that of being prime, and it could be that at least one number had to be that way without the given numbers existing of necessity. The statement would compare with 'Of the 400 people assembled in the hall, at least two must have the same birthday', where the existence of the relevant people is merely contingent. For necessity to apply to an individual number we should need something like 'The number π exists of necessity', where a number is directly specified, but if this is not to be given an analogous construal, it would appear that it falls to the objection that such a number might never have been introduced into mathematics.

If 'God necessarily exists' falls in line with 'There is necessarily a prime number between 10 and 20', it will have the force of 'Exactly one thing must be divine.' The kind of necessity here involved does not strike me as questionable. The problem lies, rather, with the truth of the proposition. I cited above an argument against the possibility of necessary existence that many would endorse and which maintains that 'existence cannot be held to be a quality which a perfect being would have to have, since it is not a quality at all. So it further follows that no existential assertion *can* be analytic' (Penelhum 1960: 184). The first sentence envisages assertions about individuals, rejecting '*A* exists' as an ascription of a quality to an individual, *A*, whereas the conclusion embraces *all* existential assertions, whether or not of this species. I see no way in which this extension can be justified, but I suspect that, paradoxically, those who reject all possibility of necessary existential propositions have not distanced themselves sufficiently from a construal of existential propositions which they would reject, such a form as 'There is a being which exists of necessity' being dismissed on the grounds just indicated, as if it compared with 'There is a being which must eventually decay' in predicating something of some being. However, if 'God necessarily exists' is not about an individual, God, but about how things must be, having the force of 'Exactly one being must be divine', it falls outside the scope of Penelhum's objection.

On the other hand, it may well be that what is sought is precisely a reading more in line with our second possibility. Just as it might be held that an abstract entity exists of necessity, thanks to its particular constitution, so God's unique nature may be thought to be the source of his necessity. Is this coherent? It was suggested above that 'has existed from all eternity' could be used in defining a possible essence, and it is not impossible that even the bare 'exists' should have this role, as when 'a real castle' is defined as 'a castle which exists'. But does not that, quite inappropriately, render 'Real castles exist' analytic? Yes, but only when read, quite innocuously, as 'Real castles are castles that exist', not when understood as 'There are real castles.' There is point to such a definition if we have a suitable contrast— real castles as against imaginary castles, say—and here we note that 'there is' is suitably enlisted with respect to either: 'There are castles that exist and castles that do not.' It is not that it is incoherent to have essence embrace existence in this way; it just does not serve as the basis for an existence proof. With respect to our current concern, recourse to such notions as those of eternity and indestructibility appears to offer greater promise in elucidating the relevant necessity, and here too number may be thought to provide a model.

Consider, then, the proposition that abstract entities are eternal and indestructible. A first reaction may be to dismiss this as so much Platonic nonsense; a more fruitful response is to ask what it means. Not, surely, what might be intended with a comparable assertion about material objects. Thus, the claim that numbers are eternal suggests that they some-how outlast the most long-lived of physical entities, and the claim that they are indestructible likewise suggests that they resist our most determined efforts to bring their existence to an end: no force, however powerful, is in the least able to make any impact upon them, but they simply go on existing into the most distant reaches of time, brushing off any threats to their continuation. But, of course, to say that numbers are eternal means only that distinctions of tense, as marked by, for instance, '. . . is prime but will cease to be so', have no application. Similarly with indestructibility. If a case can be made for speaking of numbers as indestructible—on the grounds, let us say, that definability suffices for existence—then it is not that the constitution of π or e enables either to withstand a great heat, a powerful acid, or a nuclear explosion; there is no such thing as bringing such forces to bear on a number. You cannot destroy a number, sure enough, but that means: it makes no sense to speak of destruction in its regard. Its definability remains untouched by physical forces.

If the claim that numbers are indestructible is to be interpreted in the way suggested, it may be felt that it has thereby been stripped of any real significance. The proposal was of interest only in so far as it was thought of as sustaining just those implications which we have disowned in clarifying how it may be understood. However, this interpretation is not altogether remote from Aquinas's grounds for speaking of angels and souls as necessary beings. A material being has parts, which makes for the possibility of disintegration, decomposition. A spiritual being, by contrast, is not liable to any such form of dissolution, but, once in existence, will continue in that state. It is not just a brute fact about spirits that they are, in a certain sense, indestructible, but this feature can be said to be grounded in their nature, though they did not have to exist in the first place, and even when they exist, their existence is something God could withdraw. Again, the kind of timelessness that applies with numbers mirrors the eternity commonly ascribed to God: not so much a matter of enduring through the ages as being outside time altogether; that is, being such that distinctions of tense play no part in descriptions of him.

If Aquinas wished to maintain that God's essence made for his indestructibility in a more than contingent sense, he could make out a case along these lines: God cannot be destroyed, in that he is not the kind of being which it makes sense to speak of destroying. Not a matter of some species of unimaginable toughness or hardness possessed by God, simply that a being without spatial location is (conceptually) out of the range of any of the destructive forces that occupants of the physical universe may have to face. Moreover, the lack of a material constitution means the lack of anything that might disintegrate or perish over time. What puts God out of reach of destructive forces is also, we may note, what precludes him from having a constructive role. Nor does lack of a material constitution distinguish God's necessity from the necessity which some of his creatures, notably angels, enjoy. Is it just that, as well as not having what is required for dissolution to be possible, he does not owe his existence to another? This does not tell us why he had to exist in the first place, so risks making his existence a mere brute fact, but if it makes no sense to speak of him as beginning to exist or coming into existence, then perhaps any contingency is ruled out.

But God has a rival in this respect, a rival in the form of matter, and a rival having a decided existential advantage: we know that it exists, which is more than we can say for God. Prima facie, it is easier to argue for the inescapability of something all-pervasive, as is matter, than for the inescapability of some particular individual, and when that individual has all the problematic characteristics of the deity, the case for matter, or for the physical more generally, would appear overwhelming. Indeed, one of the advantages of a term with the logic of 'matter' is that we can envisage the absence of this or that bit of matter without yielding on the thesis that the existence of matter is necessary, which makes for a seemingly lesser demand than does the claim that a particular individual exists of necessity, the claim generally had in mind when it is held that statements of existence never enjoy the necessity of logical truths.

It might well be that there had to be something, we have argued, even though there is no being of which one could say that it had to be. However, when we move to talk of stuff rather than individuals, we may lose this distinction. That is, while there is a distinction between 'There must be something' and 'There is something that must be', we do not have the same division with respect to 'There must be matter' and 'Matter must be.' True, the modal distinction may re-emerge with 'this matter', which may refer to a kind—plutonium, dark matter—or to a particular volume or particle. We could allow that there had to be matter, or matter of a certain kind, without allowing that any given quantity or item of matter had its existence of necessity. In conjunction with 'This is matter', 'Matter takes up space' licenses 'This takes up space', but 'Matter has to exist' together with 'This is matter' does not, as here construed, license 'This has to exist.' It is just: there has to be matter; something has to be material. It is only necessity as indestructibility that applies to a given volume of matter, as this persists throughout the transformations it undergoes.

7

Mind and Agency

The miscellany offered by abstractions has little to offer for our purposes, but if there is anything that can hope to dethrone matter from its position of pre-eminence, it has to be in the category of mind or spirit. We shall now consider both these notions, along with those of force and agency, which have an indispensable auxiliary role if either candidate is to be reckoned fundamental, but which are as difficult to conceive of outside space and time as is mind itself.

7.1 MAKING SENSE OF MIND

What sorts of relation may a mind bear to a body, a brain, or to matter generally? When there is felt to be a problem as to how, for instance, they may interact, there is a good chance that 'mind' is being taken to name some kind of immaterial *stuff*, mirroring the way 'matter', or a more specific term such as 'carbon' or 'salt', designates material stuff or substance. The surface grammar of the key terms is close enough for a problem to arise as to the nature of the relation between what each designates, but sufficiently different for that problem to be unsolvable.

Consider Descartes' claim that mind and body are distinct, since body is divisible whereas the mind is not. A physicalist may feel obliged to take issue with this alleged difference. However, although he could cite a way in which mind, too, is divisible, as when a person suffers from a split personality, it is not clear that this is divisibility in the same sense as applies to bodies, so not clear that his claim for mind–body identity could profit from the verbal agreement. 'Mind' relates to a whole family of terms—'thought', 'intellect', 'understanding', 'mood', 'intention', 'opinion'—which, although they are ascribed to corporeal beings, are grossly misconstrued if taken to name anything physical. But does the physicalist need to insist that what can be said of mind can be said of body? It is as if he feared that a concession on this point would have him admitting the existence of two distinct *substances*, mind and body, as indeed Descartes thought the distinction in point of divisibility to demonstrate.

The physicalist insists that a human being consists of nothing more than flesh, blood, bone, and other organic substances. Nothing more? What about the mind or soul? The 'nothing more' claim exploits an interpretation of 'what x consists of' based on its application to physical objects generally, as when it is said that a clock consists of nothing more than cog wheels, a spring, a pendulum, and so forth. The extension to human beings can be allowed, but its allowability does not show that there is no call to speak of mind, only that this is not to be numbered among the constituents of a person. There are ways of being attributable to x other than being an element of which x is composed—think of a sense of humour, of pride, of a liking for chocolate—but the 'nothing more' observation serves to delineate the area where anything that qualifies as a constituent is to be found. 'What x is' is not exhausted by finding out what goes to make up x, but what goes to make up x as one of its constituents is to be found only in this way. It is not that mind—or the soul—is such an element, but an ethereal one, an immaterial component.

In *The Blue Book*, Wittgenstein wrote:

We feel then that in the cases in which "I" is used as subject, we don't use it because we recognize a particular person by his bodily characteristics; and this creates the illusion that we use this word to refer to something bodiless, which, however, has its seat in our body. In fact *this* seems to be the real ego, the one of which it was said, "Cogito, ergo sum".—"Is there then no mind, but only a body?" Answer: The word "mind" has meaning, i.e., it has a use in our language; but saying this doesn't yet say what kind of use we make of it.

(1958: 69–70)

What kind of a use does 'mind' enjoy? A survey of the diverse contexts in which it occurs soon reveals that there is more than one use to take into account. Consider a sample of the host of idioms in which the word figures, as 'bear in mind', 'have one's mind on what one is doing', 'be of sound mind', 'speak one's mind', 'be in two minds', and 'make up one's mind'. The occurrence of 'mind' is explicable as we go from context to context, but not in such a way that we see it as making a uniform contribution throughout—as though, when we say someone is of sound mind, has changed his mind, and has his mind on what he is doing, the same item is being said to be sound, to have changed, and to be on what the person is doing. It is accordingly questionable whether we may take the term out of context and raise the question of the relation between mind and brain, say, in quite general terms. Certainly, there would appear to be no prospect of finding in these idioms a reference to any kind of 'stuff', whether material or ethereal.

True, fragmented though the usage may be, a central group of recurring patterns can be identified. Thus, a connection with intention or inclination can often be discerned: 'we were of a mind to . . .', 'I've a good mind to . . .', 'I've half a mind to . . .', 'be in two minds', 'make up one's mind', 'set one's mind on . . .'. This usage may overlap with one in which *opinion* is involved, as with 'be of the same mind', 'change one's mind', 'have a mind of one's own', 'to my mind', and 'speak one's mind'. So, making up one's mind or changing one's mind may relate to a proposed action, whence a connection with intention, or concern merely a view or opinion. Either way there is a difference from the use when intellectual prowess is at issue, as with 'a sharp (original, prosaic, brilliant, unsound) mind', or when it is a matter of general attitudes and ways of thinking—'the mediaeval mind'—and these in turn are distinguishable from the use of the term to indicate awareness of, attention to, or preoccupation with something, as with 'on one's mind', 'keep the difference in mind', 'bear in mind', 'out of sight, out of mind', 'have one's mind on one's work', or 'cast one's mind back'. There are these patterns, but, once more, the prospects of saying anything useful about 'mind' when it occurs in isolation, wrested out of the particular contexts which determine its specific use, would appear remote.

If I give you a piece of my mind then I let you know what I really think or feel. There would not appear to be any problem further to that of elucidating these latter notions, no residue which 'mind' captures and which a satisfactory elaboration will leave untouched. Likewise with having one's mind on what one is doing, where the notion of attending to something is to be probed; or, again, if I know my own mind then I am definite in my views, and if I am out of my mind my views, my reasonings, do not add up to anything rational or coherent. Note that identifying something as a mind plays no part in our attribution of qualities of mind or of psychological states, as when we say that someone has a sharp mind or a dreamy personality. Incisiveness of responses on matters of reasoning and understanding provide a basis for judgements on the former, and an inattentiveness to practical affairs a basis for the latter. Likewise with being narrow-minded, single-minded, high-minded, and so forth.

If there remain questions which centre ineliminably around mind, they will, I suspect, be questions in which 'mind' is taken to feature as the name of a special, and specially mysterious, setting or location which is host to our thoughts and mental life generally. This is the conception that may be held to lie behind such locutions as 'A thought crossed my mind' and 'It was at the forefront of her mind', as also with idioms where 'head' may be used: 'He did the calculation in his head', 'The tune kept running through her head.' And, of course, it is *true* that much can be said to happen in the mind, or in one's head. It is the significance of this way of speaking that is at issue. Here is one possibility.

With many activities it makes sense to ask where they took place or were engaged in, the likely answer specifying some public location. When the activity qualifies as mental, as with calculating, planning or daydreaming, the question of the person's whereabouts when engaged in the activity will be answerable in this way—'He thought up the scheme in the bath'—but the activity itself may not be similarly locatable. We may perform a calculation on a computer, on a blackboard, or on paper, but we may also perform it in our head. In speaking of the calculation as in our head or in our mind, we appear to be offering an alternative to a public location, but is it then appropriate to speak of a *location*? Is the way in which a thought is in one's mind analogous to the way in which objects are disposed in a space or place? There is no question of comparability with respect to the relations which may hold with the latter, when objects may be to the left or the right, above, below or behind others, but any spatial terminology we may call upon has a purely metaphorical significance. A thought is at the back of my mind if I am not giving my full attention to it; it is at the forefront of my mind if I am. Contrast the use of 'in my head' where the appropriateness of the description is determined by examining the head—'I have a tumour in my head'—with the use which is quite indifferent to what opening up the head might reveal—'I worked the answer out in my head.'

The orderings possible for publicly located things and happenings have no application to mental calculations, reflections, musings, and so forth, but the 'in' of 'in the mind' is in this respect misleading. So what, exactly, is the import of this phrase, or of 'in the head'? When something is done, or takes place, we are often interested in knowing *where*, and the phrases 'in my mind' and 'in my head' may furnish an answer when no public location can be invoked. They furnish an answer in that, thanks to the spatial preposition, they are *formally* of the right kind. In the absence of a public location we do not reject the question, saying—as we might—'My thoughts are not anywhere', yet the superficially locational answer is in reality no more positive than such a rejection; it serves to exclude anything that might literally qualify as a location, but to do so in a way that keeps it in line with the more positive forms. But does not 'in the mind' signal a transition from public space to, precisely, a private one? We have just noted how little of what characterizes a space or place is retained by 'in the mind'. The transition from public to private space is a transition from the literal to the metaphorical, from what qualifies as a space, properly speaking, to what can as well be characterized in the negative terms suggested.

As well as misconstruing 'mind' as the name of a substance, some would have it single out the subject proper to psychological acts and states: it is the mind that reflects, enquires, calculates, decides, and so forth. This is often no more than a literary affectation aimed at investing thought and the rest with greater depth—'The human mind restlessly seeks an understanding of this universe'—but it can do more damage if it is thought that 'mind' signifies the true subject of the psychological in a way that would allow it to usurp the place of the person. If what I say to you is at odds with what I actually think, you have not heard something from an observable being that an unobservable being denies; you have just not been made party to the true thoughts of the observable being. What reflects and understands is the same as what eats and sleeps—the person, not a disembodied being—but shifting the predicates from person to mind may lead us to lose sight of this common subject, deluding us into thinking we have legitimized the introduction of an entity that retains the distinctively human faculties yet has no essential need of a body. It is surely difficult to take seriously the suggestion that when you speak of knowing your own mind, of having an open mind or being of one mind with another, you are alluding to something that might enjoy an independent existence, to the point even of wandering off on its own after your death.

This misconceived move may be aided and abetted by an unwarranted use of the term 'self' analogous to the context-free misuses of 'mind'—see Bennett and Hacker (2003) for an exploration in depth of uses and misuses of both. We have no difficulty in making sense of 'self' as it occurs in 'myself', 'self-critical', 'self-seeking', and so forth, where the reference is to the person in question, not to an immaterial 'ego' which the person possesses. If I give you a self-addressed envelope, it will be an envelope addressed to *me*, the flesh and blood being who gave it to you. If you go on a self-catering holiday, you will be cooking for yourself, and that just means for *you*, not for something that might become separated from you in a way that would make the verbal separation given with 'your self' appropriate. In speaking of 'a self-satisfied person', nothing beyond the person is alluded to any more than 'a self-locking door' and 'a self-cleaning oven' introduce something in addition to door and oven.

When it is thought that a Supreme Being, by dint of his possession of a mind—or of *being* pure mind—is able to create and govern the material world, the mental attributes generally called upon are those of thought and will. Opposition to this picture is likely to involve ascribing primacy to unthinking matter, and it is useful, in support of this opposition, to consider how psychological capacities might evolve in an initially non-sentient world. We cannot even begin to sketch a process in which matter comes from mind, but we have some idea what stages might be involved in the development of psychological attributes in a material universe. As part of such an account we might give attention to the intermediate case of animals other than man. Watching an animal engaged in some elaborate purposive activity, as with a bird building its nest, we may feel impelled to suppose that the creature is capable of thought: a work of such complexity and productive of such order could not be, in our hands, a purely mindless pursuit. There is perhaps a sense in which, just on the strength of the observed behaviour, an ascription of thought to the bird may be warranted—not as a hypothesis to explain the behaviour, simply as part of a redescription of what is observed. But it does not appear that we could meaningfully advance beyond this. When making something, a human being may form conjectures, estimate probabilities, and draw conclusions, and, of course, he may give vocal expression to his thought. However, the former no less than the latter would appear to presuppose a mastery of concepts which can come only with possession of a language, and language that is far removed from anything that bird-song can furnish. But if Nature can present us with a wealth of constructive, purposive behaviour that none the less qualifies as 'mindless', and if the further, more sophisticated and intellectually demanding activities which we engage in can be accounted for once language is in place, it does not appear over-optimistic to suppose that a purely naturalistic explanation of the key faculty of thought is within our reach. And, once more, it is not as if starting with a divine mind could be part of a better explanation; such a starting point is not part of any explanation at all.

7.2 MIND AND ACTION

Divine agency is commonly modelled on human agency, but on human agency conceived of in Cartesian fashion; not a matter of physical acts as of lifting or cutting, but of anterior mental acts in which behaviour supposedly originates. Thus:

> The core concept of human action is not *movement of one's own body*, but rather *bringing about a change in the world—directly or indirectly—by an act of will, decision, or intention*. That concept can be intelligibly applied to a purely spiritual deity. It is just that we will have to think of God as bringing about changes in the "external" world directly by an act of will—not indirectly through moving His body, as in our case.

> (Alston 1985: 225)

Human action is not a matter of will, decision, or intention acting on body acting on world, so it is not as if, with God as agent, we simply omit the bodily intermediary and have him act on the world directly. Can decisions and intentions *ever* be causes of actions? That deciding to move, say, can have one's moving as an effect may be thought so evident, we have no alternative but to tailor our theory of causation to accommodate this truth (cf. Mellor 1995: 2). Actions do not just follow on decisions, they follow on as their upshot, and what can this mean if not that they are brought about by the decisions? However, it is far from clear that a decision has what it takes to cause anything. Consider the moment of decision. Sometimes this is the moment an act is initiated, as when one decides to speak, not at some future time, but then and there. Here deciding to speak differs from *merely* speaking in that it is speaking subsequent to some uncertainty or hesitation, speaking which follows on weighing up the pros and cons of doing so. In this case the deciding is assimilated into the act in a way that makes it unsuited to being the act's cause. However, this is not the kind of case that the causalist has in mind, but his concern is with occasions when there is a lapse of time between the deciding and the acting, as when you decide you will do your utmost to become famous or to follow a career as a musician.

Consider now the moment of decision as it figures in cases of this latter variety. From the time when a decision is reached we can look back to a period when we were in two minds about a course of action, and forward to a state of determination or resolution. The moment of decision is both the end point of the period of indecision and the initial point of a period of firmness of purpose, a point which, unlike these extended periods, is quite without duration. If deciding is merely making a transition to a certain frame of mind, then we have with the decision no more the cause of the action than the beginning of a movement is the cause of that movement, or the onset of old age is the cause of old age. True, the formation of an intention, the taking of a decision to do something, brings with it a systematic change in our attitudes to possibilities of action, but this is not a matter of *causing* such change; the change in attitude is just what the having of the intention consists in. We become liable to favour courses of action which may be thought to increase our chances of success, which make it easier to carry out the intention when the time comes. Similarly, our reaction to possibilities which might frustrate the intention is different from what it would have been had we not taken the decision. With the decision our pattern of responses aligns itself with the intention, this redirection in many cases being effected without our taking further decisions: we simply act in a way appropriate to the demands of the situation and in the light of the intention. To repeat, in saying this I am seeking to explain what it is to have an intention, not what intentions commonly cause. There is doubtless some indeterminacy in the matter of what intending demands, but the shift in our attitude to possibilities of action is a mark of having an intention, not something contingently related thereto, something which is seen to be bound up with the intention only by being found to be somehow generated by it. Nor, correspondingly, is the relation between deciding and the subsequent readiness to act a causal relation, but deciding just *is* becoming ready to act. With our decision we move from irresolution to resolution. The decision marks the point of transition, the beginning of the latter state rather than its cause.

This account of deciding throws some light on the relation between psychological acts and states and associated behaviour. When the deciding occurs *with* the acting, action following on deliberation gives a criterion for there having been a decision, while when an intention to act rather than immediate action is at issue, thought, in the form of a decision, impinges upon behaviour through its relation to a behavioural disposition, to a state of readiness to do certain things, the possibility that a state of mind can be at the same time of this character being what provides a bridge between the mental and the behavioural. (Here, as on the topic of animal thought, I repeat points elaborated in Rundle 1997.)

Acts of will, or volitions, have, for good reasons, fallen out of favour with philosophers, nor are they familiar in our ordinary explanations of agency, where the key role goes to bodily acts. We turn the door knob with our hand, but the turning may well be the first thing we do of relevance, not an act resulting from something else we have done, some unwitnessable performance from which the visible action flows. The unreality of any such psychological antecedent is plain enough in the numerous cases where, while our action may be voluntary, it proceeds without any inner spur, as will or volition might be thought to contribute. Think of, for instance, writing or speaking. You can be saying what you wish to say without there having been an antecedent desire which somehow instigated your speech; it is more a matter of the character of the speech itself that makes it voluntary, the expression of a desire—it is of a kind which one can control, can choose to perform, desist from, or terminate.

Hume characterized one form of free will, liberty of spontaneity, as '*a power of acting or not acting, according to the determinations of the will*' (1902: 95). If, as he and many other philosophers have supposed, the relation between will or desire and action is taken to be causal, we can consider ourselves fortunate in finding that when, say, we want to open a door, at the very least an attempt to open the door ensues, since it is in no way foreign to the notion of cause that such a desire should have issued in a quite different effect, as, say, that of taking off our shoes. But we are not at the mercy of such causal vagaries if the relation is the more intimate one whereby, if the action is free, our desires are made manifest in, rather than being causes of, what we do.

When the will is invoked, it is sometimes thought of on the model of issuing a command, as with Locke: 'a thought or preference of the mind ordering, or as it were commanding, the doing or not doing such or such a particular action' (1975: 236). Analyses along these lines prolong rather than disperse the air of unreality, and it is noteworthy that nowadays those who wish none the less to identify a psychological antecedent of action customarily turn to the notion of *trying* to furnish the necessary impetus. Arguments which would counter this move often contend that trying is too narrow a concept for this purpose. There is no trying when no effort is required, no obstacle to overcome. It would be most unusual if you had to *try* to speak before you could come up with the greeting, 'Good morning'. Likewise with a multitude of other voluntary or intentional acts. However, it is worth noting that, as far as what the agent does is concerned, this may be the same whether or not it is in place to speak of trying. I post a letter to you. If you receive it, I can say that I got in touch, but if you do not, I can say only that I tried to get in touch. In either case my action is the same, success or failure being what dictates the appropriateness or otherwise of 'try'. Of course, if some effort is involved, then we shall be able to speak of trying in either case, but if trying is to be extended to actions quite generally, including those performed without effort, or any mustering of resolve, then it would appear that all we have by way of a common feature is the initial stages of the *action*, successful or otherwise, and the initial stages of the action are quite clearly not its cause. Any ubiquitous psychological antecedent, let alone one that might be assigned a causal role, remains as far out of the picture as ever.

Those who believe in the reality of psychokinesis consider it possible to effect changes in the world merely through an act of the will—Locke's account of voluntary action, we may note, amounts to regarding it as an exercise of psychokinesis directed at one's own limbs. It is not absurd to suppose that issuing a spoken command should have an effect on things in one's environment, nor even that formulating the command to oneself should likewise have external repercussions. Neural activity associated with such an act could conceivably harness larger forces which impacted upon things beyond the brain. Whether the command is delivered out loud or said to oneself, what is difficult to account for is the specificity of the effect. If a soldier is given the command 'Attention!' or 'Stand at ease!', his understanding of the words puts him in a position to comply. Even when the words are uttered *in foro interno*, we can imagine that some sort of signal should reach an inanimate object, but a seemingly intractable difficulty remains on the side of the object, which is not possessed of the understanding which would result in its moving to the left when told to move to the left, or rotating when told to rotate. Psychokinesis is not a promising model for making sense of God's action on a mindless cosmos, and indeed the difficulties are much the same as those encountered with God's supposed role as a lawgiver. It is maintained that it needs God to formulate the relevant laws for Nature to behave as it does, but it is only light rays endowed with powers of comprehension, not to say a degree of goodwill, that might respond appropriately to the proclamation that the angle of incidence is to be equal to the angle of reflection.

While many would dispute the claim that deciding, intending, wanting, and trying cannot be invoked to show how mind might act upon matter, even allowing such interaction falls short of conceding that the conception of a bodiless agent is coherent, a conception that has been the target of much criticism—see, for instance, Gaskin (2000). Moreover, granted that the preceding observations are unlikely to win over anyone who regards mind as more fundamental than matter, it is worth emphasizing how strong the claim for mind must be if our position is to come under threat, namely, that it would be possible to have *just* a mind or minds, no physical universe whatsoever, and the claim that we cannot think away all matter, whatever else there may be, is, when set against this supposed possibility, exceedingly modest. It is surely reasonable to argue against the sufficiency of the mental both for *being* and *acting* by insisting on the necessity of the physical. As already indicated, when someone is said to have changed their mind or to have their mind on other things, there is no question of discerning a reference to something capable of enjoying an existence independent of the person; to claim that what is identified has what it takes to be an agent simply adds to the absurdity.

True, despite, or perhaps because of its ubiquity and inescapability, matter has often been in bad odour in philosophy. In Platonic terms, the material world is a world of appearances only; it is the world behind these, the world of immaterial Forms, immutable and eternal, that constitutes the true reality, the truly knowable. In the *Phaedo* (47–8) Plato suggests that a preoccupation with the bodily leads us to suppose that the objects of the invisible world are less real and less valuable than the objects of the visible world, whereas the truth is the exact opposite: the empirical world which is apprehended through the senses is deserving only of contempt. The philosopher's soul utterly despises his body (46): 'so long as we have the body accompanying our reason in its inquiries, so long as our souls are befouled by this evil admixture, we shall assuredly never fully possess that which we desire, to wit truth' (47).

Objects of the invisible world do not today enjoy the same vogue as with Plato, but matter may still be considered discredited by the association of materialism with some bankrupt moral code. This association depends on reading into 'materialism' connotations which are no part of the use which it enjoys in the present context. It is surely reasonable to hold that the supposition that reality without matter is inconceivable is in no way inconsistent with a morality which plays down the importance of material possessions and lays emphasis on the kinds of value—or at least some of them—commonly styled 'spiritual'.

7.3 SPIRITS AND FORCES

Talk of spiritual values need take us no further away from the material world than talk of intellectual or moral values, but what of talk of *spirits*? For our ancestors, there was a dimension of spirituality which did not just encompass morality, but which extended to beings which, though they might be of this world, were not subject to the constraints which a material existence imposes. Even if we are now sceptical of such a conception, our central thesis is at risk if an independent existence for such immaterial beings is as much as a logical possibility. Given the key role that *agency* is to provide, any help that *spirit* can offer will depend on the possibility of its combining with *force*, so it is the combination of the two that we shall consider.

An attempt to give substance to the notion of a being outside space and time—a spirit—has been made by I. M. Crombie, starting from the consideration that we cannot adequately describe human beings or human experience if we confine ourselves to the range of concepts adequate to describing a chair, a cabbage, or even an electronic computer. The additional concepts needed, as those of *loving, feeling* and *seeing*, have, compared with such concepts as those of *walking* or *digesting*, a relative independence of space. The need for the non-physical concepts does not mean that we are spirits, but it does enable us to conceive of a being independent of space (1957: 57–8). Crombie is undoubtedly right to insist on the need to go beyond the purely physical, but the concepts requisite for making sense of a spiritual force or agency are to be drawn, I believe, as much from the physical as from the non-physical side. Crombie thinks that the spiritual being of which we may form a conception in this way is a being whose activity is not to be thought of in terms of colliding with this, or exercising a gravitational pull on that, but I should have thought that these, and others of a like character, are just the concepts needed to flesh out the crucial notion of agency. I shall now try to show that focusing on the notion of a force requires us to come down on the side of the physical rather than the non-physical.

Imagine that objects are found to move around as if impelled by some unseen force. If this can happen to physical objects, it can happen to human beings, so let us suppose that you find yourself subjected to such a force. It will then be possible for you at least to try to resist, which means that your hand, say, will come up against something as you seek to counter the force. Your efforts may result in your becoming aware of the contours of an invisible object, as you move your hand laterally while at the same time trying to advance it. On the other hand, it may be not as when you make contact with the surface of a solid body, but more as when you struggle against the wind. Certainly, some such experience will be necessary if we are to speak of an external force. If you have no experience of encountering anything in either way, then any impediments to your intended movement, along with the movements which occur in their stead, will have to come from within you. Our interest is in the external force, and, if it should be as described, it will be nonsensical to speak of a mind, spirit, will, or soul as what is impinging upon you; it is clearly something with attributes of the physical, though something invisible, that you have come up against.

The notion of force is worth considering in greater generality. It was mentioned above that 'power' may be used with reference to a source of change, as with electricity, as well as having a more general use in which it is like 'capacity', as in 'has the power to corrode'. 'Force' is similar. It may be applied directly to an agent—as when a person is described as 'a force for good', 'a force to be reckoned with', or 'a driving force'—but its more customary application is with reference to acts rather than to agents. Indeed, talk of a force exerted just is, I should say, talk of what some agent *does*, but by way of redescription rather than explanation. That a force is operating follows from various causal truths relating to acts of pushing, pulling, and so forth.

To elaborate, the role of 'force' in designating an agent is as legitimate as is the conception of the agent designated. So, in speaking of natural forces we may be speaking of winds, lightning, volcanic eruptions, and the like. It is when 'force' purports to identify an *additional* agent, a means whereby a recognizable agent is instrumental in producing its effect, that we have a suspect use, a misconstrual which is tempting when we focus on the force in abstraction from the being which exercises it. Thus, a force is said to act upon a body, to deform a body to which it is applied, to cause a body to move; the effect of a force on a body is determined by its magnitude, direction, and point of application. Such ways of speaking may be harmless, but they suggest a hypostatization of forces, an elevation to the status of independent agents. When you push a wheelbarrow, it is your act of pushing that causes the barrow to move. You can be said to be exerting a force, but that is a way of redescribing what you do; it is not to introduce a further link in the causal chain, as though you act to produce a force which in turn acts upon the barrow. It is this confused use that is at issue when forces are thought of in animistic terms, such forces ranking along-side various unseen spiritual agents thought responsible for happenings in Nature. Indeed, not merely is a force thought to be an agent, it may be considered an agent *par excellence*, the very antithesis of inert, inactive matter. However, matter surely does not deserve to be demoted in this way if, as argued, talk of a force resolves into talk of something done by an agent, and in particular a physical agent.

Consider the claim—to be found in Kepler—that, since force has only an immaterial existence, its presence can be recognized only through its effects (see Jammer 1957: 89). This may involve a misrepresentation of the grammar of 'force' to which we have just alluded: a force not being a material agent, it has to be an immaterial agent, whereas it is not to be categorized as an agent at all. Whether or not there is this implication, it would appear that, in saying that a force—or power—can be recognized only in this indirect fashion, we are likening a force to a physical object, which might come to our attention in either way. Such a comparison is misguided. We can know of the presence of an object concealed under the carpet through the bumps which it makes, and we can also lift up the carpet to see what is responsible for the observed effects. With a force there is nothing corresponding to lifting up the carpet for the sake of a more direct verification, but we can only avail ourselves of further of its manifestations—as when making contact with a live wire persuades us that an electro-motive force is doing what we have witnessed. These, however, are not indirect indications of something of which we might be more directly apprised. There is no shortfall in our grounds for speaking of a force, but if there can be said to be a 'further existence' for which the effects of the force provide evidence, this will be the *agent* exert-ing the force. When an agent is itself described as a force, there will be the possibility of an identification of that force independently of identifying an effect attributable to it; when 'force' has a grammar that contrasts with that of physical object terms, there is no such independence.

Similar considerations can be levelled against the suggestion that forces be granted the status of theoretical entities. In the first place, there is no question of the forces in question being merely theoretical, but their reality is brought home to us in unmistakable ways. Secondly, and as already indicated, whether theoretical or actual, a force is not best placed in the category of *entities*; that would have it consorting with agents, stuffs, particles, and other objects, when it is to be aligned with such terms as 'power' and 'capacity'. If a force is described as 'mysterious', this compares with a description of an *ability* in these terms, not with that of a particle, say. An ability to bend spoons by gently rubbing them is mysterious in that we do not know how the person is able to perform the feat; likewise, a magnetic force may be mysterious in that we do not know how magnets attract and repel. As with power, Hume's all-embracing scepticism concerning our knowledge of force and energy was misplaced: 'We are ignorant, it is true, of the manner in which bodies operate on each other: Their force or energy is entirely incomprehensible' (1902: 72).

It is not that, force being less concrete than matter, it is freed from the constraints that would keep it in the physical world. Like *power* and *capacity, force* can be said to have a grammar which qualifies it as more abstract, but its application is always contingent upon the availability of an agent, and so long as we can make sense only of material agents, there is nothing here that would allow us to transcend the physical world. There is no reason to suppose that we have in the idea of a spiritual force anything which might compete with recognizable agents when explanations of existence or change are to be devised.

'Force' may be set alongside 'energy' as a term enjoying the same kind of logic, but there is also a strong tendency to reify energy, to endow the term with a grammar appropriate to the name of a substance: energy is likened to a substance that flows through empty space, matter ceasing to be the indispensable vehicle for its transport. Thus Poincaré's characterization of electromagnetic energy as 'a fluid endowed with inertia' (1900: 232), and the more colourful account offered by the physicist Oliver Lodge:

On the new plan we may label a bit of energy and trace its motion and change of form, just as we may ticket a piece of matter so as to identify it in other places under other conditions; and the route of the energy may be discussed with the same certainty that its existence was continuous as would be felt in discussing the route of some lost luggage which has turned up at a distant station in however battered and transformed a condition.

(1885: 482)

The issues raised here involve important questions of identity: just what is it that constitutes energy, or a force? We naturally look to the physicist's equations, as $e = mc^2$ or $F = ma$, to find enlightenment, but such equations must be handled with care. In mathematical and physical contexts, '$=$' symbolizes equality, but it is also read, by philosophers, as 'is identical with', a reading which can generate confusion. Equality is a species of equivalence relation which falls short of identity. A figure has two equal sides: the sides match or agree in a certain respect, in this case length. Similarly, things may be equal in weight, velocity or other features which receive a numerical measure—so, not so readily, colour or taste, say. Talk of equality is in place when we have to do, not with alternative designations of a single item—as with an identity—but of two things or quantities which are assigned a common numerical measure. Consider the formula for the volume of a sphere, $V = \frac{4}{3}\pi r^3$. This tells you what the volume is, in the sense that it enables you to calculate the volume, to assign it a measure; it does not explain what we *understand* by 'volume'. Again, pressure is measured by the force divided by the area of the surface on which it acts, but it would not be appropriate to offer $A = F/p$ as an explanation of *area*. It is the equality of quantities specified in the two ways that is at issue. Similarly with Einstein's equation relating mass and energy, $e = mc^2$. We neither duplicate nor contradict what this affirms when we add that by 'energy' is meant 'capacity for work'. Once more, the role of the equation is to show how numerical values associated with energy levels are determined. It is only if we had an identity that we could say that energy just *is* mass times the square of the speed of light in a sense which would explain what is meant by 'energy'. Contrast Einstein, 'The mass of a body is a measure of its energy content' (1905: 641), where, at least on this occasion, the character of the relevant *equation* is respected, with Russell, who embraces a simple identification: 'Mass is only a form of energy, and there is no reason why matter should not be dissolved into other forms of energy. It is energy, not matter, that is fundamental in physics' (1948: 291). The stronger identity is not proven by showing that all mass is transformable into energy, or that there is in the theory of relativity only one conservation law of mass *or* energy ('massergy'), though Max Jammer infers from this that 'mass and energy are identical, they are synonyms for the same physical substratum' (1961: 188). Of course, the relevant functional dependencies which allow us to switch to and fro between various numerical equivalences make such a construal enormously tempting. (For a more informed discussion of the interpretation of $e = mc^2$, see Lange 2002: 224–40.)

The distinction between mere equations and identities is of importance in connection with the question of the incommensurability of scientific theories. It is thought that scientific revolutions are accompanied by radical shifts in the meanings of key terms, so that it is not that the pre-revolutionary and the revolutionary theorists are advancing different views about the same things, but the apparent constancies provided by the latter are no more than verbal. Thus, the same terms, as 'mass' and 'force', may be employed both in Newtonian and in relativistic physics, but since they are not interpreted in the same way in the two theories, the followers of Einstein are not talking about the same things as their Newtonian predecessors when each speaks of *mass* or *force*.

It is, of course, true that there may be such a shift, but that there is does not follow from the consideration that the equations used to calculate the relevant quantities in the two theories result in the assignment of different values. There can be sufficient independence of the definitions and associated equations for there to be agreement in understanding but a difference in the respective calculations. Thus, it may be that the explanation which we offer of 'force' proceeds in exactly the same way in either case, a similar range of examples being invoked in illustration of the notion, and the same near-synonyms being enlisted in either case. Such a strategy may well serve to convey the meaning of the term in a way that is sufficiently general as to be indifferent to the divergences which emerge at the level of specific measurements. Not only does acceptance of $F = ma$ as an equality neither preclude nor render otiose an independent definition of 'force', but such an equality can hold even when the terms on either side relate to different categories, so when there can be no question of an explanation of the meaning of the one in terms of the other(s). A term signifying a capacity, as 'energy', has a different grammar from that of 'mass', and 'the product of mass and acceleration' cannot do duty for 'force' in such contexts as 'exert a force', 'the direction of the force', and so forth. If the equation $F = ma$ is taken to state that the meaning of 'force' is 'mass times acceleration', then we should have a short way with any attempt to apply the notion of force beyond the physical, since *mass* keeps us well and truly within that domain. That threat is diminished if the equation is taken merely as a recipe for quantifying forces, but the reliance on physical phenomena when *explaining* force continues to present an obstacle to any such extension.

Back to our main concern. Such notions as those of force and energy do not appear to allow of a non-physical application, but do we have to rely on pre-scientific interpretations of such key concepts to find an alternative to purely material existence? Is it not the case that the revolutionary ideas that have come to dominate physics have spelt the death of matter? Relativity theory has led to the abandonment of Newtonian assumptions about space and time, and the Newtonian image of matter as inert and passive, subject to the iron rule of determinism, has given way to a more dynamical, creative, chaotic conception, a mysterious domain of waves and particles in which chance rather than a rigid causation holds sway. In quantum field theory solid matter has been supplanted by the energy of the field, and in superstring theory the reality is sub-microscopic loops of invisible string. Think, too, of black holes, gravitational waves, and anti-matter. All a far cry from the matter of common sense.

It is true that a radically different conceptual scheme may recommend itself in describing and explaining the physical world. We customarily think of bodies as having the boundaries which sight and touch ascribe to them. Since, on this view, bodies may be separated by empty space, we have a problem understanding how one such body might have an influence on another. Suppose, however, that we think of bodies as extending as far as their influence is felt. Instead of action at a distance, we shall then have overlapping areas of influence, a conception which preserves locality. The seemingly empty space will be pervaded by the electromagnetic field, physical objects being particular concentrations of energy within that field.

However, fruitful though this conception may be, it would be wrong to take the possibility of such a scheme as showing the unreality of physical objects, with the field the only reality. It is not as if we have to do with a discredited empirical hypothesis—such familiar items as chairs and tables being one and all to be reckoned as illusory—but our expectations as to what we shall encounter describable in the old terminology will not have altered one iota. Moreover, it has to be shown that the proposed alternative is coherent, and in particular that we are not required to speak of the energy of the field in just those physical object terms which, in adopting the new scheme, we seek to abjure. Thus, we have seen that talk of energy is not, as it were, self-sufficient, but that, so long as we conceive of it as a *capacity*, it is in need of something of which it is a capacity. If, now, talk of energy as moving, flowing, being transferred or transformed, requires that we treat energy as some form of reidentifiable stuff, now here, now there, divided into parcels enjoying their own individuality, then we have inappropriately imposed the old scheme on the new. This is simply an illustration of one of our recurring themes: the inescapability of a physical universe does not mean that every noun has the grammar of a name for a kind of physical object. Finally, and more generally, however remarkable and unexpected new ways of looking at the world may be, nothing beyond physical reality has been shown to exist—no rehabilitation of spiritual forces, paranormal agents, magical properties, or the like.

So broad is the notion of being or existence, the only limit that can be imposed on what can be is to be found in the demand for consistency or coherence that any existential claim must satisfy. The notion is itself totally indifferent to *kinds* of thing, so that it would be wrong to favour one kind rather than another, wrong to read some particular qualification, whether in the genus of *material* or of *immaterial*, into that notion. No form of existence seems privileged, all seem thinkable away. In particular, there appears at first blush to be no compelling reason why a material universe should have existed. However, this point notwithstanding, there are forms or modes of existence that are derivative or dependent. For instance, there cannot be pain without consciousness, nor consciousness without a conscious subject. The thesis that nothing can exist in the absence of a material universe does not imply the nonsensical view that everything is material, but we can hold that if anything exists, matter exists, on the grounds that it is only in matter that the necessary independent existence is to be found. And that is our thesis.

8
Time and Explanation

Our conclusion that the universe cannot be said to have come into existence left it open whether it has existed for an infinite or only a finite time, and the same question arises with respect to its future: no event is describable as the universe's ceasing to exist, but are finite and infinite futures both possibilities? Causal series within the universe have been central to cosmological arguments for the existence of God, and while beginnings of such series need not be as problematic as a beginning of the universe, here too the question arises as to whether a series had a first member or can be followed back interminably, with in either case a question as to how the series can be satisfactorily explained. It is of interest to see if we can make any headway on these issues. More generally, they are issues which lead us to ask whether there can be any ultimate explanations, whether the regress of explanations can ever be brought to a satisfactory end.

8.1 TIME AND INFINITY

The bewilderment which the mere fact of existence engenders and which prompts the question 'Why is there something rather than nothing?' is matched by the bewilderment felt when we imagine objects coming into existence from nowhere when there is an already existing setting to receive them; so, molecules coming into existence in the way envisaged by a theory of continuous creation may well strike us as incomprehensible— though that is not to say that it is logically impossible; or, indeed, that an act of creation out of nothing is any the less opaque. But we are not confronted with any such happenings with respect to the universe itself, our talk of a beginning of existence having given way to talk of the universe as being temporally bounded. Uncaused beginnings are mysterious, but not a mystery we have to face in this instance; there is no *event*—the beginning of the universe—to be explained, events being possible only *in* time. Instead, we are left, not with a cosmic happening in search of a cause, but with an enquiry after conditions which would warrant a certain description, viz. 'of finite duration'.

A universe that has existed for an infinite time is, of course, not one which had a first moment of time, but it would also appear that a universe which has been in existence for only a finite time need not have had a first moment, as in the Hartle–Hawking cosmology. We thus have two possibilities, a bounded or an unbounded temporal series and, since the considerations which rule out a beginning of the universe appear likewise to rule out its ceasing to be, the two possibilities arise with respect to the future as well as to the past. Our question now is whether, physical theory aside, we have any reason to favour one or other of the two possibilities in either case.

The more familiar problems are associated with unbounded series; in particular, it is felt that there is some incoherence in the supposition of a past history of infinite duration. Likewise, too, with series of acts or events, as arise with, for instance, versions of the cosmological argument which contend that causal chains cannot go on for ever back in time, but must be grounded in an initial efficient cause. More generally, all the series of changes which we encounter raise the questions: Can this process be traced back, if only in thought, through a period of infinite time? Can it be supposed to continue infinitely far into the future? In either case it may be held that we have to do with two possibilities, depending on whether the infinity is actual or potential. We shall now consider what each involves.

The notion of the potentially infinite may be called upon to characterize a process or development that can be extended indefinitely. If that is its use, it may well be considered misleading; it is misleading, in so far as there is no question of an infinity that can become actual. Indeed, if the only way an infinity can be actual is by becoming actual, we may surely conclude that such an infinity cannot exist. Talk of *becoming* places the relevant series in time, but while any increments to a finite temporal series will leave it larger, it will still only be finite. Certainly, we do better to omit the reference to infinity altogether and settle for some expression such as 'indefinitely extendible'. Is a similarly innocuous reading available for 'actually infinite'? Consider the most easily handled case, that of numbers. Wittgenstein wrote: 'The infinite number series is only the infinite possibility of finite series of numbers. It is senseless to speak of the whole infinite number series, as if it, too, were an extension. . . . The signs themselves only contain the possibility and not the reality of their repetition' (1975: §144). This may be read as restricting the infinity of the numbers to no more than a potential infinity, but it could also be taken, not as a denial of an actual infinity, but as telling us what such an infinity comes to: an actual infinity of numbers is to be understood in terms of the indefinite extendibility of a sequence of numerical signs. There may be only finitely many signs at any time, but that does not mean that we are obliged to speak in the same way of numbers.

The infinity of the numbers may be given this relatively unproblematic interpretation, but we should still hold out for the infinity's being actual, as soon emerges if we consider what a merely potential infinity would be in mathematics. For the finitist mathematician, the notion of infinity is that of a structure in growth. The conception of a completed infinity is incoherent; we have to do always with a potential infinity only, never an actual infinity. This is not a satisfactory formulation if it is implied that, at any time, there are in existence only as many numbers as have been 'constructed' at that time, so that the number of odd numbers, say, could vary from day to day. On the other hand, if the membership of a series is determined by a choice rather than by a rule, as with the intuitionist's free choice sequences, then there will indeed be only those elements that have resulted from choices to date. Here, we note, we have an essentially temporal procedure—that of making successive choices—but when our generating principle is a law, as with the series of odd numbers, temporal constraints do not operate, any restrictions being definitional: does the law in question unambiguously determine the membership of the series? If it does, and if it provides a specification of infinitely many numbers, then that is what we have, actually and literally. Indeed, it is the notion of a merely *potential* infinity that, because of its involvement with temporal notions, is of only dubious application to such a series as that of the odd numbers.

When we turn to infinity as this may be thought realized in the physical world, whether in spatial or temporal terms, the problems become more severe. Can there be, in any sense, infinitely many days? Not the most appropriate temporal unit for these cosmic questions, it is true, but it is a convenient measure to adopt; all we ask of our unit is that a series of them either terminate or be divergent. Our answer to the question is likely to differ depending on whether we look to the past or to the future. If to the future, then any infinity is naturally considered to be potential only, 'There will be infinitely many days after today' being thought of in terms of indefinite extendibility: whatever future day is envisaged, we can suppose it to be succeeded by another, where the succeeding is, of course, something that will only then take place, not something that has in some sense already occurred. With the past, by contrast, the temporal succession, whether finite or infinite, may be held to be a given, so, if infinite, a matter of an actual infinity.

We may be right to query the possibility that the universe should have existed for an infinite time, but we have to take care that our objections do not simply consist in drawing attention to the peculiar logic of the infinite, to those of its features which are definitive, or at least distinctive, of the concept. Consider aleph-zero—in symbols, $\aleph_0$—which may be defined as the number which gives the answer to the question, how many natural numbers are there? Series of objects being defined as equal if they can be put into a one-one correspondence with one another, we can say that there are just as many odd numbers as there are natural numbers, each series having $\aleph_0$ members. This shows that a set may have just as many members as one of its proper subsets, but while such an eventuality is ruled out for finite sets, it is simply one of the features characteristic of infinite sets. How might a charge of incoherence be rebutted? That is not difficult. The claim that, in the domain of the infinite, the whole may be no greater than a proper part, is as well defined as is the mapping on the basis of which it is explained, the mapping which in this instance pairs 0 with 1, 1 with 3, 2 with 5, and in general n with $2n + 1$. The only objection to the informal description is that it may be ill chosen, but as a redescription of an admissible mapping it cannot be dismissed as incoherent. Again, if n is any natural number, n plus $\aleph_0$ is equal to $\aleph_0$, and, however large n may be, even multiplying $\aleph_0$ by n still leaves us with $\aleph_0$. The acceptance of such equations obliges us to prize apart concepts which usually coincide, as 'having another member added (subtracted)' usually goes hand in hand with 'increasing (decreasing) in number', but again it is easy to see the rationale for the severance.

What holds for operations with such numbers carries over to operations with totalities, if such there be, of which these numbers give the measure. The results may strike us as paradoxical, but that is not to say that they are incoherent. Understandably, however, the latter is a conclusion that has been drawn. Thus, a beginning of the world has frequently been held to be inescapable on the grounds that, if the world has already been in existence for an infinite time, we have an infinity that is being continually augmented, which is absurd; likewise, if some heavenly body should perform many revolutions for each revolution of some other heavenly body, then, if the former should have revolved infinitely many times, the latter will have revolved many more times that infinite number, which is again held to be impossible. However, while we can allow that any series of days which receives $\aleph_0$ as its measure continues to have that measure with the addition of further days, and that n times $\aleph_0$ is still $\aleph_0$, the coherence of the arithmetic of transfinite cardinals is no guarantee that $\aleph_0$ has any such application in the first place. It is there, rather than in the arithmetic, that the problem lies.

Another faulty argument rests on the claim that, if there have been infinitely many days, then some day will have occurred an infinite time ago. The implication that two days could be separated by an infinity of intermediate days is to be rejected, but we can accept an infinity of past days without allowing that any such day is anything other than finitely distant in the past. Again, though, rejecting this argument does not mean that the supposition of a past infinity is logically irreproachable.

Before seeing whether we may come down more decisively either for or against the supposition, let us consider whether it is right to regard past and future as asymmetric, a potential infinity being the most that future times may enjoy, even if an actual infinity is a possibility for the past. Given the general difficulty in finding asymmetries in the relations of temporal succession and temporal precedence, the question is of interest beyond the present issue. Think of today as designated by t_0, and with successions of days to left and to right, but with no indication given as to which succession is future, which past. Thus:

$$\ldots x_5, x_4, x_3, x_2, x_1, t_0, y_1, y_2, y_3, y_4, y_5, \ldots$$

Are there any relevant conclusions that can be drawn with respect to the series of *ys*—or *xs*—only if we know which of past or future that series represents? The temporal direction is undoubtedly crucial if the issue is one of what we are in fact capable of coming to *know*, but our question is one of ontology rather than epistemology, and here the asymmetry is less clear. Certainly, it is not established by the usual, woefully lame, arguments which seek to show that the events of the past, having occurred, are real, that they actually exist, whereas those of the future, having not yet taken place, are neither. This style of argument combines a triviality with a falsehood. The triviality is that past events have occurred, future events have not. The falsehood is that the past, unlike the future, is real, that it actually exists. This is false, in that only current events *are* real, actually exist now; yesterday's—of which we have extensive knowledge—*were* so, and tomorrow's—which are currently largely conjectural—*will be* so. Compare the observation that what is distinctive of the present is that it is then, and only then, that all our thought, action and experience take place. That is true, but it does not point to a significant difference between the present and the past and future. If a thought *takes* place, then of course it takes place in the present; that does not mean there have been no past thoughts; it is simply that any such *took* place.

The only way I can see to favour past rather than future events with talk of actuality or reality relates to the greater likelihood of knowledge with respect to the former. We say that something has actually happened when, for instance, it was thought to have happened and, after some uncertainty, it turns out that it indeed has. To say that yesterday's storm has actually occurred purports to put the matter beyond all doubt; and here there is a possible contrast with future happenings: we do not at present know—or, at least, we do not have the same direct kind of knowledge—that there will be a storm tomorrow, so the scope for saying that a storm actually will occur is that much more limited. But again, it is not *present* actuality that accrues to the past storm.

Leave aside the matter of what is currently knowable and we have total symmetry: both past and future contrast with the present; present events are actual; of past events we can say only that they were, of future events we can say only that they will be. The propositions thought to support a difference turn out to be empty tautologies—what has happened has happened—or an epistemic notion has been smuggled in to enable an inappropriate differentiation of past and future. I am witnessing a lightning flash. The flash is real, actual, unlike the last flash of the summer, which *was* real, actual, and unlike the first flash of the winter, which *will be* real, actual. Future flashes are not laid up somewhere, waiting their moment to put in an appearance, but nor have past flashes secured a lasting reality; as though, having occurred, they are here to stay, an extant totality augmented with every storm. They have one and all had their day, made their fleeting appearance and gone for ever. It hardly needs saying that, in making these observations, I am not advancing a *theory* of time, but nor am I repeating common-sense beliefs which a physical or philosophical theory might overturn. That happenings which are over and done with or which are yet to occur are not real now is a matter, not of such a belief, but of a *grammatical* truth.

Again, consider the claim that the past, in opposition to the future, is *fixed*, that it can accordingly be known, but not changed, whereas the future, by contrast, is open, determinable by us, that there is as yet nothing there to know. But, clearly, we cannot change the future any more than we can change the past, talk of changing being in place when something which is so and so is made to be otherwise. We cannot say of the future that things *are* so and so, and will be altered, and in so far as we can say that they *will* be so and so, we cannot as yet change them. That is a possibility only once they are present. Clearly, too, it is not true that, with respect to the past, there *is* something 'there' to be known; on the other hand, if we say, as we might, that we know what has happened, there is sense and symmetry in talk of knowing what will happen. It makes sense to speak of having intentions for the future, but not for the past, not because the past is fixed and the future is not, but because 'bring about' has an exclusively future orientation.

It is sometimes held that the question whether the future is real depends on whether statements about the future made in the present are determinately true or false. So, if you had said 'There will be a forest fire in July', and a forest fire is now, in July, in progress, then on one view what you said was true when you said it, while on another view it had at that point no determinate truth value. Suppose we opt for the first view. In what sense does that mean that the forest fire was real at the time when you said what you said, when it was not July and no forest was burning? Not having then taken place, what could it possibly mean to say that such a fire *was* none the less *then* real? Surely, there can be no more to the realist's position than is given with the proposal that a future-tense proposition be considered to have been true if things turn out as predicted, a proposal we may endorse or reject with no fear as to consequences either way.

So, epistemological considerations aside, past and future appear to be on a par in terms of their contrast to the present. How can we speak of infinity with respect to either? Consider first the future. The indefinite extendibility of a series of signs suffices for an actual infinity of numbers, but once time enters an actual infinity cannot be secured so readily: while allowing that the series of days stretching ahead should be indefinitely extendible, we should not wish to speak on this basis of an eventual infinity of future days. But consider. If it is true that for every day yet to come there will be a day that follows, then there will be infinitely many days. What is potential about this infinity? Any future day is at only a finite remove from today, but there will be, we are supposing, infinitely many such. If any day you care to nominate will have a tomorrow, then no natural number will be without its corresponding day; the number of natural numbers being infinite, it follows that we are committed to an actual infinity of future days. On the other hand, at no time will there ever have been more than a finite number of days starting from the present. So where now is the infinity?

The proposition 'There will be infinitely many days' is not a proposition that could prove true; there is no point of time at which it will be possible to say that things have turned out as predicted. Such and such will be so only if there is some future time at which it is so. The points of time at which something may become a future reality are each and every one of them only finitely far off into the future, and this is not changed by the consideration that there are infinitely many such points. There are infinitely many, in the sense that we have infinitely many possibilities to choose from in specifying a future date, but that is not to say that infinitely many such points will come to pass. The only point of time at which it would be appropriate to say that an infinite period had elapsed would be one that is infinitely distant from the present, and there can be no such point.

But, granted that no being in time could have any knowledge thereof, might it none the less not be *true* that the universe will go on for ever, that there is an actual infinity of times stretching into the future? This looks to be an abuse of 'actual' of a kind already noted, but there is indeed a further possibility, and one which does not presuppose a future perspective from which the proposition will be seen to have been confirmed, as is apparent from our claim that there will never be a time at which it can be said that there have been infinitely many days since today. This is clearly not being envisaged as something that will be affirmable only when the period signified by *never* has been traversed. Consider 'The galaxies will never recede at a speed greater than that of light.' This is not a proposition which awaits finding out what happens at or by the appointed time, but we can have reasons here and now for affirming it, a speed greater than light being ruled out by well-grounded theoretical considerations. Can such considerations be held to short-circuit what would otherwise have to be established year by year over an infinite future time? No. It makes no sense to speak of the generalization proving true on each of infinitely many future days, so, a case-by-case verification having been ruled out, no sense to have some other procedure achieve this for us. So what does the proposition mean? Simply, 'We can rule out any recession of the galaxies at a speed greater than light', a form of words which implies nothing as to the temporal span to be traversed.

If the considerations just advanced are on target, we come down in favour of no more than a potential infinity of future times, in the sense that we can suppose the future history of the universe to have any finite measure we please. Whatever number of days we envisage as giving the future measure of the universe, we can conceive of it lasting longer, but we cannot conceive of it lasting longer than every such period. Compare: anyone who bought a ticket in the lottery can be supposed to be the winner, but we cannot suppose that everyone should be the winner. How does it stand with respect to the past? We cannot now think in terms of what is possible for a journey backwards in time which would mirror a journey forwards, but we may ask whether, and in what sense, it is possible to go in thought infinitely far back into the past, and with this perspective it is in place to repeat the considerations which arose with respect to the future. For any past day you care to specify, we can suppose that it had a predecessor, and there are indefinitely many days you can specify, but there is no such thing as going back infinitely far, no day on which it could have been said that today was then infinitely far in the future. So, there have not been infinitely many days, and there will not have been that number.

If this reasoning is correct, it is no more a possibility that the universe has existed for infinitely many past days than that it should exist for infinitely many future days. However, this symmetry may still be challenged. For instance, Richard Sorabji agrees that 'an infinity of *future* years starting from now would always remain potential and never be completed' (1983: 221), but he considers there to be a disanalogy between the past and the future, in that past years do not start from now, but only our *thoughts* about them, should we choose to think of past years in reverse order. We may say that the past years have been gone through, and accordingly assign them a *finish*, but we are not thereby assigning them *two* termini, and this leaves us free to think of them as forming a traversed series which is more than an extendible finitude. By contrast, any future series which takes its starting point from a given point of time and which we can think of as having been gone through will have a finish as well as a start: 'It is not future years *as such* which have a different infinity from past years, but future years which have been *traversed*, for the traversed ones will have *two* termini' (ibid., 222).

But this does not show that we can speak of infinitely many past years as having been traversed; only that, if we do, we are not to assign the traversal a starting point, only an end point. Starting from the present we can go forward not only in thought, but we can live through a future succession of years. Whether in thought or in reality, however, we can advance only a finite distance, however far that may be. Any traversing of the past, thought of as, say, encountering or living through a succession of years, can, of course, only terminate, not begin, in the present, but while there can be no literal movement back through time, any movement currently terminating can be redescribed as extending back: the meteor which has just struck the earth was *n* miles distant an hour ago, *m* miles distant an hour before that, and so on. But any such extension, any phase of the meteor's history, can only be finite. There could be no point in the meteor's history that was separated from the present by an infinite passage of time.

So far, the supposition of a symmetry between past and future is favoured, with in either case no more than a potential infinity of days to be allowed for. However, in rejecting the possibility of an actual infinity of times, past or future, it is not clear what, more positively, has been established. The consideration that the only meaningful measures of future temporal stretches are finite does not mean that the universe will *cease* to exist after a finite time. How could it have that implication? The age of the universe is always the age of the universe at some point of time; we are not dealing with a *fixed* quantity, a quantity that cannot subsequently be exceeded. When someone speaks of the future history of the universe, we can always ask: its history up to when? The universe will continue in being for only a finite time in the sense that on any occasion on which one might say that it has continued in being it will be possible to add 'for a finite time', but while the only continuations of the universe's history are finite, this need not be coupled with the claim that one of them will be terminal. Symmetrically, the only backwards projections of the universe are finite, but this does not mean that one of them was initial, that it had no predecessor.

Consider further the future case. We have here a form of words which looks to be an instance of the law of excluded middle, namely: either the universe will continue in being for only a finite time, or it will never end. And, having rejected the possibility that the universe should go on for ever, we must surely embrace the first disjunct. However, that step fails to take into account the appropriate interpretation of the second disjunct. We can refuse a construal of 'The universe will never end' as a prediction awaiting fulfilment at some future point of time, but, while there is no such point, that does not mean that this form of words allows of no acceptable reading, since we granted that theoretical grounds might be available for ruling out in advance some future happening—in this case, a last day, an end to the universe. With that reading, however, our disjunction comes to the claim that either there will be a last day, or the supposition of a last day can be excluded. Suppose there are no compelling grounds for ruling out a last day, that this is not a supposition that leads to absurdity. Does that mean that a last day will be assured? Surely not. The two disjuncts are not, despite initial appearances, one another's contradictories, and we are not looking at an instance of the law of excluded middle. True, at any future time there will have been only finitely many days, and it is only such truths, truths that are so at some time, that are allowable, but this does not imply that there will be a last day. In so far as the claim that the universe will never end is interpreted as suggested, we may be able to say that it will go on for ever, but not in the sense that it will go on for an infinite time—that it will eventually *have* gone on for ever.

It is natural to query this reasoning in the following way. 'The universe will go on for ever' surely equates to 'We can place no limit on the future duration of the universe', a reading which maintains the legitimate construal of 'indefinitely extendible', but which is contradicted by 'We can place a limit on the future duration of the universe', a proposition that commits us to 'The universe will end one day', contrary to what has been claimed. However, the suggested paraphrase is incorrect. 'We can place no limit on the future duration of the universe' is consistent with the universe's none the less ceasing to exist; something stronger is needed, and we have captured this with 'A cessation of the universe can be ruled out.'

Have we perhaps overlooked a further possibility? Is not the relevant alternative to there being a last day simply that the universe will keep on going—not an alternative that embodies the rejected perspective? Certainly, with respect to some future day we can say that either that day will be the last or the universe will keep going on that day. The difficulty comes when we try to generate a more general reading: Either some day will be the last or the universe will keep on going. This cannot be: either some day will be the last or the universe will keep going on that day. There is no 'that day'. It has to be: or there will never be a last day, which takes us to our first reading: or the supposition of a last day can be excluded. Someone might argue: We are not in a position to name the day when the universe will come to an end, but for all that it *must*. What, after all, is the alternative? That it will go on for ever? But this we have ruled out: there is no such thing as going on for ever. Well, there is no such thing as going on for ever if that means that at some point the universe will have achieved that feat, but it can be said that it will go on for ever in the sense that it will keep on going, something that can be seen to be true from day to day, but never more than that, never the more final terminus supposedly given with 'will *have* gone on for ever'. There may never be a last day—the supposition may be refutable—but, for all that, at any time there will have been only a finite number of days to that point. The only perspectives we can meaningfully consider are at a finite remove from the present, even though we have an unlimited number of possibilities to choose from.

Likewise with respect to the past and the matching disjunction: either the universe began to exist or it has been in existence for an infinite time. So, either the universe began to exist, or we can rule out a beginning. Ruling out a beginning means ruling out each proposition of the form 'The universe began *n* years ago', these being the only genuine possibilities, infinitely many of them though there are. But suppose that we cannot rule out each and every one of them. That does not imply that the universe began to exist. The only meaningful measures we can assign to the universe, whether as regards its past or its future duration, are finite. But that does not mean that one such measure, at present unknown, gives the future final age, or length of history to date, of the universe. Only that, *if* the universe began or will end, its duration will be measurable in this way. So you are saying that it may go on for ever, and may have been in existence for all eternity? What else might this *if* imply? I am saying that, whatever day you may conjecture as being the last, or the first, may not be so.

Propositions such as 'The universe will never end' have been taken as the focus of debate between the realist and the anti-realist, the former seeing in such forms of words the depiction of a possibility which, while we could never know that it was realized, is none the less genuine, the latter maintaining that any question of truth is ruled out by this very circumstance. Neither is our position. With respect to 'The galaxies will never recede at a speed greater than that of light', we noted that there was a coherent interpretation, though not one which implied a failure of such a recession over an infinite period of time, and there is likewise a coherent interpretation, and one on which the proposition could be known to be true, for 'The universe will never end.' Indeed, one of our claims has been that the notions of beginning and ceasing to exist are inapplicable to the universe. However, there is not another reading which is sufficiently coherent that we might think to reject it on the grounds that the state of affairs conjectured transcends anything we could come to know. Nor, as noted, is there any violation of the law of excluded middle. These points are elaborated in Rundle (1990: ch. 12).

8.2 CAUSAL SERIES AND EXPLANATION

Let us now relate these temporal considerations to questions concerning the explanation of causal series within the universe. To suppose that a series of changes extends indefinitely into the past, with no point of time when an initial change got under way, is to admit a series for which any final explanation is seemingly denied us. To take an example anticipated above, consider a watch with a mainspring which sets in motion a succession of gear-wheels. An explanation of the rotation of the last wheel in the succession can be supplied, but not if we can no longer appeal to the mainspring. Supposing this to be removed, it will not help if we suppose there to be *more* gear-wheels in the succession, and this is true whatever the number, even an infinity of gear-wheels being no substitute for the mainspring. In contrast to the succession of men begetting men, this is an instance of a *per se* causal series: one wheel moves another in virtue of being itself moved, whereas one man does not beget another in virtue of being himself begotten—grandfather's begetting of father is not the cause of father's begetting of son. Is the demand for a first member more pressing in the former case? If x moves y which then moves z, y's moving of z is in a sense the same event as its being moved by x, but while this brings cause and effect closer than in the *per accidens* case, it is not evident what repercussions this has for a first member of the series. On the other hand, that is of no great account if there is just as much reason to posit a first member whether the ordering of causes is *per se* or *per accidens*. Certainly, it is difficult to rest content with a series which simply presents us with change after change as we go back in time, no member having a degree of independence or self-sufficiency which would differentiate it from the others. The problem is not solely one for the theist. When the series starts with God there is an added problem posed by a succession of causes in which such disparate items as God and the physical changes which he induces are held to be linked in a homogeneous relationship, but a problem remains even if we stay within the universe.

However, the possibilities which the example of the watch invites us to compare are perhaps not quite as we might at first think. The series which takes us back to the mainspring may strike us as less problematic than one in which our search for an explanation simply finds us repeatedly referred back to an earlier happening, no ultimate explanation ever being in sight, but does the explanation which brings this series to an end fare any better? Have we not simply traded an unending series for one which originates in an as yet unexplained cause? If the mainspring had causal antecedents, then in envisaging it as removed we are just introducing a gap in the chain of causes; if it had no causal antecedents, there is no accounting, causally, for its existence. Imagining our series of gear-wheels as extending back indefinitely appears at least to remove the gap, this supposition having the advantage that we have a cause for any member of the series we care to single out. Hume, for one, would consider this enough: 'Did I show you the particular causes of each individual in a collection of twenty particles of matter, I should think it very unreasonable, should you afterwards ask me, what was the cause of the whole twenty. This is sufficiently explained in explaining the cause of the parts' (1947: 190–1).

But what of an infinite series? According to some versions of the cosmological argument, a series of dependent existents cannot extend infinitely back into the past, but must terminate in an originating cause. Our own argument has been the seemingly more paradoxical one that, while there cannot be such a series, it does not follow that any causal series must have had a first member. The analogue in the future case is not paradoxical. In postulating a series proceeding indefinitely into the future, we can contemplate an arbitrarily large number of members: whatever number you opt for, we shall allow that the series to the date then envisaged should have at least that number of members, but not that the series will have a member on every one of the infinitely many of the future days possible. The important consideration is that we do not have to allow that the series must stop at some point in time, yet in refusing to go along with the insistence that it must come to an end we are not subscribing to the 'possibility' that it may go on for ever, in a sense that implies that at some time it will have done so. Given that we have found difficulties in the idea that everything may one day cease to exist, it is of some significance that we can rule out a future of infinite duration without requiring an eventual end to the universe.

If the past is symmetric, we shall be allowing that any finite extension back in time can be countenanced, and also that the series did not have to start at some point, that there did not have to be a first day or a first member of the series. It is whether the symmetry extends this far that is contentious. When considering what may have happened in the past, we can consider only what may have taken place within some finite time before the present, whether determinately or indeterminately specified— '12,000,000 years ago', 'at some past time'. Just as there is no limit to the number of future periods dating from now that can be contemplated, so there is no limit to the number of past periods that can be envisaged leading up to the present. Whatever future day you specify, you can always suppose that it is followed by another day, and whatever past day you specify, you can always suppose that it was preceded by another day. The series cannot extend infinitely far into the future, but that does not mean that it will end some day. It cannot extend infinitely far back in time, but that does not mean that it began one day. But we may well not be happy with this alleged symmetry. We may be prepared to rule out both a future and a past infinity of members of a causal series, but while that leaves it indeterminate how many members will follow, and, in particular, whether there will be a last, we feel that it is determinate just how many have preceded, and whether there was a first. Our instincts here may be correct, but we have not seen a way to defend them. Still, whether or not we have the kind of past–future symmetry considered, it does appear that an explanatory asymmetry remains. It is of no great concern if a future series simply peters out, all change generated by series having ceased. But when confronted with a change, the demands of explanation appear to require us to posit a further *prior* change, cessation in this direction being explanatorily problematic.

In view of the counter-intuitive character of some of the preceding observations, it is worth pointing out that the basic existential issues are independent of the matter of the duration of the universe, or of causal series within it. This can be seen by considering the question left in the air with Hume's assertion that the cause of a collection is sufficiently explained by explaining the causes of its parts. It appears that, if the series extends infinitely far into the past, then we have an explanation of every one of the successive individual particles, but since we have argued that such an infinite extension is impossible, we do not have in this way an explanation of each particle. On the other hand, since—our counter-intuitive conclusion—this impossibility does not mean that the series must have had a first member, it is not clear how things stand on the question of a comprehensive explanation.

There are two cases to consider, depending on whether or not the series is supposed to have had a first member. If there is no first member, it would appear that every member of the series can be accounted for in terms of the action of its predecessor, and to insist that, none the less, the series as a whole remains in need of explanation, appears simply to discount this consideration. However, much depends on how 'the series as a whole' is being understood. Thus, Swinburne claims that, whether the age of the universe is finite or infinite, 'If the only causes of its past states are prior past states, the set of past states as a whole will have no cause and so no explanation' (1979: 124). Talk of a *set* can be taken in more than one way. If it is as with, say, a set of glasses or a set of knives and forks, then in speaking of the set we are speaking of nothing more than the objects which go to make it up. We have to do, not with an abstract object, but with some thing or things which we can place on the table. To the claim that, while each member of the succession has a preceding cause, the whole formed by the members is in need of a cause, Hume replied by casting doubt on the propriety of forming such a whole: 'the uniting of these parts into a whole, like the uniting of distinct counties into one kingdom, or several distinct members into one body, is performed by an arbitrary act of the mind, and has no influence on the nature of things' (1947: 190). An objection along these lines is perhaps to the point when the whole is as with a set in the sense indicated, the glasses, say, being deemed to form or constitute a set in virtue of some feature which, while not necessarily arbitrary, may be said to have 'no influence on the nature of things'. More important, however, is the consideration that nothing over and above the members of the set or succession has to be acknowledged. On the other hand, if 'set' is understood as in set theory, where we are required to make sense of an empty set, then, as Swinburne's argument requires, a set can be taken to be something over and above its members. The set of states will then be not simply the states but something which contains them, but, just as a set of glasses, in this sense, will not be something you can place on the table, so too a set of states will not, as an abstract object, present us with a question as to its causation. Indeed, it will not be an appropriate term of any such relation.

However, all is not lost for those who consider Hume to be too undemanding in what he requires for an explanation, there being a far more satisfactory way of showing that something remains to be accounted for in our succession of causes. If each member of the succession fully explains the existence of what it engenders, we have a complete explanation of the totality of individual members and therewith of the series which they comprise, but what we represent as a matter of bringing into existence is a process which only partially accounts for the being of what is generated. The assumed causal explanations bear upon the successive transformations of matter, but they fail to account for the matter that persists throughout these changes, matter of which we may say: this might not have existed, essentially the same question being posed by 'How has it come about that this matter exists?' at whatever point in the series it is raised, so long as the same matter is being indicated. Indeed, it would be extraordinary if a complete explanation of the existence of C_{n+1} were to be had by appealing to its causation by its predecessor, C_n, since this would mean that C_n acted, not by transforming matter, but by creating matter out of nothing. There is some irony in the thought that a commitment to sanctioning creation *ex nihilo* is the lot of those who, like Hume, regard causation within the relevant series as sufficient to account for the existence of each of its members.

If there is no first member of the series, and if for every member we rule out creation *ex nihilo*, then we are left with something, the persisting matter, which does raise a question as to its possible origination which is not answered by accounting for the successive changes. On the other hand, if causation is confined to such series, if there is no question of invoking a transcendent cause, then something other than a causal explanation will have to be sought for the persisting matter. We reach the same conclusion if we consider a series having a first member. That member will not, of course, have a causal ancestor within the series, and again, causation being found only in the changes involved in one thing acting upon another, there is no question of a non-physical cause, but the existence of matter that will have started to transform from that point will still be in need of explanation. So, whether we have a first member or not, an explanation of the existence of the series is called for which is not causal. Or so it would seem. If there is no coming to be of the material universe, its being is always a matter of its continuing to be, and since continuing in being is not something that requires explanation, the fact that the physical universe exists is not, it would appear, a fact in need of explanation. But we may surely ask whether there had to be something of this nature, something that continues to be. If 'x might not have existed' implies 'There is a time at which x might not have existed', then, since there is no time at which the universe might not have existed, it is not possible that the universe should not have existed, so it exists of necessity. If this is accepted, then, while a *causal* explanation is not wanted, it does not matter whether we say that the existence of the universe is in no need of explanation, or that an explanation is to be found in the unthinkability of its non-existence.

8.3 AN END TO EXPLANATIONS

A physical universe may be a necessity, but is there any ultimate explanation of the successive transformations through which it has persisted? We shall now follow up this theme in general terms, beginning with a closer look at the demand for explanation. First, there are two kinds of explanation to consider. Suppose we ask why a building collapsed, and are told that the collapse was due to an earthquake. We may then ask what led to the earthquake, and receive an explanation citing movement along a fracture in the earth's crust. The source of this movement may then be traced, and so on back through the series of causes which have culminated in the present happening. The other form of regress may have the same starting point, but take us to successively more general explanations. So, the collapse was due to an earthquake, but why is it that earthquakes result in such collapses? Because, let us say, the movement of the ground is sufficient to topple a structure made as this was. And why is it sufficient? Laws relating to the strength of materials may now be cited, and so on back through yet more general laws, culminating perhaps in basic laws which pose the question why the fundamental constants which figure in them have the values they have. Here, conceivably, evolutionary considerations may, as suggested earlier, have a part to play, the constants having settled down to their current value as a result of their greater stability *vis-à-vis* values which resulted in various more transient physical states. We shall now consider further the demand for explanation, especially as this arises with series of causes.

On the one hand, the intuitive appeal of the principle of sufficient reason encourages us in our search for explanations. In Leibniz's formulation, 'nothing happens without a reason why it should be so, rather than otherwise' (Alexander 1956: 16). As was argued above, an insistence that causation of *E* by *C* on a given occasion implies like behaviour whenever relevant conditions are repeated is more properly based on this principle than on our bare conception of causation, so it enjoys a fundamental role in reasonings concerning causes. According to the principle, which has played a central role in proofs of the existence of God, there is an explanation for the occurrence of any event, or the existence of any thing, yet the uncompromising universality of explanations implied is considered by many to be ultimately self-defeating. This is the message in the following passage from Flew, which he offers as showing that the principle of sufficient reason is demonstrably false:

It is often thought, by naturalists as well as by theists, that it is an unavoidable defect in every naturalistic system, and one which—if only it happened to be true—theism could remedy, that in any such naturalistic system the most fundamental laws of matter and energy cannot be susceptible of any further explanation. Yet this is not, if the system is true, a defect; nor is it one which, even if theism were true, theism could remedy. For it is not a contingent fact about one sort of system, but a logical truth about all explanations of facts. The ultimate facts about God would have to be, for precisely the same reason, equally inexplicable. In each and every case we must necessarily find at the end of every explanatory road some ultimates which have simply to be accepted as the fundamental truths about the way things are. And this itself is a contention, not about the lamentable contingent facts of the human condition, but about what follows necessarily from the nature of explanation.

Flew (1966: 83)

In so far as the thesis is that ultimate facts are not *further* explicable, this is unexceptionable, but if the claim is that explanation must ultimately terminate in unexplained and inexplicable truths, we have a substantive, and less easily resolvable, issue. There is, after all, another possibility, namely, that we should reach a point where the demand for an explanation is seen to be misconceived. This would make for an end to explanations without imperilling the principle of sufficient reason, since that principle can reasonably be taken as requiring no more than that, whenever it *makes sense* to ask for an explanation, there should be one. If at some point the demand is seen to be unfounded, it is not so much that, since explanations must come to an end, we shall inescapably be left with something inexplicable; rather, what we are left with is something which simply does not need explaining.

Lack of an explanation is worrying when we are confronted with the sort of phenomenon for which there *could* be an explanation—as when something falls, shatters, or melts—but where an explanation eludes us, cases in which it will be difficult to say that there is no explanation, rather than simply that we have not as yet succeeded in finding one. A contrast is provided when the demand is seen to be misplaced. Coincidences provide a suitable illustration. Suppose that *A* occurs at midday and that *B*, coincidentally, occurs at the same time. There is a sense in which, if we can explain why each occurred at midday, we can explain why they occurred then, at the same time. But explaining why two events occurred at the same time may often involve a richer explanation, one which could have adjusted to the time of occurrence of each, had this been different. Indeed, with an explanation of this form it may be that we explain why the events occurred, or had to occur, simultaneously, without explaining why they occurred precisely when they did. If, on the other hand, it is a matter merely of a coincidence, success in explaining why the events occurred at the same time is derivative upon the consideration that we explain why A occurred when it did, and, independently, why B occurred when it did. Since the point of time is the same for each, we explain why they occurred at that, the same time. The individual times come first, with sameness a consequence forming no part of the explanation, whereas in the other case the sameness is part of what is explained, and explained in greater generality. The type of explanation we might initially seek is seen to be inappropriate to the phenomena in question, so its lack is of no concern.

A more interesting and more relevant example concerns the persistence of states. As already argued, continuing in existence, or continuing to be of such and such a character, is not in general something that requires explanation. That fact itself requires explanation, however, and we found this in the consideration that persistence in being or continuation of a state is not an instance of change in the relevant sense. So, why do laws of Nature continue to hold? Why do bodies continue to behave in such and such a regular fashion? To the extent that there is no change, no intrusion of a disruptive factor, there is nothing to explain. True, *persistence* has connotations of *doing* something—think of a persistent salesman; likewise, too, with *ageing*, where a visible process of change may be involved. However, the austere notion of persisting or enduring, pared down to its purely temporal character, can be readily appreciated as involving no change beyond one of relation, a relation of co-presence with genuine changes, as of some regular process which may be enlisted to give a measure of time passing. A celebrated example of a form of change which invites comparison with persistence in being is that of persistence in motion, and we shall shortly turn this likeness to our purposes.

It was suggested that lack of an explanation is troubling when the phenomenon in question is one which *could* be explained, and the lack remains of concern even when it is acknowledged that reasons must come to an end, since we should like to know why they come to an end when they do. Moreover, while there is no question of arbitrarily terminating a causal series of which the universe as a whole is a member, there are still causal series within the universe to deal with, series which, whether having a beginning or not, pose a problem. So, nothing got the Big Bang—if such there was—under way, but we may still wonder how change is to be explained. The series of events that has culminated in the present state of the universe may or may not have had a beginning. Under either supposition we should like to have some inkling of a possible explanation of that series. We can account for the substrate of the changes—the inescapable physical reality—but what of the changes themselves? What sorts of things does it make sense to posit in answer to the question how things got going? What could have instituted the changes that have led to the current state of the universe?

It is of some interest if one of the fundamental changes is that of expansion or inflation, since expansion is a form of motion, and, on the usual interpretation of Newton's First Law of Motion, continuing in motion is not a phenomenon that is in need of causal explanation any more than, in general, is persisting in being, whether this is a matter of continuing to exist, or continuing to be so and so—as dry, cold, upright or at rest. Newton's First Law runs: Every body remains in a state of rest or of uniform motion in a straight line unless acted upon by a net force. We are inclined to see an asymmetry between the two conditions, motion and rest, but since, according to Newton, a body perseveres in a new state solely by the force of inertia, it is in virtue of the same property of matter that a body both persists in motion and persists in a state of rest—though physicists would not now speak of a *force* in this connection. What sets a body in motion is what accounts for the *moving*, a continuing state, not just for the *beginning* of this state, the transition from rest to motion.

That no cause is needed to account for continuing in motion is of importance with respect to the problem of explaining causal series within the universe. Suppose we have a stream of particles. With particles in motion we have the possibility of particles in collision, and hence of causation, the original energy being preserved but redistributed. The paths of bodies intersect, resulting in impact, displacement, momentum imparted, forces redirected; discontinuous changes. The continuation in motion which led to such causation does not require explanation, but there is, of course, the question of what got the motion under way. I have suggested that when we are considering existence on a cosmic scale, there is no question of a beginning of existence, but the nearest we can get to this is by talking of a finite duration of the universe. Likewise with beginnings of movement, or of change generally, as when the expansion of the universe from a minute highly compressed volume of matter is at issue. In order for it to be possible to speak of something as beginning to move, or to expand or inflate, there must have been an antecedent state of rest. However, if there is no time at which a particle was not moving, then it did not begin to move, and in this case there is accordingly no beginning of movement to be explained. So, we have a simple pattern: we meet with causation in the form of collisions between moving particles; however, not only are the continuing motions of the particles which led to these collisions in no need of explanation, but in the fundamental cosmic cases that concern us, there is no origination of motion, hence no origination requiring explanation.

We may reinforce this argument in the following way. It is natural to suppose that, while rest does not call for a cause, motion does, but what most clearly requires a cause is beginning to move—and, symmetrically, coming to rest. Mere motion is seen as symmetrical with rest through the consideration that, when two bodies A and B are moving relatively to one another, one can equally regard A as moving and B as at rest, or B as moving and A as at rest. Essentially, what it takes for there to be motion is simply that A be changing its position relative to B. Which of A and B, if either, we deem at rest is of lesser account, but since being at rest does not require a causal explanation, and since either body can be deemed at rest, neither is in a state that demands a cause. No cause is needed beyond that which resulted in the two bodies moving relatively to one another.

However, this argument has to confront the consideration that the body which is said to move is the body which is *made* to move. So long as we respect this consideration, we are in general not at liberty to regard A or B indifferently as the body in motion. On the other hand, in the context with which we are now concerned, where the particles in question were not made to move, there is symmetry: movement is now no more in need of a causal explanation than is rest.

When bodies interact in the way suggested, we shall, then, have causal relations generated from states of affairs of a different order as far as what, if anything, they demand by way of explanation. The consequent interactions give rise to much greater complexity, but perhaps the situation is fundamentally the same as when causation is not there to be coped with. It is rather that the introduction of causation on such a ubiquitous scale distorts our vision: we see it as posing the fundamental existential questions, when the myriad causal happenings are merely a confusing by-product of the more fundamental and simpler state of affairs, now obscured. If changes involved in the Big Bang were merely relational changes, they will not provoke the kinds of query which seem inevitable given our place in the subsequent history of the universe. And, we have argued, there can have been no beginning of change, no static universe in which the seconds ticked by prior to the dawning of the first event.

The pattern of explanation here, or at least that aspect which underlies the reasoning which buttresses Newton's First Law, is of considerable importance. There is, for instance, scope for applying it to the conservation of matter-energy. So long as the relevant conservation law is logically contingent, we are seemingly faced with an irresolvable explanatory dilemma:

Either the regress of explanation terminates in a most fundamental law or it does not. If there is a deepest law, it will be logically contingent, and so the fact that it holds rather than not doing so will be a brute fact. If the regress does not terminate, then for every law in the infinite hierarchy there is a deeper law from which it can be deduced. In this case, however, the whole hierarchy will be logically contingent, and so the question of why it holds rather than some other hierarchy will arise. So if only scientific explanation is allowed, the fact that this particular infinite hierarchy of contingent laws holds will be a brute inexplicable fact. Therefore, on the assumption that scientific laws are logically contingent and are explained by being deduced from other laws, there are bound to be inexplicable brute facts if only scientific explanation is allowed.

(Quinn 1993: 607)

Philip Quinn considers that such explanatory problems are 'too big, so to speak, for science to solve', but he holds that, if the theistic doctrine of creation and conservation is true, they have solutions in terms of agent-causation: 'The reason why there is a certain amount of matter-energy and not some other amount or none at all is that God so wills it, and the explanation of why matter-energy is conserved is that God conserves it' (ibid.). While it is questionable whether this solution would advance our understanding, many would agree with the statement of the problem, and it is not clear what shape a non-theistic solution might take. However, no change in total energy would appear to be on a par with no change in a state of rest, the absence of change in either case meaning that there is simply nothing requiring explanation. Suppose we have a body, x, which, like the sun, is seething with activity, and a body, y, which is totally static. Must x pose a greater problem than y? Each, perhaps, raises a question as to why it exists, but if, with x, there was never a transition from rest to motion, no further question need be posed by x's character as continually changing. In particular, it need not be that there is energy to be accounted for in x that is not to be found in y, but, as is claimed for the universe as a whole, the sum of energy could be zero: 'The law of gravitation insures that the negative potential energy of gravitation between the masses in the universe must always be equal in magnitude but opposite in effect to the sum of the mc^2 energies associated with each of the individual masses. The total is therefore always exactly zero!' (Barrow 1994: 112). It is not always clear what we are to infer from the supposition that quantities cancel in this way.

A universe that is in balance in a certain respect is still not nothing, still very much something that needs to be accounted for. However, in so far as the undoubted changes in the universe are consistent with no change overall, there is a case for saying that no change remains to be explained.

Explanatory regresses can surely be satisfactorily handled only if at some point the question of a possible explanation does not arise, and this can be found to be so without our having to yield on the status of the relevant law as logically contingent. It would not seem that a series of explanations of physical facts could terminate in a logical truth. It is not logic, surely, that guarantees that, for instance, the basic physical constants should have had just the values they have. On the other hand, if we never get beyond a contingent truth, we seemingly never get beyond a brute fact: things might have been otherwise; that they are as they are remains ultimately inexplicable. How do matters stand if the terminus is a truth which for some reason does not call for explanation? Take once more the question why bodies, once in existence, continue to exist. It is not logically necessary that they should continue, but that they do none the less requires no explanation; it is only when they cease to exist that there is something to be accounted for. We may say, 'That's just the way things are', by way of acknowledging that there is no terminus in a logical truth, but not as an admission that something in need of explanation remains unexplained. Further promising candidates for this approach are provided by conclusions arrived at by thought experiments, as with Galileo's argument to show that all bodies fall at the same rate, regardless of their weight.

While there may be no grounding in a logical truth, that is not to say that there is no place for necessity in our explanations. True, if we are dealing with contingent truths, then explanations from which they can be deduced cannot be necessary. If whatever commits us to a logical impossibility is itself logically impossible, then we cannot have a contingent proposition Q following from a necessary proposition P, since if Q happened to be false we should be committed to a logical impossibility in the form of the negation of P, which surely makes Q itself logically impossible. However, it could none the less turn out that what was to be explained was an *a posteriori* necessity. So, we can determine the ratio of two masses by comparing their velocities when subjected to a force—as when propelled, say—and we can determine their ratios by weighing them. The mass determined in the first way—the inertial mass—is found to be equal to the mass determined in the second way—the gravitational mass. This equality is satisfactorily explained if it can be shown that inertial and gravitational mass are the same property, and if the Kripkean considerations touched upon above in connection with the identity of individuals can be extended to property identity, our explanation will rest upon an identity that is *a posteriori* necessary.

To return, finally, to our main theme, it is of interest to see how our attempt at establishing the self-sufficiency of the universe both mirrors and departs from considerations which figure in arguments for a divine creator. Whether in speaking of God or of the universe, we are at risk of making misconceived projections of our language: what makes sense with respect to things within the universe may cease to do so when God, or the universe as a whole, is at issue. To some extent, this has made for a *via negativa* in speaking about the latter, but the failure of certain descriptions to apply to the universe, as with 'came into existence' and 'was caused to be', has been part of the resolution of our problem rather than the source of a difficulty. The question why there is something rather than nothing is surely not to be answered by specifying a cause, but the question why the *universe* exists might appear, initially, to be answerable only in this way. However, just as questions concerning where and when having as their subject-matter the universe as a whole are often seen to be improper, so, if our argument has been on target, *why* can be added to *where* and *when*. The changes found in Nature, and their causation, are, like the size of the universe or its rate of expansion, simply internal features of the universe having no more than physical significance. Indeed, the claim that there might have been nothing seems likewise to be a projection of a way of speaking beyond the bounds of its meaningful application. So, we may wonder: how could we as much as have had the idea that there might have been nothing if, as here argued, this is not a genuine possibility? By generalizing, I suggest, on such reports as 'There is nothing in the cupboard', 'There is nothing on the table' and 'There is nothing between the earth and the moon.' 'There is nothing' demands the kind of completion which the less comprehensive forms provide, but any such completion, even 'There is nothing anywhere', leaves us with something.

Whereas theological discourse features descriptions of God which, like those which would place him in the category of *persons*, are at best of uncertain intelligibility, much remains that can meaningfully be said about the universe, as cosmology testifies. However, we have found that the notion of necessary existence is not to be jettisoned, as is customary in dismissing arguments for a creator, but it proves to play a key role in answering, and in answering in a logically satisfying way, our initial query, why is there something rather than nothing? Nor do we find any reason to abandon the principle of sufficient reason. If there has to be a physical reality, then that there is such is, it could be said, self-explanatory—better: something that is not in need of explanation—however much an explanation is needed for why, more specifically, the universe is as we find it. And if, as seems possible, questions concerning fundamental changes in the evolution of the universe can be laid to rest by showing that the apparent need for explanation is no more than apparent, we are on the way to giving a comprehensive yet purely naturalistic account of the fundamental facts of existence.

It is natural for a theist to be drawn to a tripartite classification of reality—as physical, spiritual, and abstract. Priority may go to the first two categories, abstractions being held to enjoy no more than a derivative or secondary status, if they count as real at all; on the other hand, a more Platonic conception, one which would people God's mind with such items, may accord them a greater standing. Either way, anything purely abstract would be considered to fall short of both the physical and the spiritual when it comes to being an agent of change. However, the force of our argument has been both to dissociate the notion of agency from the non-physical, and to suggest that any notion of necessity as this might apply to God would align him with things as insubstantial as abstractions. The view is sometimes expressed that, while we may not be able to prove that God exists, it cannot be shown that he does not. There is both need and room for faith. Given the way the very concept of God appears to contain the seeds of his destruction, this view reveals an excess of optimism, and indeed our argument rules out the existence of God in at least two ways. First, if reality without matter is unthinkable, then God does not enjoy the position of supreme existential independence that his nature requires: there is something other than him which must exist. Second, if the only genuine substances are material substances, if there is no place for immaterial agents, then there is no place for God. And that, I should have thought, is the right conclusion. If God does not exist, it surely does not just happen that this is so, but it will be because there is some incoherence in the very idea of a being that transcends space and time yet is capable of action on, or in producing, the material world.

In the popular mind, the great debate in which the preceding questions of existence arise is one between science and religion. It is true that, on occasions, scientific considerations can provide an appropriate corrective to a religious belief. That is so when, for instance, we are dealing with forms of superstition which look to supernatural causes when the possibility of more mundane explanations has not been properly explored, though even here there is a risk that viewing the alternatives as religious and scientific risks making science as well as religion party to a confusion. It is not that, say, creationism is a better theory than evolution by natural selection; it is, rather, that creationism is not a theory at all. That is something that is exposed not by scientific but by philosophical argument, as are the errors in attempts to prove a divine origin of the universe. Nor is it that religion may have a role where science has nothing to say, as with questions concerning an after-life or the meaning of this life. More generally, the resolution of our queries has been seen to come from philosophy rather than from science. True, the kinds of question which physicists address at this level overlap with those which can be reckoned philosophical, questions of meaning being inescapable for cosmologists as well as for philosophers, but showing how presuppositions behind a question have to be abandoned, that the question itself is to be rejected as resting on an illusion, is a distinctively philosophical task.

References

Alexander, H. G. (1956). *The Leibniz–Clarke Correspondence*. Manchester: Manchester University Press.

Alston, William P. (1985). 'Functionalism and Theological Language', *American Philosophical Quarterly*, Vol. 22, No. 3.

Anscombe, G. E. M. and Geach, P. T. (1961). *Three Philosophers*. Oxford: Blackwell.

Aquinas, Thomas (1945). *Summa Theologiae*, Part I, in *Basic Writings of Saint Thomas Aquinas*, Vol. I, ed. Anton C. Pegis. New York: Random House.

—— (1955). *On the Truth of the Catholic Faith: Summa contra Gentiles*, trans. Anton C. Pegis. New York: Doubleday.

Aristotle (1987) *Poetics*, trans. with a Commentary by Stephen Halliwell. London: Duckworth.

Atkins, P. W. (1994). *Creation Revisited: The Origin of Space, Time and the Universe*. Harmondsworth: Penguin.

Augustine, St, of Hippo (1972). *Concerning the City of God against the Pagans*, trans. Henry Bettenson. London: Penguin Books.

Ayer, A. J. (1952). *Language, Truth and Logic*. New York: Dover, 2nd edn.

—— ed. (1959). *Logical Positivism*. Glencoe: Free Press.

Baldwin, Thomas (1996). 'There might be Nothing', *Analysis*, Vol. 56, No. 4.

Barrow, John D. (1988). *The World within the World*. Oxford: Oxford University Press.

—— (1994). *The Origin of the Universe*. New York: BasicBooks.

—— (2000). *The Book of Nothing*. London: Jonathan Cape.

—— and Tipler, Frank J. (1986). *The Anthropic Cosmological Principle*. Oxford: Oxford University Press.

Benacerraf, Paul (1965). 'What Numbers Could Not Be', *Philosophical Review*, Vol. 74, No. 1.

Bennett, M. R. and Hacker, P. M. S. (2003). *Philosophical Foundations of Neuroscience*. Oxford: Blackwell.

Berkeley, G. (1975). *Philosophical Works, Including the Works on Vision*, Introduction and Notes by M. R. Ayers. London: Dent.

Blanshard, Brand (1974). *Reason and Belief*. London: George Allen & Unwin.

Carter, B. (1974). 'The Anthropic Principle and Large Number Coincidences', in M. Longair, ed., *Confrontation of Cosmological Theories with Observation*. Dordrecht: D. Reidel.

Cicero, Marcus Tullius (1997). *The Nature of the Gods*, trans. P. G. Walsh. Oxford: Oxford University Press.

Collins, C. B. and Hawking, S. W. (1973). 'Why is the Universe Isotropic?', *Astrophysics Journal*, Vol. 180.

Comte, Auguste (1957). *A General View of Positivism*, trans. J. H. Bridges. New York: Robert Speller and Sons.

Coplestone, F. C. (1955). *Aquinas*. Harmondsworth: Penguin Books.

Craig, William Lane (1998). 'The Tensed vs. Tenseless Theory of Time: A Watershed for the Conception of Divine Eternity', in *Questions of Time and Tense*, ed. Robin Le Poidevin. Oxford: Clarendon Press.

Crease, Robert, and Mann, Charles (1986). *The Second Creation*. New York: Macmillan.

Crombie, I. M. (1957). 'The Possibility of Theological Statements', in Basil Mitchell, ed., *Faith and Logic*. London: George Allen & Unwin.

——(1987). 'Eternity and Omnitemporality', in *The Rationality of Religious Belief: Essays in Honour of Basil Mitchell*, ed. William J. Abraham and Steven W. Holtzer. Oxford: Clarendon Press.

Davies, Paul (1995). *About Time: Einstein's Unfinished Revolution*. London: Penguin Books.

Dretske, Fred (1977). 'Laws of Nature', *Philosophy of Science*, Vol. 44.

Duhem, Pierre (1954). *The Aim and Structure of Physical Theory*, trans. P. Wiener. Princeton: Princeton University Press.

Dummett, Michael (1978). 'Can an Effect Precede its Cause?', in *Truth and Other Enigmas*. London: Duckworth.

Earman, John (1976). 'Causation: A Matter of Life and Death', *The Journal of Philosophy*, Vol. 73, No. 1.

Einstein, Albert (1905). 'Ist die Trägheit eines Körpers von seinem Energieinhalt abhängig?', *Annalen der Physik*, Vol. 18.

Ewing, A. C. (1932). 'A Defence of Causality', *Proceedings of the Aristotelian Society*, Vol. 33.

Fackenheim, Emil L. (1964). 'On the Eclipse of God', *Commentary*, Vol. 37, No. 6.

Flew, A. (1955). 'Theology and Falsification', in *New Essays in Philosophical Theology*, ed. Anthony Flew and Alasdair MacIntyre. London: SCM Press. Reprinted in Mitchell 1971. Page numbers as in reprint.

——(1966). *God and Philosophy*. London: Hutchinson.

Fogelin, Robert J. (1990). 'A Reading of Aquinas's Five Ways', *American Philosophical Quarterly*, Vol. 27, No. 4.

Foster, John (1983). 'Induction, Explanation and Natural Necessity', *Proceedings of the Aristotelian Society*, Vol. 83.

Frege, Gottlob (1980). *The Foundations of Arithmetic*, trans. J. L. Austin, 2nd revised edn. Oxford: Blackwell.

Ganssle, Gregory E., ed. (2001). *God and Time: Four Views*. Carlisle: Paternoster Press.

—— and Woodruff, David M., eds. (2002). *God and Time: Essays on the Divine Nature*. Oxford: Oxford University Press.

Gaskin, J. C. A. (1988). *Hume's Philosophy of Religion*, 2nd edn. London: Macmillan.

—— (2000). 'Gods, Ghosts and Curious Persons', *Philosophical Writings*, No. 13.

Geach, P. T. (1955). 'Form and Existence', *Proceedings of the Aristotelian Society*, Vol. 55.

—— (1969). *God and the Soul*. London: Routledge & Kegan Paul.

Harré, Rom (1986). *Varieties of Realism: A Rationale for the Natural Sciences*. Oxford: Blackwell.

Hawking, Stephen W. (1988). *A Brief History of Time: From the Big Bang to Black Holes*. London and New York: Bantam.

—— (2001). *The Universe in a Nutshell*. London and New York: Bantam.

Helm, Paul (1989). 'Omniscience and Eternity', *Proceedings of the Aristotelian Society*, Supp. Vol. 63.

Hume, David (1888). *A Treatise of Human Nature*, ed. L. A. Selby-Bigge. Oxford: Clarendon Press.

—— (1902). *An Enquiry Concerning Human Understanding*, ed. L. A. Selby-Bigge. Oxford: Clarendon Press.

—— (1947). *Dialogues Concerning Natural Religion*, 2nd edn, ed. N. Kemp Smith. Edinburgh: Thomas Nelson.

Jacobson, Anne Jaap (1984). 'Does Hume Hold a Regularity Theory of Causality?', *History of Philosophy Quarterly*, Vol. 1, No. 1.

Jammer, Max (1957). *Concepts of Force: A Study in the Foundations of Dynamics*. Cambridge: Harvard University Press.

—— (1961). *Concepts of Mass in Classical and Modern Physics*. Cambridge: Harvard University Press.

Kenny, Anthony (1969). *The Five Ways: St. Thomas Aquinas' Proofs of God's Existence*. London: Routledge & Kegan Paul.

Kretzmann, Norman (1999). *The Metaphysics of Creation: Aquinas's Natural Theology in Summa contra gentiles II*. Oxford: Clarendon Press.

Kripke, S. (1980). *Naming and Necessity*. Oxford: Blackwell.

Lange, Marc (2002). *An Introduction to the Philosophy of Physics: Locality, Fields, Energy, and Mass*. Oxford and Malden: Blackwell.

Leftow, Brian (1991). *Time and Eternity*. Ithaca and London: Cornell University Press.

Leslie, John (1989). *Universes*. London and New York: Routledge.

Locke, John (1975). *An Essay Concerning Human Understanding*, ed. Peter H. Nidditch. Oxford: Clarendon Press.

Lodge, Oliver (1885). 'On the identity of energy in connection with Mr Poynting's paper on the transfer of energy in an electromagnetic field; and on the fundamental forms of energy', *Philosophical Magazine*, Vol. 19.

Lowe, E. J. (1996). 'Why is there Anything at all?', *Proceedings of the Aristotelian Society*, Supp. Vol. 70.

Mackie, J. L. (1974). *The Cement of the Universe: A Study of Causation*. Oxford: Clarendon Press.

——(1982). *The Miracle of Theism*. Oxford: Clarendon Press.

Malcolm, Norman (1960). 'Anselm's Ontological Arguments', *The Philosophical Review*, Vol. 69.

——(1963). *Knowledge and Certainty: Essays and Lectures*. Englewood Cliffs: Prentice-Hall.

McGinn, C. (1991). *The Problem of Consciousness*. Oxford: Blackwell.

Mellor, D. H. (1995). *The Facts of Causation*. London and New York: Routledge.

Mitchell, Basil, ed. (1971). *The Philosophy of Religion*. Oxford: Oxford University Press.

Nielsen, Kai (1982). *An Introduction to the Philosophy of Religion*. London: Macmillan.

Penelhum, Terence (1960). 'Divine Necessity', *Mind*, Vol. 69, reprinted in Mitchell 1971. Page numbers as in reprint.

Penrose, Roger (1990). *The Emperor's New Mind*. Vintage: London.

Plantinga, Alvin (1967). *God and Other Minds: A Study of the Rational Justification of Belief in God*. Ithaca and London: Cornell University Press.

Plato (1972). *Phaedo*, trans with an Introduction and Commentary by R. Hackworth. Cambridge: University Press.

Poincaré, Jules Henri (1900). 'La théorie de Lorentz et le principe de réaction', *Archives Néerlandaises des sciences exactes et naturelles*, Vol. 2.

Polkinghorne, John (1990). *Science and Creation: The Search for Understanding*. Boston: Shambhala.

Putnam, Hilary (1975). 'The Meaning of "Meaning"', in *Mind, Language and Reality: Philosophical Papers*, Vol. 2. Cambridge: Cambridge University Press.

Quine, W. V. (1961). 'Two Dogmas of Empiricism' in *From a Logical Point of View*, revised edn. Cambridge: Harvard University Press.

——(1981). *Theories and Things*. Cambridge: Harvard University Press.

Quinn, Philip L. (1993). 'Creation, Conservation, and the Big Bang', in *Philosophical Problems of the Internal and External Worlds: Essays on the Philosophy of Adolf Grünbaum*, ed. John Earman, Allen I. Janis, Gerald J. Massey, and Nicholas Rescher. University of Pittsburgh Press/Universitätsverlag Konstanz.

Rees, Martin (1999). *Just Six Numbers: The Deep Forces that Shape the Universe*. London: Weidenfeld & Nicolson.

Robertson, H. P. (1959). 'Geometry as a Branch of Physics', in *Albert Einstein: Philosopher-Scientist*, Vol. 1, ed. Paul Arthur Schilpp. New York: Harper.

Ross, James F. (1980). 'Creation', *The Journal of Philosophy*, Vol. 77, No. 10.

Rundle, Bede (1979). *Grammar in Philosophy*. Oxford: Clarendon Press.

——(1990). *Wittgenstein and Contemporary Philosophy of Language*. Oxford: Blackwell.

—— (1997). *Mind in Action*. Oxford: Clarendon Press.

—— (2001). 'Objects and Attitudes', *Language and Communication*, Vol. 21, No. 2.

Russell, Bertrand (1948). *Human Knowledge: Its Scope and Limits*. New York: Simon & Schuster.

—— and Coplestone, F. C. (1964). 'A Debate on the Existence of God', reprinted in J. Hick, ed., *The Existence of God*. London: Macmillan.

Schlesinger, George N. (1988). *New Perspectives on Old-Time Religion*. Oxford: Clarendon Press.

Smart, J. J. C. (1955). 'The Existence of God', in *New Essays in Philosophical Theology*, ed. Anthony Flew and Alasdair MacIntyre. London: SCM Press.

—— and Haldane J. J. (1996). *Atheism and Theism*. Oxford and Malden: Blackwell.

Smolin, Lee (1997). *The Life of the Cosmos*. London: Weidenfield & Nicolson.

Sorabji, Richard (1983). *Time, Creation and the Continuum: Theories in Antiquity and the Early Middle Ages*. London: Duckworth.

Spinoza, Baruch (1910). *Ethics*. London: J. M. Dent and Sons.

Stebbing, L. Susan (1950). *A Modern Introduction to Logic*, 7th edn. London: Methuen.

Stove, D. C. (1978). 'Part IX of Hume's *Dialogues*', *The Philosophical Quarterly*, Vol. 28.

Strawson, Galen (1989). *The Secret Connexion: Causation, Realism, and David Hume*. Oxford: Clarendon Press.

Swinburne, Richard (1979). *The Existence of God*. Oxford: Clarendon Press.

—— (1990). 'The Limits of Explanation', in *Explanation and its Limits*, ed. Dudley Knowles. Cambridge: Cambridge University Press.

Thorne, Kip S. (1994). *Black Holes and Time Warps: Einstein's Outrageous Legacy*. Norton: New York.

Waismann, F. (1965). *The Principles of Linguistic Philosophy*, ed. R. Harré. London: Macmillan.

Walsh, W. H. (1963). *Metaphysics*. London: Hutchinson University Library.

Ward, Keith (1996). *God, Chance and Necessity*. Oxford: Oneworld.

Wisdom, J. (1944). 'Gods', *Proceedings of the Aristotelian Society*, Vol. 45.

Wittgenstein, L. (1958). *The Blue and Brown Books*. Oxford: Blackwell.

—— (1968). 'Notes for Lectures on "Private Experience" and "Sense Data"', ed. R. Rhees, *The Philosophical Review*, Vol. 77.

—— (1970). *Lectures and Conversations on Aesthetics, Psychology and Religious Belief*, ed. C. Barrett. Oxford: Blackwell.

—— (1975). *Philosophical Remarks*, ed. R. Rhees, trans. R. Hargreaves and R. White. Oxford: Blackwell.

—— (1978). *Remarks on the Foundations of Mathematics*, ed. G. H. von Wright, R. Rhees, G. E. M. Anscombe, trans. G. E. M. Anscombe, revised edn. Oxford: Blackwell.

—— (1979a). *Wittgenstein and the Vienna Circle*, conversations recorded by F. Waismann, ed. B. F. McGuinness, trans. J. Schulte and B. F. McGuinness. Oxford: Blackwell.

Wittgenstein, L. (1979b). *Wittgenstein's Lectures, Cambridge 1932–35, from the Notes of Alice Ambrose and Margaret MacDonald*, ed. A. Ambrose. Oxford: Blackwell.

—— (1980). *Remarks on the Philosophy of Psychology*, Vol. I, ed. G. E. M. Anscombe and G. H. von Wright, trans. G. E. M. Anscombe. Oxford: Blackwell.

—— (1992). *Last Writings on the Philosophy of Psychology*, Vol. II, ed. G. H. von Wright and H. Nyman, trans. C. G. Luckhardt and M. A. E. Aue. Oxford: Blackwell.

Worthing, Mark William (1996). *God, Creation, and Contemporary Physics*. Minneapolis: Fortress Press.

Index